STR		ALC	
SHI	1/02	ALM	
SHM		SDL	
KTN		HEN	
WEL		SOU	
HRB		SOM	

WORKING FOR
VICTORY

WORKING FOR
VICTORY

A DIARY OF LIFE IN A
SECOND WORLD WAR FACTORY

EDITED AND INTRODUCED BY
SUE BRULEY

SUTTON PUBLISHING
IMPERIAL WAR MUSEUM

First published in 2001 by
Sutton Publishing Limited · Phoenix Mill
Thrupp · Stroud · Gloucestershire · GL5 2BU

Copyright © Sue Bruley, 2001

British Library Cataloguing in Publication Data
A catalogue record for this book is available from the British Library

ISBN 0 7509 2516 7

Typeset in 10/12 pt New Baskerville.
Typesetting and origination by
Sutton Publishing Limited.
Printed and bound in England by
J.H. Haynes & Co. Ltd, Sparkford.

In memory of Kathleen Church-Bliss and Elsie Whiteman,

centre lathe turners at Morrisons 1942–45,

who wrote this diary.

Contents

List of Illustrations

Acknowledgements

Many people have made a contribution towards the publication of this diary, and generally sustaining me through the period of this research. As I cannot mention everyone by name I would like to start by thanking everyone collectively for their kindness and co-operation. Of the people I need to name specifically Alison Speirs must come at the top of the list, as she gave permission to publish the diaries and gave me a great deal of practical help, including supplying several of the photographs. Jocelyn Hemming produced a first rate typescript from the original handwritten diaries. This work was funded by the Imperial War Museum and the University of Portsmouth. Ligia Kasanin and Gail Stewart Bye helped to proof-read the typescript and spurred me on to finish the book.

My oral respondents: Ken Peters, Audrey Clark, Gordon 'Bing' Crosby and Ken Thoroughgood gave me other views of Morrisons in wartime and helped to put names to the photographs; Jane Salusbury and Alison Speirs illuminated me on the family lives of Kathleen and Elsie. Audrey Clark and Ken Peters also supplied several photographs and Ken Thoroughgood produced a plan of the factory floor which has been reproduced in the book. I have also benefitted from the letters and visual material kindly sent into the *Croydon Guardian* in response to my appeal for information, particularly Joe Askew who wrote at great length from New Zealand, and phone conversations from members of the Whiteman and Church-Bliss families.

My grateful thanks are also due to Roderick Suddaby and other staff in the Documents Department at the Imperial War Museum; Malcom Taylor of the Vaughan Williams Memorial Library; the English Folk Dance and Song Society; Gary Ransom of Janes Publications Image Library; Tom Sansum and other members of the Croydon Airport Society; Steve Roud, Local Studies, Croydon Central Library and Fred Milsom for help with the technical terms.

My colleagues at the University of Portsmouth have been very supportive throughout this project. I am particularly grateful to Brad Beaven, with whom I had fruitful discussions on the Home Front, and James Thomas, who proof-read the edited manuscript and gave valuable advice on the final shape of the book. Thanks must also go to Christopher Feeney and Sutton Publishing for having confidence in this book.

I would like to mention several members of my family. My brother Steve helped with the art work in the factory plan and produced some of the photographs. My mother started my interest in women's war work by telling me about her wartime experiences in a radio factory. She is one of the many unsung heroines of the Second World War. My children, Eric, Charlotte and Rowan, have been a constant reminder to me that there is life outside of work. I hope now that they will see that there was a point to all those hours at the word processor.

People, Places and 'Things':
Explanatory Notes

Hundreds of people are mentioned in the diary. This list only includes those who are mentioned several times or who have some overall significance. (Public figures who appear incidentally are given a brief note in the text, if known.) Within each thematic group the list has been compiled alphabetically using the first name most commonly applied.

THE DIARISTS
Elsie Whiteman/E/Els
Kathleen Church-Bliss/K/Kat
Both originally lived in a house called 'Benacre' in Milford, Surrey. Moved to 15 Duppas Hill Road, Croydon, February 1942, and later moved to 25 Duppas Hill Road.

FAMILY, FRIENDS AND DUPPAS HILL ROAD PEOPLE
'Auntie' – elderly folk dance friend of Elsie, rents Elsie's house next door to
    Benacre
Mrs Bellwood – landlady, 15 Duppas Hill Road
Mr Bellwood/Norman/Papa Bellwood – landlord, also fire watch warden
Mrs Brookes – landlady, 25 Duppas Hill Road
Billy Brown – young boy from Morrisons, uses Duppas Hill Road shelter
Eric – Elsie's brother, lives in the Midlands
Mum/Ma/Mother – Kathleen's well-connected mother
Millie and Ronald – Elsie's sister and brother-in-law. Ronald is a senior civil servant
Madge – Elsie's sister
Phyl (Phyliss) and Phillip – Elsie's sister and brother-in-law
Tommy Adkins – old friend (see epilogue)

TRAINING CENTRE, CROYDON
Teachers:
Mr Dalton
Mr Lloyd/'Bacchus'
Mr King/'Poppa King'

Trainees:
'James Harcourt'
John Bailey, also at Waddon

'Margery Kahn'
Nelly Vivian/'Greasy Locks'/'N.'
'Marlene Dietrich'
Perce Harvey

TRAINING CENTRE, WADDON
Teachers/Instructors:
Mr Evans
Mr Hyde/Gestapo Hyde/may also be Tony
Mr Powney/Old Powney/Old P./Old Beast/Old B./Lazy Old Bugger
Mr Williams/George/'Gawge'

Trainees:
Andre
Bert
'Drummond Sutherland'
Fred Feeley
Tubby Davey/Ronny

MORRISONS
Above the shop floor:
Miss Barr – probably liaison officer between Morrisons and the National Service
   Office/on Lateness and Absentee Committee, takes minutes at works council
Mr Biffo – conducts/compères factory orchestra
Miss Corney – women's welfare supervisor
Mr Davies – personnel manager, on Lateness and Absentee Committee
Mr Heseltine – deputy works manager
Mr Hurst – works manager, on works council
Captain Lines – manager/director
Mr McGiveney – sometimes described as managing director, on works council
Mr Overton – production manager
Mr Payne – in charge of welfare, also responsible for the orchestra
Mr Proctor – also described as Managing Director/the 'Well Scrubbed Pig'/
   Captain of the Factory Home Guard
Mr Young – director, chairman of works council

On the shop floor:
Anne Smith – shop stewardess, No. 2 Factory
Mrs Barford – Nellie, worker in No. 2 Factory, elected to works council
Bradford – George/Gentle George/Pussy/Assistant Foreman
Bert Runacres – on works council
Catford – Peter, young machine shop worker, shares canteen table with K and E,
   affair with Peccadillo
Cayzer – inspector, active in AEU
Costello – Bernard, on works council
Dennis Ellis – young helper to Fred in machine shop, same table as K and E in
   canteen

Eddie Cook – chargehand in automatics
Eddie Wratten – shares canteen table with K and E, marries Ivy Barney
Fred Lundy – setter and chargehand in machine shop/'Sir Hubert Stanley'
George Baker – chargehand
George Ross – on Sick Benefit Committee/Communist
'Godfrey Tearle' – Harry May/inspector on nights
Grace Dobson – 'Details' department, on works council
Graham – Welby/inspector
Mrs Hazelgrove – Peggy/Old Mother Riley/OMR/machine shop worker
Hilda Greenwood – machine shop worker/'moaning Minnie'/affair with Rapley
Hilda Carter – Mrs Carter/machine shop worker
The 'Hippo' – 'hippopotamus'/elderly worker on milling machines
Mrs Israel – machine shop worker
Jock – Jock Ure/elderly sweeper/factory poet
Joe Phillips – elderly worker/dinnertime friend
Jim Sawyer – Head of Inspection Bench (AID)
Jimmy Dale – shop steward/communist/on works council
Ivy Barney – inspector/machine shop/shares canteen table with K and E/marries
    Eddie Wratten
Ken Peters – young worker in machine shop/on works council
Kilby – Manchester Kilby/Little Kilby/machine shop worker/becomes third
    nurse
Lancashire – young man/tool room worker/on works council
Laurie Charman – machine shop worker/Laurie and husband Ron become
friends with E and K
Lavender – chargehand
Len Quirk – chargehand/capstan lathes
The Lizard – Inspector/Holliday
Lou – Fat Cooky/miller/shares canteen table with E and K
Mrs Margetson – middle-aged machine-shop worker
Mrs Marley – 'Parachute Marley'/'Gaudy Image'/becomes lady surpervisor at
    Waddon
May Nolan – miller/union activist
Moroney – Joe/inspector No. 2 Factory/AEU branch chairman/ on works
    council
Muriel Young – machine shop worker/girlfriend of Reg Green
Nancy Deacon – machine shop worker
N. Graham – probably machine shop worker, shares canteen table with K and E
Peccadillo – Blondie Avery/Audrey/works on drills/affair with Catford
Peter Joseph – inspector
Pierrot – Jim the Pierrot/inspector
Rachel Thurgood – machine shop worker
Mr Rapley – foreman/machine shop
Reg Green – machine shop worker/boyfriend of Muriel Young
Sally Fillingham – young woman worker/factory talent show performer
Stan Wallace – setter and chargehand/machine shop/becomes friend of E and K

Mr Tickle – rate-fixer
Wax Doll – young woman worker in tool making/the Pierette/Glamour
    Girl/affair with Pierrot
Webster – nurse/becomes women's welfare supervisor
Wolatile – young woman worker/Eileen/probably machine shop

ENGINEERING TERMS/TOOLS USED IN THE TEXT

aileron – movable control surface on the wing of an aircraft
capstan lathe – a multi-operational lathe, capable of high rates of production
centre lathe – produces small numbers of parts to high standards of accuracy,
    hence 'centre lathe turning'
chuck – the part of a machine tool that holds either the work piece or a cutting
    tool. Found on lathes and drilling machines
chuck key – tool used to tighten the chuck so that it holds either the work piece
    or a tool tightly to prevent it moving
Idle Time – hourly pay only, no bonus
micrometer – hand tool for accurate measurement of parts down to a
    thousandth of an inch
millers – semi-skilled operators for metal cutting machines
millwrights – skilled workers who erect and maintain machines and plant (fitters
    are similar, usually working on smaller machines)
reamer – hand tool for finishing holes to an exact size, after drilling
scribing block – used by fitters and toolmakers to mark out the desired shape on
    a piece of metal
setter – sets up machines for capstan and centre lathe workers and supervises
    them
tin bashers – workers who use hand tools, rollers and wheels to shape flat sheets
    of metal into complex three dimensional shapes

MONEY AND MEASUREMENTS
20 shillings (20*s*) = 20/- = £1
1*s* = 12*d* = 1/-
2/12/6 in the text = £2 12*s* 6*d*
21*s* = 1 guinea
12" = 12 in = 1 ft = 1'
a 'thou' = 1,000th of an inch

ABBREVIATIONS USED IN THE TEXT
AEU   Amalgamated Engineering Union
AID   Aircraft Inspection Department (run by MAP)
ATS   Auxiliary Territorial Service
ARP   Air Raid Precautions
CI   Chief instructor (ACI – probably a different version of same)
EFDS   English Folk Dance Society (later became English Folk Dance and
           Song Society, EFDSS)

ENSA	Entertainments National Service Association
FAP	First Aid Post
NFS	National Fire Service
NSO	National Service Office/Officer
MAP	Ministry of Aircraft Production
m/c	machine shop
MO	Medical Officer
OMR	Old Mother Riley (see above)
P-Planes	pilotless aircraft carrying 'buzz bombs' or 'flying bombs'/V1s.
REME	Royal Electrical and Mechanical Engineers

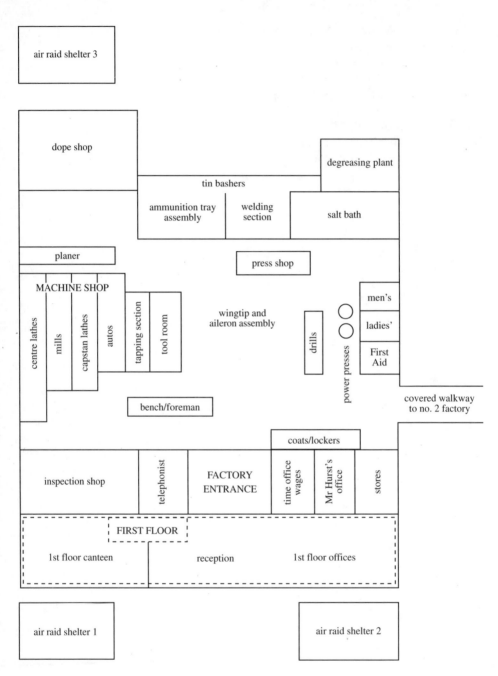

Plan of Morrisons' No. 1 Factory. *(Drawn by Stephen Bruley from a sketch by Ken Thoroughgood)*

Introduction

As the collective memory of the Second World War recedes, written documents, particularly diaries and other memoirs, will be increasingly used by historians for evidence of life on the Home Front. Diaries are an especially important source for their detailed recall and immediate response to events. The joint diary of Elsie Whiteman and Kathleen Church-Bliss, from February 1942 to November 1944, is undoubtedly one of the best examples of the war diary genre. It is written by two middle-aged women of considerable means who exchanged a comfortable and pleasant life in the Surrey countryside for the grime and exhaustion of factory labour in Croydon. Their diary, recounting first life at the government training centre and then at Morrisons, bursts with wit and humour and the minutiae of wartime tragedies and hardships. This introduction aims to place it in a war setting, provide some background detail on Morrisons and some biographical information on the two women diarists, and to outline the key historiographical aspects of the diary.

The demands of modern warfare produced far-reaching effects on British society during the Second World War. Unprecedented state intervention touched the lives of every citizen, particularly the working population. From March 1941 labour was effectively controlled by the state through the Essential Work Order and other government initiatives. Men of military age were conscripted into the services, with the exception of those deemed to be in essential war industries, or 'reserved' occupations. Engineering, particularly aircraft manufacture which was crucial to the war effort, fell within this category. Female labour was also regulated, so adult women were required to register for some sort of war service, although women with dependents were exempt. Through their labour organisations, workers formally surrendered the right to withhold their labour (though unofficial strikes did still occur, though rarely). Employers, in turn, lost the right to dismiss labour, which gave workers a sense of security that they had never experienced during the lean years between the wars. Consequently, the deferential attitude towards management evaporated as workers gained a new confidence in the war years. The downside of this was that once in industry workers could not leave unless they obtained official release (rarely granted until close to the end of the war), and shifts were often exhausting with extensive overtime routinely demanded. Government, realising that 'happy workers are productive workers' promoted welfare reform. Issues such as safety, lighting, ventilation, canteens, nurseries and 'shopping time' for mothers began to be addressed. The government also encouraged the formation of 'Joint Production Committees' or similar bodies where workers and managers could discuss ways of enhancing output, although the effectiveness of these committees is questionable.[1]

The expansion of war industries was facilitated by the extensive use of female labour. This was especially so in aircraft manufacture where women's labour rose from 7 per cent to 40 per cent between 1935 and 1944, representing nearly ¾ million women.[2] This was made possible by a series of 'dilution' agreements between the Associated Engineering union (AEU, traditionally for skilled men only, but which had already accepted semi-skilled men as members), engineering employers and the government. Women were allowed to undertake work previously thought of as 'boys' or 'youth' labour, and could, in theory, progress to performing work graded as skilled or semi-skilled male labour for equal pay rates, if they could work at the stipulated pace and not require extra supervision. In practice, however, such work was usually regraded and labelled 'women's work' so that women were very rarely in a position to be able to claim equal pay.[3] In any case, these agreements were defined as temporary and for the duration of the war only, so women had no permanent claim to the posts they held. One of the ways in which the government promoted female labour was through the opening up of the Government Training Centres to women (previously only domestic service training had been available to them). Although specialist training courses were almost impossible to obtain, many women did gain access to sixteen-week basic engineering courses. However, once in industry women were denied opportunities available to male trainees, as managers did not expect to employ semi-skilled women.[4] As a result, the sixteen-week courses for women were curtailed to four or eight weeks in 1942. In practice, the majority of female entrants to industry went straight from the labour exchange to a firm and were assigned to low grade, unskilled labour with little or no opportunity to progress.

Morrisons Engineering Works was situated on the Purley Way, Croydon, close to Waddon Station.[5] At this time the most significant local feature was Croydon airport, which was situated close to Morrisons, and is referred to as 'the aerodrome' in the diary (it closed in 1959). Morrisons was only one of many light engineering firms in the area at this time. A photograph of the new factory (see plate section) dated 1938, places its origins in the pre-war boom in aircraft manufacture. Morrisons produced components for aircraft built by Vickers in Weybridge, Surrey. The company worked on parts for Lancasters, Hurricanes, Wellingtons and Spitfires. The striking rise in engineering trades in the late 1930s was accompanied by technological change and the erosion of skilled labour.[6] The aircraft industry was no exception to this and most of the new firms connected with the industry, such as Morrisons, employed large numbers of semi-skilled men and very few skilled engineers. Increasingly, mass production techniques were utilised and labour was employed on a timed bonus system. Women were very much part of this fast-expanding workforce, although mainly employed on unskilled assembly work before the outbreak of war in 1939.[7] Morrisons' management did not officially recognise trade unions in the factory, but there is much evidence of union activity among both men and women.

Morrisons grew at a spectacular rate during the war years. Its workforce expanded from about 150 to nearly 500 by 1942 and about 600 in 1944.[8] The Croydon factory took over the neighbouring site and the two buildings became known as No. 1 and No. 2 Factories. In addition, Morrisons established factories in Preston and Peterborough. Most of Morrisons' male workers were not enlisted as they were in reserved occupations, but it was impossible to recruit extra male labour, so it was women who made up the shortfall, making the firm's rapid growth possible. At its peak more than half of Morrisons' workforce were women.[9] According to the diary, the great majority of these women were married. The women entered areas of the factory, such as the drilling and tapping centre, a capstan lathes and the tool room, which had all previously been the exclusive provinces of men.

Our mirror into the Morrison factory was created by the writing of two of these new women workers. Kathleen Church-Bliss and Elsie Whiteman were both mature women of some means from affluent London families. Kathleen, a direct descendant of Sir Charles Barry, architect of the Houses of Parliament, was born in 1900 and brought up in Tite Street, Chelsea.[10] She had no siblings and enjoyed a close and affectionate relationship with her lawyer father. At thirteen she became a boarder at Wycombe Abbey School, Buckinghamshire, where her grandfather was chairman of the governors. Despite being extremely bright she did not go to university and appears to have been destined to stay at home with her demanding mother, particularly after her father's death in 1923. She found an outlet, however, in the folk dance and song movement; 'All these lovely new friends and the glorious music became my life.'[11]

Elsie Whiteman was five years older than Kathleen and came from a large, prosperous family based in west London, in Elgin Crescent, Notting Hill.[12] Her mother died while Elsie was still a child. Her father made his money in milk distribution and retired early. After being privately educated Elsie trained as a teacher, specialising in Physical Training. Her great passion was dancing and she, too, was drawn into the folk dance and song movement in the early 1920s. This movement centred around the English Folk Dance Society (EFDS), which had its headquarters at Cecil Sharp House, in Camden, north London. Both Kathleen and Elsie became involved as teachers and organisers for the society, and in 1927 they met and became close friends. Both women enjoyed a wide circle of friends in the EFDS, including men. There is no evidence that either of them had any romantic involvements with men. This does not necessarily mean that they chose not to form relationships with the opposite sex, as the young men of their generation were scarce as a direct result of the First World War. In social activities of the 1920s, it was common for women to greatly outnumber men, so EFDS events would normally feature women dancing with women, as well as men and women dancing together. While attempts to categorise the sexuality of Kathleen and Elsie should be resisted, readers of the diary will not fail to notice the intensity of the relationship between the two. This is very much in the tradition of a 'romantic friendship.'

In 1935 Kathleen bought a Tudor farmhouse, 'Benacre', in Milford, Surrey and moved in with Elsie. At a later date Elsie bought the house next door, but she never lived there and rented the house out to an older folk dance friend who is referred to as 'Auntie' in the diary. The house was on the old A3 from London to Portsmouth and was opened by the two women as a cafe/restaurant for passing motorists and cyclists. Elsie Whiteman's niece remembers visiting

Benacre as a small child and thought it was a 'lovely place'.[13] Kathleen did not entirely escape from her mother, as at some point she appears to have established herself at the Undershaw Hotel in Hindhead, not far from Milford. Kathleen and Elsie ran the business successfully for six years. Then, in August 1941 they made a decision to close the teashop and volunteer for war work in engineering. It took several months for the two women to complete arrangements for letting out the house and moving to Croydon, where they embarked on a government training course in machine operating in February 1942. From there they entered Morrisons' No. 1 Factory as centre lathe operators in June 1942.

Undoubtedly, patriotism played a part in this decision. It is clear from the diary itself and interviews with surviving relatives that both women were keen to support the war effort, and munitions work would be a very visible expression of this. The outcome of the war was by no means certain at this point, and Britain stood alone to face a hostile, Nazi-dominated Europe. The fact that they left it so late to volunteer, however, indicates that there were other influences at work. With so many men enlisted and petrol only available to those on legitimate war work, it is likely that the business was in decline, as there cannot have been much passing trade from day trippers. More significantly, the compulsory registration of women for war work meant that at regular intervals a new and older cohort of women were called into service. In less than a year Kathleen's age group would be included and later Elsie would also have to register, as, eventually, the scheme covered women up to fifty years old. By volunteering for munitions and stipulating that they wished to stay together Kathleen and Elsie avoided the separation which would ensue if they waited for events to take their course. There were also, however, plenty of women of their social standing and age who avoided arduous factory labour. A regular commitment to the Women's Voluntary Service (WVS), for example, would have almost certainly given them exemption from registration and enabled them to remain at home. The decision to enter a munitions factory was partly taken in a spirit of adventure. The idea to keep a diary and make a detailed account of their experiences in the training centre and later at Morrisons has to be seen in this light. They thought of themselves as social explorers, not unlike the great social investigators of the late Victorian and Edwardian eras. It seems likely that the two women hoped that one day the diary would reach a wider audience. This was, however, a very hazy notion as they were aware that, due to the sensitive nature of the material, publication would be impossible for many years. As the diary reveals, they did circulate early volumes privately, while still at Morrisons, and were eager to hear reactions to their factory experiences from family and friends.

Unlike the Land Army, service women or housewives, very few women in war industries recorded their experiences. Considering the hours that they worked, and the fact that many of them had family responsibilities, this is hardly surprising. There is a large volume of Mass Observation material relating to industry, but mostly this is the work of middle-class observers rather than of the workers themselves.[14] Kathleen and Elsie, although not working class, lived and worked as industrial workers during this time and felt all the pressures of factory life in wartime. We have tended to look to oral history for evidence of industrial women's conscientiousness. This has led to a generalisation of the younger women's experiences and a relative neglect of the older woman worker.[15] This category was, in fact, incredibly important to the war effort. The largest group of new women workers in wartime were aged thirty-five to forty-five.[16] At the time of their entry into industry Kathleen was forty-two and Elsie forty-seven.[17] As a record of the experiences of older, single women the diary provides a unique insight into the perspective of a hitherto marginalised group.[18]

What appears in this volume is an edited version of the diaries. Substantial cuts have had to be made to create a readable book of manageable length. The full manuscript is available to researchers at the Imperial War Museum. The essence of factory life has been retained as its central focus. Peripheral activities, such as domestic events, lengthy descriptions of weekend or evening excursions, or routine contact with family and friends outside the factory have been reduced or eliminated. The two women were energetically social and maintained contact with a very wide network of friends and family throughout this period, despite their work commitments. Much of the details of these encounters has been edited out. Elsie and Kathleen took it in turns to write the diary and never wrote directly in the first person. Sometimes it is obvious which one has written a particular entry, but this is by no means always the case. As the main aim of publishing the diary is historical rather than literary, a decision was made to leave the diary as it stands and not to attempt to identify individual contributions.

The observations which Kathleen and Elsie made about the people around them are extremely colourful and vivid. Many of the factory and training-centre characters were given nicknames: 'Lizard', 'Pussy', 'Wax Doll', 'Greasy Locks', 'Hippo'. Sometimes these names correspond to film stars: Marlene Dietrich, Godfrey Tearle. Readers will have to appreciate that unrecognisable words or words detached from their usual context are just part of Kathleen's style and not typing errors. The words 'fradged', 'fubsy', 'rorty', 'argufy', 'chy-iked', 'gubation' and 'distrait' are among those which appear to be invented. Someone was said to be 'very piano'. Management, at the training centre and Morrisons, received some of the harshest descriptions; 'a well scrubbed pig', 'dried up little horror', 'group of vultures'. We can be reasonably sure that the more imaginative language in the diary was the work of Kathleen as it corresponds to some earlier writing of hers.[19] There are a few references which are frankly anti-semitic such as 'jew-boy'. While this must be acknowledged, it should be seen as typical of the class background of the two women at this time. Other terms are used which would not be regarded as acceptable today, for example, 'bitch' and 'bastard'. The diary also reflects Kathleen and Elsie's volatile moods. Their 'setter', Stan, for instance, is praised to the hilt when things are going well, but on 'off' days he is subjected to vitriolic condemnation.

The diary provides a remarkable insight into wartime factory life. The immediacy of the diary format and the wonderfully expressive and detailed writing creates a powerful evocation of the feelings and atmosphere of the period. The nightly outpourings of Kathleen and Elsie overflow with detailed accounts of gender divisions at work and the firm's stumbling attempts at workplace democracy. The range of their observations also takes in factory culture, wartime bureaucracy, morale and reaction to official propaganda, factory welfare, 'social mixing', intrusions into personal life and the effects of mass bombing.[20] Efforts have been made to contact other workers at Morrisons during the war. Several oral history interviews have been conducted and much of the factual material contained in the diary has been verified.[21] Something of what Kathleen and Elsie's work colleagues thought of them is known. Ken Thoroughgood, a young man in the press shop at the time, thought they were a 'toffee nosed pair' and didn't have much to do with them.[22] Another young worker, Ken Peters, kept his distance at first, but got to know and appreciate Kathleen through her promotion of welfare inside the factory.[23] It is evident from the diary that both women earned a great deal of respect from other workers and that many colleagues genuinely warmed to them during their time in the factory. This was particularly so of Kathleen who became an effective spokesperson for the workers' interests on the factory works council.

Ultimately, the diary must be read as the work of the two women concerned and written from their perspective: following Elsie and Kathleen through the ups and downs of wartime life. They eagerly recounted all the comings and goings in the machine shop and took a surprising amount of interest in factory gossip. The diary followed the progress of the war closely. Elsie and Kathleen took immense pride in seeing photographs of aircraft, especially if components were visible which they had had some experience of working on. Sometimes their accounts are deliberately meant to be humorous, and lively encounters and situations were relayed in a strikingly funny and light-hearted manner. At other times there are powerful and emotional descriptions, particularly around the time of the V1 bombs (known as Doodle-bugs or flying bombs) in the summer of 1944, which are enthralling and exciting. The factory characters and incidents depicted in the diary are described so graphically that the images almost leap from the page. By connecting with real people in real situations the war becomes an overwhelmingly human experience.

Postwar British society has grown accustomed to the notion of the Second World War as a 'people's war', with implications of social levelling and equality of sacrifice. The government deliberately fostered this idea during the war to enhance social cohesion and to boost morale.[24] Reading the diary, it is clear that such rosy and simplistic notions of the war are only part of the picture. In particular, it is apparent that the idea of 'working for victory' is much more complex than the popular image of the war implies. Similarly, the descriptions of life under sustained bomb attacks are infinitely more nuanced than the stereotypical images of cockneys cheerfully putting up with all manner of horrors. The diary has a great deal to say, some of which exemplifies the 'people's war' spirit and some of which sits very uncomfortably with this concept. Hopefully, publication of the diary will help to foster a more balanced and realistic view of the war. Scholars will quickly appreciate the journal of Kathleen Church-Bliss and Elsie Whiteman to be one of the most significant documents to emerge from the Home Front in Britain during the Second World War.

The diary comes to an abrupt halt in the autumn of 1944, reflecting both exhaustion with war work and disenchantment on the part of Kathleen and Elsie, who were, by this time, pressing for release from factory work. Once the tide had turned and victory was assured the idea of 'working for the duration' lost its moral force. The factory adventure had worn thin and both women lost motivation and interest in writing the diary. As far as possible, the story of Morrisons and the lives of the two women diarists from November 1944 has been pieced together for the epilogue.

Editor's Note
Comments and explanations in parentheses are those of the diarists, and those in square brackets have been added by the editor.

CHAPTER ONE

Training

1942
Friday February 6
[K and E started looking for accommodation in Croydon. This proved very difficult as many houses were blitzed and no longer habitable. Also, K and E were hoping to find a landlady who would 'keep house' for them, but they soon found that the local landladies were unwilling to clean their rooms, wash the bedding, prepare fires etc. After a long search they accepted two 'gloomy cells' on the top floor of a house not far from the training centre.]

Sunday 15 February
Arrived at 15 Duppas Hill Road in car laden from floor to ceiling with bedding and suitcases. Many journeys up and down to bring in our unbelievable number of suitcases and when all at last were brought up we set to work to organise our arrangements. We found that the double bed in our second cell seemed to be entirely composed of bumps – with a lumpy feather 'duvet' atop. We did not fancy this so made up the large single divan in our sitting-room and shall see how two can manage on it. Nice electric hot-plate and griller and a wilting geranium plant and a large aspidistra, a nice little fire which burns the legs but doesn't warm the room much. We tried the portable wireless and found it excellent, and after a picnic lunch stepped out to the Britannia Works to time the distance – about 20 minutes walk. After unpacking & tea we listened to Churchill. The fall of Singapore. And so to the smallest double bed in the world, but well enough with all our own bedding.

Monday 16 February
To get to work by 9 a.m. we rose at 7 a.m. and did our breakfast & one or two household jobs and then off by 8.30 to Industry. Here 7 others were added to us – all in their 20's – and we were herded from here to there by the lady supervisor ('Come along you girls'). We were interviewed by the assistant manager and K and E have been put to Machine Operating tho' we asked for Fitting. After that we got our clocking cards and overalls and caps and schoolbooks and then returned to the lady supervisor who told us we could go home and must be ready by 7 a.m. tomorrow. The shifts are 7 a.m. – 2 p.m., lunch 11–11.30 – and alternate weeks 2.30 p.m. – 9.30 p.m., hot meal at 5 p.m. Saturdays 7–12 (early shift) and 12–5 (late shift). So that every other weekend is a long weekend from 12 Saturday till 12 p.m. the following Monday and the intervening weekend exceedingly brief.

One girl we like – Mrs Crisp, young and rather a naughty one we should suppose. Conscripted. Another pale one with greasy black hair we also like. Then there is 'Margery Kahn' [*film star?*] and 'Marlene Dietrich' [*German/US film star*] who are smart and hale from Clapham. Of these we shall only be with Greasy Locks, as she is a machine operator and the others are to be fitters – but perhaps we shall all be matey at lunch. We don't like the look of the different forlorn bodies we see lying in the Rest Room each time we go in.

Tuesday 17 February
Rose at 5 a.m. and arrived at the G.T. [*Government Training*] school at 6.39. Found that we were the first but for the firewatchers and people trickled in till after 7 a.m. The lady supervisor walked about, calling out ineffectually at intervals: 'Show willing, girls.' Finally, she collected us new trainees and took us off to the chief instructor. He led us to a Machine Operating Room and left us there. At last a harassed-looking young pimp of a teacher came up, and mumbled at us in a language we didn't understand & everybody couldn't hear above the noise of the machines. He snatched up a bundle of drawings and we followed him to a lecture room, where he said we might as well copy some of the drawings as no machines were vacant and no one was free to teach us anything in our workroom. So we laboriously drew a capstan lathe for about an hour and also drew several small tools. Then another teacher came in and said he wanted our room, so rather cold & hungry we trailed back to our work room, casting envious eyes at the empty tea trolley which had never visited us in the lecture room. Finally someone told us to go to a capstan lathe and the lad there would tell us something and he did – a nice little jew-boy, a friendly alien we should think, very young and a born teacher. He told us quite a bit, but hadn't got the metal material to show us very much practical. Then a bell rang and we tacked on to the back of a teacher's lecturing group over our heads, but we understood some of it, and so back to our little jew-boy where we put a ½" thread on to both ends of a metal rod. E was in the middle of hers when the bell rang for lunch, and everyone charged off – from 11–11.30. to such a lunch! – a nice canteen and well organised, plentiful food, very badly cooked. E could not eat hers, in spite of only toast & tea at 6. o'c. – sausage patty with uncooked dough pastry, elastic mashed potatoes, burnt gravy and heaps of hard green peas, followed by a huge slab of uneatable white stodge pudding and sauce. Back to our little jew-boy, rather late, but nobody seemed to notice. The machine was now out of order, so to amuse us he took us along to the Store Room, and got out some tools and showed us how they worked. Still no sign of teacher. Then a little middle-aged man like James Harcourt [*actor*] wanted to use the lathe to cut some 2" lengths of steel, so we stood and watched him for some time. Still no teacher came near us, and at the stroke of 1.30 the machine went off and everyone started clearing up and clearing off. We remained wearily patient till we were given our cards and departed, having taken 7 hours to learn what we might have acquired in one.

Wednesday 18 February
We watched 'James Harcourt' set up the capstan lathe, which was helpful, and cut off bits of metal. After a bit he let us each have a go – but E unfortunately

broke the tool – so went in search of teacher (Mr Dalton) who ground it and explained how it had happened.

So we began again, but by this time the band kept on coming off the roller and stopping the machine. Various trainees tried and failed to get it better and Miss Greasy Locks (Vivian) succeeded in getting her hand pinched between the band and the roller – but was not hurt much. Then Mr Douch (another teacher) came to help with the band and seemed to think it was a very derelict machine. By this time we had had lunch and returned. We only tried sandwiches today and they were quite good. Then someone else came round for the War Savings Prize sweep and then at 1.20 people began to tidy up because it was Pay Day. So we dismantled the tools and came away past queues of people waiting for their money.

The men trainees are all very kind and helpful and James Harcourt means well, but doesn't know enough to be much use to us and is very slow. There is a strange-looking elderly woman who seems to be rather a show piece. She walks and looks like a stage 'char', but seems a great character. She has just completed her 8-weeks course and is passing out to an aircraft factory on Monday. She says she has never wasted so much time in all her life!

Mrs Bellwood, our landlady, has been very kind in our rooms and now arranges to have the fire lit & the room done for us. She opines that tho' K may stay the course, poor E looks too delicate. We are not typical trainees anyway she says and ought to be supervisors.

Thursday 19 February
Today was an altogether different thing. We again arrived very early and hadn't long to wait before Mr Douch, after a chat with our pimp teacher, Mr Dalton, and a bit of head jerking in our direction, came and took us over as pupils. He sent Els to 'that fellow at the "shaper" who would show her how to work it' and K and Miss Vivian went off with himself. They spent the rest of the morning flushed & excited. He set them to work a hacksaw and saw through an inch rod of metal and then they played about with rules and calipers for a long time, and then went off with Mr Douch to the central lathe. Els was not quite so lucky, but learned a bit nevertheless. Her 'fellow' Geoff rapidly named the parts and controls of the 'shape' and then set to work to cut a small piece of metal in half and then make a sort of groove in one side of it. When he had finished he discovered he had made the groove in the wrong side of it and went off to another class leaving Els with a job of work to continue. But, unfortunately, the machine went wrong so she called another woman trainee to help and she spent a long time putting it right by trial & error, and it worked all right for a little and then went wrong again, and so on all the morning, but Elsie did learn something about the machine, so does not regard it as a wasted day. Kathleen & Miss Vivian and Mr Douch had a lovely time at the central lathe and seem to be quite at their ease with it. Mr Douch then gathered the new trainees round him and gave us some easy fractions and decimals which we were quite able to keep up with. Kathleen acquired great merit with Mr Douch by making a brush out of a bit of wire and a piece of cotton waste.

Friday 20 February
E & K both found that some parts of their machine seemed to be missing, so the early part of the morning was spent hunting for the missing parts and Els found that part of her machine was missing altogether and so tacked on to K and Mr Douch, who were assembling the lathe. At last E's missing piece appeared so she set to work to try and assemble her shaper and with the aid of Geoff got a fresh metal (her yesterday's work having completely disappeared) and started off 'shaping' again. K and Miss Vivian were messing about with their central lathe. We had no sooner got nicely to work when Mr Douch stopped and sent us off to the lecture room. Here quite a number of new trainees were gathered together and were addressed by one man on ARP and mumbled a welcome by the assistant manager, a dried up little horror. Then the education officer delivered a long jubation and we committed ourselves to knowing decimals, fractions and elementary geometry, but nothing of the metric system or square roots. By this time we had had 2 hours of talk and it was 11. o'c. so we went off to lunch. When we got back to our workroom we were sent off again to the lecture room where Mr Dalton took us for another two hours on tools and their uses – with many diagrams & explanations delivered so quickly that we wilted from exhaustion. It was after 1.30 by now (K & E had acquired merit by being able to decimalise $\frac{1}{64}$ – the result of prep last night!) and K & E went off to get health cards from the office.

Saturday 21 February
Quite a good and busy morning and a new little teacher man came and peered at Els' machine and we think he is the teacher who has been absent. On another visit Els nabbed him to explain about the intricacies of the machine. She has been wanting to know how the wheels go round every day, but no trainee seems capable of giving more than a monosyllabic reply to any question. However Mr Lloyd, the new teacher, explained very clearly and with thought, Els may master it in time.

Having been in 'Industry' one week we mentally review the situation. The work began pretty badly with hours of doing nothing, but since we have been set to work we have been enthralled and happy. We haven't heard one educated voice, trainees, teachers or office staff and mercifully our own Kensington voices don't seem to have excited comment. They think we are sisters because we speak alike. We think they are all an extraordinarily nice crowd and we are rapidly getting used to their abrupt and terse phraseology. If asked any question they reply in one word if possible and do not amplify at all. Looking round the groups of teacher and pupils they look exceedingly matey; for heads have to be brought close together for voices to be heard above the noise of the machines.

Mr Dalton, who seems to be the chief teacher in our room, is said to be exceedingly clever and can certainly draw diagrams quicker than a flash. He is, however, completely illiterate and can hardly talk at all. This perhaps accounts for his tremendously abrupt manner and he is certainly a man of few words.

We are shocked beyond measure at the dreadful food and think something should be done about it, because it is such a wicked waste and the trainees really need a good meal. We are surprised how little we notice the noise of the machines, and all our years of long standing have accustomed our legs to this sort of life. The other trainees moan about their feet. Our hands, unfortunately, at the end of only one week, look like the hands of mechanics, which we are sorry about.

Monday 23 February
Mr Douch was away but Mr Davies was very kind to K & Greasy Locks and taught them how to use the scriber's gauge as the chuck of their machine had been damaged. Els continued with Mr Lloyd and spent hours shaping down a block of metal in order to learn to take sufficiently fine strokes. Kathleen did grand things fitting a metal rod into a ring, which she did not quite perfect.

Tuesday 24 February
A long & tiring day and we don't like the afternoon shift. Els learnt some more from Mr Lloyd, but got very tired working the machine by hand to 'get conversant'. K and Greasy Locks spent all day fitting rings onto metal rods to $\frac{1}{1,000}$", not very successfully. Els had her machine all to herself all day. Moved into the large double bed, the small one being so cramped & hard.

Wednesday 25 February
Hateful late shift again. K was Mr Dalton's 'Golden Girl' and he spent most of the day muttering incomprehensible instructions to her, while she smiled vaguely as she could neither hear nor understand. But he set her up a lovely 'poker' for her to 'turn' for him and he gave her a private lesson in the micrometer, which she elucidated afterwards by reference to the text book. Els continued her cutting exercise and then Mr Lloyd gave the beginners a lesson on the 'mike' which K had already mastered.

Thursday 26 February
Mr Lloyd put Els to work on her old shaper again and she had a quiet 4 hours with no interruption or interference from anyone. After lunch Mr Lloyd suddenly taught her to grind tools and also to use the hacksaw, at which task she was Prize Girl. Having made a successful tool she was sent off miles away to the blacksmith's shop to have it hardened & tempered, and so finally back to work where E & Joyce Lillywhite went to work once more on the shaper. Meanwhile, K & Nelly Vivian had been underdogs on their lathe to Miss Francis, an advanced trainee, and spent the day turning Mr Dalton's poker.

After lunch Miss Francis made an elaborate-shaped rod and K and Nelly were allowed to work the machine only occasionally so had rather a dull time. In the 'lecturette' we had an elementary lesson on decimals which were quite too much for Nelly. We left at 4.30 – Els to prepare supper and K to buy the rations, but nearly all the shops were shut. Industry and civil life don't seem to combine.

K does not care very much for Miss Francis, who seems a rather self-centred and sulky young woman. When bored she sits down and reads a novel. However, she and Nelly are both passionately fond of music and both sing at concerts and both 'like the classical'. At the end of the day there was a great exchange of snaps of fiancés.

Friday 27 February
Els and Joyce Lillywhite were set to work again when the damaged tool had been repaired, but they hadn't been at it long before Mr King, an elderly Scottish teacher, took it away and set them to work on an angle iron. It was a rather slow day for Els, as the work progressed slowly, & Joyce seemed disinclined to take any intelligent interest, which was rather trying as Mr King took endless pains with them. When bored Joyce leans against the machine and smiles slowly & amiably in the direction of any man – so they, needs must, come & have a word with such a bonny milkmaid. Els didn't learn much today of the engineering, but she can do Joyce's accent and delivery quite a treat.

K and Nelly had a lovely day on the lathe, Miss Francis being out of the way on a test. They finished turning a most complicated affair and were complimented on it by teacher. They did a tremendous lot of 'mike' work to Elsie's envy. They really felt they had accomplished something by the end of the day. In the afternoon in the 'lecturette' period, there was a reshuffle of teachers and pupils – and E & K found they belonged to Mr King. He's a nice old thing and a very patient teacher tho' not perhaps quite so clear & quick as Mr Lloyd. During the day Poppa King was visited by two lustrous Russian jewesses, blonde and brunette, who came to say 'good-bye' before departing to a new job. He told E that they were the best pupils he had ever had and had completed the course in 12 weeks. Nelly Vivian is good and quick at the work – but the decimals and fractions seem to her abracadabra.

Saturday 28 February
We both got quietly on with our respective jobs and Mr King told Els that if she and K want to keep together they must learn to work the same machine. E intimated that K would not care to change her lathe for E's mangy shaper and he said it (the lathe) was the better thing to be thoroughly conversant with as it led to more, and he would see the chief instructor about it, to get us united to the same group. So E hopes to join K on Monday.

We forgot to mention that we were paid on Wednesday £2/3/- each plus 24s/- settling in allowance. We all assembled in clocking order in various workshops, and filed past 2 pay desks, where our numbers and names were called out and our pay envelopes handed to us. It felt like receiving the first earnings of one's life. Today is the end of our second week, which has gone fast, and we have enjoyed it.

We have got to know a lot more about our fellow workers. Joyce Lillywhite was a housemaid near Horsham. Nelly Vivian considers her rather babyish, which she certainly is. Then there is Perce Harvey who doesn't really like engineering at all and pines to be back as butler in Cadogan Square. He is a great snob and keeps telling us that he is not used to this sort of work. Mr King tells us that milling is the best paid and most skilled of the machine jobs and there is a large demand for them. He doesn't in the least know whether the trainees who have just come in will have the opportunity of doing the 16-week course; as Croydon closes in 8 weeks. He thinks 8 weeks will be most unsatisfactory as it is impossible to make his pupils conversant with all the machines in that time. 'James Harcourt' has left us now and gone to London.

We see Mrs Crisp (the nice girl we liked the first day) sometimes in the canteen. She says that 'Marlene Dietrich' & 'Marjorie Kahn' are very cocky. They were both shop girls, Mrs Crisp was a dressmaker. These are all fitters and they seem to spend all their time filing.

Mr Dalton, our first teacher, has now passed on to Waddon, for which we are not sorry, as we couldn't understand or hear a word he says. We did rather admire him in his lecture the other day. He was explaining at great length, the working of the micrometer and two girls at the back were chatting together. He continued through the hubbub for a second or two and then suddenly leaned over at them & said in a furious voice 'Do you know how to read the micrometer?' When they replied 'yes' he snapped at them 'Then kindly allow me to read mine' and continued the lecture in a deathly hush.

Monday 2 March
Infuriating day for both of us. Mr King has left us for another department and E and K are now both under Mr Lloyd who is so sick of all this chopping and changing that he seems unable to take any interest in anyone. Nothing has yet been said about E and K uniting on the same machine. E and Joyce went on with their shaper and K and Nelly finished their second 'cottonreel' – not very accurately. The whole work of the department was disorganised by a Tool Inspection at 1 p.m. when every tool in the place was called in for an inventory, and after being out of action for about an hour they were checked by the accountant. All the teachers seemed nearly demented rushing around for missing spanners and rulers and were very disinclined to pay any attention even to any of the trainees who had work they could get on with. K and E were pained to note that on their form 'Short Course' was written, so there seems no option of a longer one, which is rather disappointing. We feel we shall never learn anything nor get anyone to take any interest in any questions we want to ask about our future plans. Certainly the centre is not well organised.

Tuesday 3 March
K found that her machine which had been going queer the day before, was now incapable of being stopped and as it seemed extremely dangerous she reported it to Mr Lloyd who said he would put her on another machine where she spent the rest of the day. K had a beauty chorus of 4 pallid girls who did not seem to want to take turns on her lathe, and as no one gave them any work today they sat all day watching K and grumbling. Mr Lloyd was very much taken up with setting a laborious test for Perce Harvey. E and Joyce Lillywhite went on with their job, which they finished at about 3, and although it didn't look a particularly good fit Mr Lloyd seemed to think it was quite alright for an exercise.

This morning the Undoubtedly Honourable Mrs Campbell [*lady supervisor*] came into our room, and as she was concerning herself with the unemployed position of the beauty chorus at K's lathe, K thought that now was the time to tell her our troubles, so she told, and Mrs C. said she would see what she could do. She had a word with Mr Lloyd and then came over to Els and said that Mr Lloyd's instructions were that we should all learn something about each machine. Those who were intelligent and showed ability might be recommended for an extended course so really 'it is up to you girls' [*she said*] and departed with a society smile. Mrs C. really is very nice and does seem to take an interest in everyone and we hope she will take action.

Wednesday 4 March

K and Nelly learnt to bore while Els was set to get conversant with a 'planer'. This she found fairly similar to the old shaper and was soon allowed to go off to the central lathe. She was enthralled by a very good lesson on 'centring' from a little lame teacher and would have been happy to watch Gibbon working the lathe for hours. But she and K had to go to Education for 2 hours in the afternoon.

We received our 2nd week's wages today and had a visit from 'Tony' – our Mr Hyde, the ACI. He wished to meet us both and asked if we would like to do the 16-week course. We both said we would, and he said it should be arranged. We think we have to thank Mr King and the Hon. Mrs C. for this.

Nelly Vivian is really rather shocked by Elsie's little Joyce – whom she says is an outrageous little flirt. E has watched her for days, while she smiles 'cowlikely' at every man in range and gathers them all about her for a chat to relieve the tedium of industry. Nelly has vouchsafed that she considers no girl who is engaged, should ever go out with any other man and that any girl who does so must be a pretty low sort.

This was all *à propos* of the nice Irish girl, Miss O'Connor, in our room. She is engaged to a man who is now away, and goes out a good bit with 'other fellows'. She has angled for an invitation to Nelly's digs, as she has learnt that there is generally a good deal of fun going on there – with plenty of male companionship. Nelly's young man has flatly refused to have her invited as he considers she can't be a decent girl if she wants to meet other fellows when she already has one of her own. We are intrigued with these fine shades of morality and fear that few of us would pass muster. Perhaps there is something to be said for spinsterdom as it gives one a little latitude.

Perce Harvey has passed his test, which is not surprising, as Mr Lloyd did all the complicated calculations for him and all Perce had to do was to drill 6 holes.

Thursday 5 March

Met John Bailey on our way to work. He has also been promoted to the 16-week course, so we shall have a friend when we move on to Waddon. He said he had noticed that we were very keen and got on with the job.

When we got into our room there was no sign of Mr Lloyd who didn't appear all day. K and Nelly got on with their work, and Els spent 2 hours watching Gibbon fail to centre his job which he learned so successfully. However, the little lame teacher took him off it and set him to work, which Els watched all day and began her repeat of it in the last 20 minutes, so was reluctant to stop at closing time.

K and Nelly were looked after by Mr Davies, who was very kind and helpful and even complimentary. He took them, and Els tacked on, to see the grinding room as they showed an intelligent interest.

Tomorrow we must practise reading the Heighth [*sic*] Gauge, which we were shown today.

Friday 6 March
Els spent all the morning and the greater part of the afternoon on her first practical work on the lathe. She worked slowly and laboriously and by 3 p.m. the job was finished and to her delight it was found to be an exact measurement – no spare thousanths either way. Teacher was astonished and told her that if she could do exact work like this she was worth her weight in gold – especially in these days. Els forebore to mention that she had taken about 5½ hours over it!

When K and Nelly heard of the triumph they were so indignant that they were determined to do the same and eventually after about 3 hours they also got exact measurements. This was indeed necessary to their *amour propre*, as earlier in the day, in an absent-minded moment, Nelly had taken off $\frac{14}{1,000}$ of an inch where no 'tolerance' at all had been allowed and they were slightly in disgrace. They were also today given a 'real job' from the grinding department – being required to make a recess ¼" wide & ¼" deep in a marvellous slimy silver-looking bar of steel. When given it the teacher said casually 'It won't take long, will it?' but 3 hours elapsed before it was ready, though it certainly was exact.

Saturday 7 March
Another infuriating tool inventory this morning as Mr Lloyd was leaving. This again meant that very little work was done while the teachers rushed round after missing tools. K and Nelly had an exciting lesson in outside screw cutting and happily made a large six-inch screw. Els didn't have a very exciting morning tho' she learnt about tapering.

This now the end of our third week and we are still enjoying it very much – or even more. We now think that a lot can be learned in a Training Centre by those who want to learn and that a great deal of idling can be done undetected by those who haven't enough initiative to find jobs for themselves.

Today was farewell to Mr Lloyd as he is taking his red nose and sharp tongue and general air of 'Bacchus-cum-Henry Lytton' [*actor*] to the Hounslow Centre. Elsie will miss him, though his mocking speech is not generally liked. However, it will remove one embarrassment from K. She & Nelly shout indiscretions to one another through the roar of the machinery and K has lived in dread that one day the machinery will suddenly stop and she will be left screaming in the hush that follows: 'Our Mr Lloyd looks as if he has been on a blind.' Nelly went off looking so smart today in a fur coat and fur gloves. Usually she looks like a draggled film star with her white face & large red mouth and lustrous black eyes and long greasy black locks. We also dressed up smart today in order to have lunch at the Civic Restaurant.

We think that industrial workers take immense pains with their hair. There are coils and whorls in every direction. We shall certainly have to join the hatless brigade when the weather improves, as it cannot be good for hair to be kept for 8 hours a day under a stuffy little industry cotton cap.

Monday 9 March
Yet another change! We had just set up our work in the nursery and said howdy to our new teacher who replaced Bacchus Lloyd when Tony arrived and told us that we and Nelly were to go into the other classroom. So we unpacked our work, and cleaned up our machines and hung about for an hour. Then Tony came again & swept us off – clasping Nelly by the elbow all the way and calling her 'my dear'. The room we found ourselves in seemed to be Super Advanced and we felt very shy, especially Els who has only spent 2 days on the lathe. However, our teacher is a dear, a middle-aged man named McEvoy, and we are glad also to see Poppa King is there to look after us.

Nelly has had a row with her young man and has given him back his ring! It was all because he was jealous at the attention paid her by some other fellow.

Tuesday 10 March
Started off today on a different machine. The usual game with 'centring' the work. After lunch we were told we had to go off to 'Tool Grinding', so Nelly decided to play truant from school, and set off with great gusto and some success on the tools. However, she was fetched away by the Education Officer's scout, and according to her own story did as little as possible for the remainder of the education period out of pique. K had a miserable afternoon getting more and more depressed and dirtier and dirtier, and has not been so unhappy since she came here. She was praised again and told she had made a good tool. However, only in the last five minutes did she really understand what tool she was supposed to have been making! We have to spend tomorrow also in the tool department and K feels like playing truant.

Wednesday 11 March
More tool grinding, but K not so depressed as all went better today. It appears that nobody likes the grinding & everyone has to be forced to do their 'three days' hard. Elsie['s] tool was 'commended' and went into the show shelf. However, she thinks she has met her Waterloo in her present tool. Education in the afternoon – rather boring but quite pleasant to sit down.

Thursday 12 March
Began with tool grinding again until the electric lights failed. We were told they would not be repaired today so went back to our central lathe, thankfully. Mr McEvoy told us we should probably be going to Waddon in a few days time. We felt very gloomy at the prospect as we have settled in nicely in our new room and like Mr McEvoy immensely. Had a fairly successful morning on the lathe & were not quite so slow as usual, but also not quite so accurate! After lunch prepared to continue – but were sent back to the tool-grinding as the lights were mended. Els made a very good tool and was commended by Mr Harland. When she explained it had taken her hours to make it Mr Harland said that didn't

matter, as it was correct in the end. He said that trainees often get the centre a bad reputation, because when they get into the factories they rush their jobs and spoil them. It is much better to be slow than inaccurate. K is delighted with her afternoon's work, as she managed to get the teacher more or less to complete the tool for her. She showed it to him about 1½ hours later, and he did not recognise his own handiwork & told her it was OK and a well ground tool! She didn't confess and hoped this will help her get a satisfactory report on her tool-grinding course. Alas, we have one more day on the beastly grindstones. We forgot to mention that Nelly and her boyfriend have made up their quarrel. He was waiting for her when she got home on Monday night and they are now all friends again & the ring replaced.

Friday 13 March
Returned once more to tools. A long and fairly successful morning. Nelly suffered from unutterable boredom – having lost her beginner's luck, and enquired the time about every 20 minutes. Elsie again acquired merit for her tools and was told she would get 100 per cent for tools. She also repaired one of K's tools which then passed muster and will again help her report! K had to help teacher with the arithmetic and was much more ready than he was with the calculation, but of tool grinding she reckons she neither knows nor cares about. It was Black Friday when she learnt at lunchtime that there was a further session of tool-grinding in the afternoon. The luncheon interval passed in sulky grumbling by K & Nelly and the hours seemed to stretch interminably to 4.30.

At the end of the afternoon our papers were filled up to say we had completed the tool grinding course & we rushed back thankfully to Mr McEvoy to tell him to expect us tomorrow.

Elsie has quite upset Mr Harland's belief that women cannot make tools. He has told her several times that her tools are good and that women generally can't do tools. Now he says he can't make it out, as if she can do it, why can't others?

Saturday 14 March
We had a very unsatisfactory morning. Spent a lot of time with Poppa King re-grinding and hardening a tool which broke off almost at the first touch. When we came back from this we found a notice to say that we . . . were to go to Waddon on Monday so were gloomier than ever. It seems to be very unsettling for all these people to have the place closing down on them. He was pleased when we said we were sorry to leave as we had been told it was the best centre. We have now been a month in 'Industry' and rather wonder what we have learned in the time, as we have changed teachers 8 times. We have moments of feeling we have learned a great deal, but more frequent moments of realising the awful gaps there must be in our knowledge. We are told that anyway they have better machines at Waddon.

Monday 16 March
Nelly still absent. Spent a quiet morning on the lathe and were told we had to go to Waddon after lunch. Said goodbye all round to our kind teachers, and

departed with a horde of others to Waddon. Nobody seemed to know anything about us, and finally we were taken off to a building, where a little man welcomed us, and told the machine operators they were all going on night shift so could go home and come back on Tuesday night at 10 p.m.

We were glad to see that little Mrs Crisp and 'Margery Kahn' & 'Marlene' have also come to Waddon, but as they are Fitters they have gone on another shift so we shan't meet them at all.

Tuesday 17 March
We had another little troubled sleep before setting out for work at 9.30 p.m. and as the distance is short we got there about 9.45 & found no signs of life. However, we penetrated to the time keeper's office for our clocking cards . . . he took us along to the lady supervisor, a nice-looking young Irish girl. The dressing room accommodation is good, but the lavatories and wash basins poor with no hot water, the lavatories rather like loose boxes. After this we were taken to the chief instructor, who obviously wasn't expecting us, and took us off to the Nursery where we were handed over to a nice Scotchman. When K saw Teacher toying with something that looked like work for a 'shaper' she hastened to say that we had worked on the centre lathe and had done 4 weeks so he sent us off again to the CI, who then took us to another department, where we were handed over to a Mr Williams to whom we tried to explain, without much success, how much we knew. He had no machines to spare for us, but, ultimately, found a derelict old lathe and we set to work on that. The whole centre is one huge open workshop . . . roofed in with corrugated iron & glass. The different sections are divided by wooden handrails, and on night shift only one portion is lighted as only machine operators seem to work at night. The CI sits in a little glass cage up one end and before long one becomes drowsy with inhaling the breathed air of the previous shifts, as the blackout causes all the windows and doors to be shut. The machines are all packed tightly together, staggered like cars in a car park and one works one's way through the maze when going in search of equipment. The noise is not so great as at Croydon, and we shall have to be careful not to scream our indiscretions at the tops of our voices as we have been in the habit of doing.

Mr Williams set us an exercise and we laboriously slogged away at this for the rest of the 8½ hours, as we do not leave until 6.30 a.m. On the dot of midnight everyone trooped off to the canteen for tea and sandwiches a ¼ hour's break. The next break is at 2.30 a.m. when we have half an hour for a hot meal. The food is not much better than at Croydon as the caterer is the same, but the cooking is a little better. Tea is free of charge during the break, and 2 cups of this brew gave E violent indigestion for the rest of the night. We were overcome by a desire for sleep from about 2.30 onwards, and it seemed the longest night we've ever known, and this in spite of the fact that we were interested in our job. The tea trolley at 5 a.m. just revived us slightly but made the indigestion worse still.

Having been Queen Smugs at Croydon and built up for ourselves a reputation for keenness and eagerness and a desire to learn, we now find we are back at zero and it will be all to do again! K began well by commenting on how fascinating lathe work is to our teacher. He was surprised and delighted with this as he says many women consider it hard labour and only learn under protest. We are two of the only 3 women lathe workers in a section full of men. They all seem very nice & friendly.

Wednesday 18 March
We made ourselves a good meal before we started off, as we thought we had done badly for food last night, also a brew of lovely coffee to take in a thermos. This because we didn't think we could drink the indigestion tea and would need some stimulus during the night.

Not a very happy night. We don't know whether our teacher was tired, but he took no interest in us at all. We got on with one job, but the lathe seemed to be going very badly, and none of the tools seemed quite as they should be, and the work did not progress at all encouragingly – so we got gloomier and gloomier as each hour advanced, and do not feel that we shall ever learn anything. All the ex-Croydons seem miserable. Perhaps it is the effect of night shift and will improve next week, but the lack of ventilation saps our vitality. The lecture was right over our heads and adds to our depression. Everybody in our section has been there about 13 weeks, and we can't help thinking we have been placed in the wrong grade.

The section next door to us is composed entirely of girls working capstan lathes. They cause us a lot of amusement, as after about 3 hours they appear to do nothing but sit about.

Thursday 19 March
We have just read 'Night Shift', [*novel by B.I.L. Holden, published in London, 1941, set around the experiences of a woman munition worker*] a very clever book, particularly poignant to us at the moment. The authoress catches the atmosphere of gloom most marvellously. It is a most depressing picture, tho', of course, written at the time when the raids were at their height, which would make a difference. But in spite of this, we do not think it rings quite true, as our experience is that the young are gay and singing and running about even at the end of a long night. We should judge the authoress to be a middle-aged woman, and with the inevitable mental aloofness of a woman working outside her own class.

Resolved before we left to have a good meal and take sandwiches in preference to buying their beastly food. Also to have a word with our teacher and ask if we were not in too high a grade as all the others in our section have done 12 or 13 weeks. [*After a struggle, K and E and others from Croydon were allowed to join the course at a lower grade.*]

Then we all trailed back and we were put in the intermediate section, where we have an elderly instructor, who is very nice and helpful and friendly. For the rest of the night our spirits rose and we now don't think it will be so bad at Waddon after all. We spent the night preparing two pieces of metal for an elementary exercise and are rather appalled to find how desperately slow we are and how very spotty our teacher has been at Croydon. We found that 3 boys who had only been in training 3 weeks had today taken their first test. We know we couldn't have done it in the allotted 5 hours.

Our new section seems very friendly and helpful. The lads came and leant over our lathe and talked to us, and helped us change the heavy chuck and also cleared up the machine for us afterwards. They have most engaging manners. There are also 3 girls, part of a contingent of nine sent by their factory for a 6-weeks course.

The night passed much more quickly than the previous ones, though zero hour was about 4 a.m. when the lathe seems to acquire the motion of a ship and one isn't quite sure which part of it is moving. However, the trolley comes round at 5 a.m. and we sat for a few minutes and drank our coffee and biscuits. We had no 'lecturette' from our teacher, as he thinks it is a farce on night shift, and that we are better employed sitting quiet for a quarter of an hour. The discipline at Waddon is stricter than at Croydon and no one may leave their section for any purpose whatsoever without written permission from the instructor. We have not laid eyes on the lady supervisor since our first interview with her. We wonder what she does for her eight hours duty, as no one ever seems to go in the cloakroom except during the breaks.

Friday 20 March
We got 'upsides' with the square root. K, who had never done it at school, quickly understood the theory, and Els laboriously mastered the theory of it, and the method came back readily from the mists of the past, the purpose of it never having been explained in youth. At the centre we set to work, but no teacher appeared, and it later transpired that he had fallen down and cut his head on the cement. He arrived later and sat in a corner looking very shaken and white and no one dared approach to ask questions. He later retired and lay down, so we continued by trial and error for 8 hours getting more depressed as the night dragged on. We learn that the first test here has to be done in 5 hours. It would take us more like 5 days, hence our depression.

Saturday 21 March
We have now been a week at Waddon, and at present we are exceedingly depressed by it and by our own spotty knowledge & sketchy instruction.

Nelly Vivian seems to have passed out of our life and we miss her accounts of her visits to the 'pitchers' with the boyfriend.

Monday 23 March
We are on the afternoon shift this week, which all seemed much less tiring with daylight and plenty of fresh air. Our elderly teacher, Mr Powney, thoroughly deserves the description of 'lazy bugger' given him by one of our nice boys. He drifts out of the section for long spells, and when there wants nothing so much as to be left alone. This is a sad change after our nice instructors at Croydon, & very damping to our ardour. The evening passed quickly however, though we are still more than depressed. Our teacher was too lazy to give us any lecturette so we all sat round gloomily. We take off our hats to the people in the section who all seem to work very conscientiously in spite of lack of encouragement from the teacher.

Tuesday 24 March

Spent the evening doing odd jobs and an hour's prep: went off cheerfully to the afternoon shift, which seems child's play after the long and stuffy night shift. Our teacher was doing a job for the CI so we didn't see much of him as he worked quietly at his own job. 'Bert', the nicest of our lads, says his family simply won't believe him when he says teacher doesn't bother to teach anything. We got on with our job quite happily and were not so depressed, though Els had a mishap at the end and cut off several 'thou' more than she should have, and finished up by moving a wrong lever and taking off a great cut and pushing the belt of the pulley also slightly cutting her finger. Not as ashamed as perhaps she should have been. We actually had a lecture from old Powney – the first since we have been there.

Wednesday 25 March

Hadn't been long at it before we had to line up in clock order to get our pay. This took some time, as we couldn't find our place, and after this we went to see the placing officer to make sure that they understood that we were to be placed together in a factory, as the Croydon officer had promised this when we enrolled. His tone was that the Croydon officer was rash to promise something he wouldn't have to fulfil, and he would promise nothing, though said he would do his best for us. This is rather unsatisfactory as we have no intention of going separately, and we think it may be best to write to the Manager about it, as in Interviews in Industry they have a way of talking through you and not listening to your case at all.

We were told that after break we were to go to Education, so after a nice sandwich meal out of doors we made our way to 'school' in company with about 30 others. The education officer is a dear little man, kindly and keen & a welcome change from the ed. officer at Croydon. He set us a test of 16 sums working up to square root and areas of Os. We were delighted to find that we could more than hold our own in this company and were finished long before the others and had an additional problem set, so were elated for the first time since we have been in Waddon.

Returning to our section we found the hour lecture was in progress and Mr Powney explained to us the Vernier protractor. We asked anxiously what we had missed and were told by the other trainees that they had learned no more than we had done in the last two minutes. If our lazy old Powney doesn't lecture during the ¼ hour lecturette we are going to ply him with questions so that he has to lecture in self defence.

Thursday 26 March

Elsie's birthday. Nothing much happened in Industry and we actually had a lecture from Lazy Powney. We finished our exercise which had taken us a week to do, and Powney never even troubled to look at it, but he and we signed a paper to say we had done it. He set us another exercise – what encouragement for the beginner! The funny little ed. officer (whom we learn was an ex-carpenter and prisoner of war in the last war – we think it likely he learned his mathematics then) came and stared at us over our lathe and barked 'Twenty each – You're quits'. When we asked him what it meant he said 'all twenty sums right – you were the 2 best' and departed.

Friday 27 March

Powney actually gave another lecture. We think perhaps that as our boys are due to go up into another section, he is apprehensive that they may not know all that they should and is making up for lost time.

Saturday 28 March

Started work again at 12.30 to finish at 5.30 p.m. Nothing very exciting happened in the centre, but we do feel we are learning something, even with so little encouragement from our teacher. They closed all the windows and blacked out long before they need, so K began to feel somewhat sick before the end, as on night shift.

We have now finished our second week at Waddon and have found it much less exhausting than night shift. Owing to our taking our own sandwiches and eating them out of doors, we have not got to know so many people as at Croydon, though we have got to know some of our ex-Croydonites better. We have an occasional crack [*chat*] with John Bailey.

'Lil' & 'Eileen' & 'Ireen' are our three little girls from the factory in our section. Lil is devoted to work, and is evidently the perfect daughter. She is cursed with the worst complexion we have ever seen, but is a very nice little soul. Eileen is like a small version of Dora Judd [*actress?*]: dapper, neat, brisk and saucy. 'Ireen' is as thin as a rail & as muscularly strong as a lion. She rushes about with heavy metal chucks as though they weighed nothing. She does everything at the run, and her stringy little arms flail about at her work. She looks a little peaky by the end of the day, but by the time she has put on a fresh layer of make-up she looks as spry as ever she did and is ready to run away from work in her trousers and high heeled shoes.

We think the spirit of the place is not so good as Croydon, though the trainees work harder and gossip less, possibly due to the stricter discipline of the students. The staff on the other hand compare most unfavourably. The majority of them appear to be dispirited and bored & able to be lazy if they want to. At Croydon, Tony used to range round from shop to shop all day long and always noticed if teachers or pupils were late or absent, whereas this man does not come round. We have heard several students complain of their teachers and have only heard three admired.

The chief instructor at Croydon was very nice and everybody liked him, whereas Mr Simpson, the Waddon CI, is a horror.

Monday 30 March

Got up at 5 a.m. to be at work by 7 a.m. Got on with our work and halfway through the morning Bert and Fred were moved up to the next grade, so that left a vacant machine. Els asked if she could transfer to this, so now we have a lathe each, which is much more absorbing than taking it in turns. The lazy old

Powney said he was feeling 'Mondayish' so wouldn't give us a lecture – so K maliciously asked him intelligent questions and before he knew where he was he was lecturing away gaily in self defence. Finishing work at 2 p.m. makes the day seem almost like a half-holiday.

Tuesday 31 March
K in the 'Slough of Despond' [*Pilgrim's Progress*] as nothing went right. Els getting on very slowly. The 'lazy old Bugger', as he is conversationally referred to by our nice boys, never came near us excepting when fetched in desperation by Kathleen and he didn't really help her at all.

Lil, the most friendly and the plainest of the girls in our section, was in a towering rage. She could get no help out of Powney either and was 'using language'. She is such a good little thing that she must have been far gone.

Wednesday 1 April
All were made April Fools by Irene, which amused us rather, as she usually never bothers to speak at all. We suggested she should make wicked old Powney a Fool but she said, very rightly, she was afraid he wouldn't take it and would probably report her to the CI for insubordination!

K found on arrival that her lathe was broken so was unable to work on it all day. Els finished her job at 10 a.m. and when she asked for a new exercise Powney said there was no metal of the required size and just walked away. She asked him twice more about it and he finally got an old piece of metal, but did not arrange to have it sawn off for her, so Els did no more work that day. However she gave K her lathe and K had a successful time 'roughing down' her piece in heavy cuts and felt she was really learning something. We had a lecture on 'speeds' of metals in which the old man took ¾ hour to say what could have been taught in 5 minutes. For the rest he just gossiped about factories.

Thursday 2 April
K's lathe mended about 10 a.m. and she got on with her exercise. She thought she was doing it well and quickly and accurately, but old Powney discovered the work had 'a taper' and he was very scathing. K who had been very cock-a-hoop all the morning, was then cast into gloom and went about declaring she was going to give up the whole course. Els had also had a very bad morning and could get no help from old P so she wanted to give it up too! So they made a pretty pair. We thought of going to the CI and saying that we think we are 'unteachable'. And if the CI should say he had had no complaint from our instructor, we should then reply that he couldn't possibly know as he never teaches us anything nor examines our work! Last week old P spent 2 days engrossed in making a 'sleeve' on the only good lathe in the room and another whole day making some special tool and couldn't bother about any of the trainees. This week he has spent 2 days almost exclusively teaching Eileen screw-cutting and the rest of us can just go hang. K has made rather [*good?*] friends with the queer, lazy, sad-looking teacher in the next section.

'Muriel Miller' and the 'Soldier's Wife', two ex-Croydon trainees who have had a very nice time in the Waddon Nursery, are now blaspheming in our section like everyone else. They can't get Powney to help them or take any interest in them. They say pathetically that they suppose they won't learn any more now.

Friday 3 April
Elsie spent the whole 7 hours trying to get a taper corrected in her exercise. She almost succeeded by the end of the day, but then of course the machine will be dismantled so she will have to start all over again tomorrow! She wishes she had gone straight into a factory on repetition work, where the fact that she is abnormally slow and stupid would not be remarked by her. K had quite a good day and finished her exercise. Old Powney never looked at it, but gave her another piece of metal for another exercise. She and Lil were held up for the lack of a drill-chuck and waited about 1½ hours for it. Finally, Evans went round trying to find one for them and one was forthcoming at last, about ¼ hour before the end of the morning. Old Powney spent the whole day with Eileen, teaching her how to make a large bolt & screw and finally helped her make a lovely little centre punch which he took away and hardened for her. He gave no attention whatsoever to anyone else, but had a lovely day with his darling Eileen. K insisted that he should come and look at her new work for half a minute which he did, and then drifted back again immediately.

Saturday 4 April
Again a very depressing slow morning. Elsie in black despair and more depressed than she had been before. K got on alright but the old beast took no interest in either of us except to talk to K as if she [*was*] a half-wit when she asked him a technical question about her work.

Tuesday 7 April
On night shift again and a better night as the ventilation was improved. André, the funny little Frenchman who has lately joined our sector, does not let Powney get away with his discouraging teaching but argues with him vociferously. He also caresses the hand when micrometers pass from one to another and gives us pokes of amusement when we hold indignation meetings about the 'lazy old bugger'.

Wednesday 8 April
Had no sooner arrived than we saw Tony's face in the CI's cage, so our spirits rose. All the Croydon trainees seemed delighted that he has come and hope he will be on our shift permanently. K said to Mr Powney that we were glad to see Mr Hyde, and he replied, 'oh! do you like him, he has come with a bad reputation'. K said very smugly 'he always notices if you are not where you ought to be.' Tony came into our section several times and had a long chow [*chat*] with K's Mr Evans, and old Powney certainly did a bit more work, and came to each of us unasked once. But his visit to Elsie was too much for him and he clasped his head melodramatically and complained of head-ache and was not good for much else, and couldn't rise to a lecturette. But we have high hopes that Tony may persecute him into action.

Thursday 9 April

The workroom rather stuffier tonight, and our good day's rest availed us nothing as we were in black despair by the end of the shift. Kathleen spent a long time setting up her work, and when she started the machine found that some internal part of the machine was missing, so all her work was wasted. All this while Els was plodding on in her melancholy ox-like way with her work. The only amusing thing in the evening was when Tony arrived to look at K's broken machine and he and Powney hung over it with her for some time. He had already asked K in front of Powney how 'we ladies' were getting on, and she had said in a superficial society way – 'We are enjoying it very much, thank you'. K said 'It isn't nearly so nice as your place at Croydon', and he agreed that it was a great pity it had closed down. He also came spying round during the lecturette, and found a line of chattering females sitting at the far end of a bench from Powney who was mumbling something about tools to the two new men.

K was moved on to another lathe, and spent the whole of the rest of the time failing to centre her work. Els was also gloomy, but managed to get a little done in the end.

Reeny became expansive tonight and told me how Eileen is Powney's favourite and he never teaches anyone else. It's just the same with the foreman at the works. He opens her pay packet and puts in extra wages!! We can hardly believe this story.

Friday 10 April

Rather fitful sleep. We lay laughing hysterically at the poor spiritless things we have become, and when we found we couldn't sleep any more, got up and went out.

Not such a bad night, though K was enraged with Powney for not helping at the crucial moment which would have enabled her to finish her work during the shift.

Monday 13 April

Work went quite well today. Powney was disinclined for anything but to tell us how ill he felt with incipient bronchitis, and he departed at 7. o'c. to some engagement, so we were left to Mr Evans for the rest of the evening. K was told she would have to do her test tomorrow, and that all our section would have to do them by the end of the week, which is causing rather a flutter.

During the interval we chatted to the little Frenchman André, who, we learn, used to be a jockey; it took him 5 weeks to get to England after the Fall of France and he wants to stay as short a time in Waddon as possible so that he may get down to the real business of making shells at once.

Tuesday 14 April

Went to Waddon where the first person we saw outside was Nelly Vivian whom we were delighted to see. She has had a marvellous time at Croydon being the only central lathe operator with 7 teachers to give her their undivided attention. She seems to have learnt a tremendous lot – and Mr Hyde said she must finish the 16- week course so he obviously thinks her good.

K and Eileen had to do their test today. Eileen found her lathe all ready for her, but K had to dismantle hers before she could begin. When she had, with difficulty, got the 3-jawed chuck on, she found that part of the 'steady' was missing. This involved taking off the chuck, & putting on another and starting all over again. K nearly in tears by this time as Eileen was well away. Powney, mercifully, was away ill and the whole atmosphere of the section was lightened with Mr Evans in charge. He helped K prepare her work and said she could have extra time on account of her false start. All went well during the test and when once set up seemed to progress pretty rapidly and was finally completed in under the required 5 hours. The only mishap was when the 'traverse' suddenly got jammed and took a gouge out of one portion, but fortunately not much. Eileen also had trouble on one occasion, but the finished article looked extremely good. We had lunch with Nelly out of doors and she kept us amused with tales of Croydon. She seems to have had a *succès fou* [*big hit*] with all the instructors, and Mr McEvoy made her a ring and Mr Heggity made her a cigarette lighter-cum-watch case – all most beautifully made.

Wednesday 15 April

K had no work to do today, but Els practised hard on a piece of old metal and felt she had learnt something. The old Beast was back again, saying he still felt ill, but he took no notice of anyone, and the usual state of gloom descended again on our Depressed Area. He was surprised to learn that Eileen and K had done their tests, but never asked K how she had got on, or made any friendly comment.

K lost her pink card and there was a fearful to-do about this. After several interviews with Tony and Mr Varrow, who both seemed to think it was a matter of national importance and would cause an inquest by the Manager and possibly Questions asked in the House, the card finally was found in another section, so all was peace.

Thursday 16 April

Els got on with her practice and learnt quite by chance, late in the day, that she was to do her test tomorrow on a machine which she had never worked. She did manage to get ½ hour on it at the end of the shift, but did not get very conversant. Lil and Rene were the victims 'on test' today. Rene got on fast, in a blazing temper with Powney who interfered and barked at her that everything she did was wrong. However, most of the time he was out of the sector altogether and took no interest in either of them. Poor Lil really is the slowest worker in the world, and at the end of the shift her test was done by the skin of her teeth and desperately inaccurate in places. She is a strange mixture of extreme caution in action and extreme inaccuracy in measurement. However, she was delighted to have it finished, and was all smiles by the end of the shift, though we doubt if the test will pass muster.

The days of 'no lectures' seem to have departed with the advent of Tony, and Powney obviously keeps a wary eye out for him. In the middle of Lil's test he suddenly taught her an entirely new method of 'shouldering' with the gauge.

This ensures absolute accuracy of length. It was the first we had seen or heard of any such method, and later when K said to Powney that she wished she had known of it before doing her test, his only comment was 'Mr Evans should have shown you!!!'

To give the old B his due he did give a very good and clear lecture on the Vernier scale today. The best we've heard from any of the teachers, which only shows he could be good if he wasn't so lazy.

Friday 17 April
Els and André did their test today. André spent the greater part of the time getting his work parallel and didn't finish his test by the end of the shift, so is to finish tomorrow. Els had a number of mishaps, '& buggered it all up' pretty completely so she was not very proud of her effort, and is still more convinced, if she needed more convincing, that she is the squarest peg in the roundest hole.

Saturday 18 April
The whole section had a completely idle air as the Old B gave no one any work to do. Everyone walked round chatting and only André got on & finished his test. E and K decided to teach themselves 'drilling' so got hold of some metal and went to work on a lathe and taught themselves a good deal.

Monday 20 April
Not so depressed today. We got on with work by ourselves, and taught ourselves 'tapering'. Tony came up and had a few words and asked us how we progressed. We said it was very slow and he promised to lend us a book. We explained that we never knew the real reason why things went wrong and he said that the instructor was there to tell us these things! K made an almost audible giggle. Old Powney was quite sunny today & smiled amiably when Violet Belton broke one [*of*] his tools. He always seems pleasanter when someone has a mishap. We suppose it sets up his *amour propre* [*self respect*]. He spent most of the day either away from the section altogether or else making a special tool on the best lathe.

Tuesday 21 April
Set to work to teach ourselves some more when Eileen came rushing to us with 'The order for the release'. Six of us are to leave Powney to go up to the next section, so we dismantled our work and hung about for ½ hour, grins of delight chasing one another across our faces, while the less fortunate congratulated with heartfelt sympathy and hoped that some new trainees would come in very soon to release them.

Eileen and Irene and Audrie went off to Mr Tooley, while K and E and Lil went to Mr Williams, shepherded there by Tony who murmured 'Are you happier now?' and departed smiling wickedly.

We spent our day mainly watching Nelly Vivian who is in this section. She teases Mr Williams and is generally beloved. We don't think her knowledge is quite so remarkable as all her tales led us to believe. She appears to be quite a good operator, but we doubt whether she understands the theory of what she is about.

Lil got a lathe and set to work with help from Bert, whom we learn to our amazement is 43!

We had a rather sardonic lecture from Mr Williams, but K acquired merit,
because she was able to explain to him how she arrived at her answer when he
posed an arithmetical problem at her. Mr Williams has a most amazing manner.
His accent is difficult to understand and he questions every statement you make
to shake your confidence in your own assertion. However, he is really pleased if
you are unshaken as K was in the end. Just before the end we got a lathe and
Mr Williams finished a job of work while we watched him.

Wednesday 22 April
We set to work on a job and got on alright. Had a lecture which made us resolved
to buy a book on trigonometry. Nellie heard to her disgust that she has to do her
first test tomorrow, but Mr Williams said 'Never mind, I'll do it for you.'

Thursday 23 April
We finished our job, but every tool we wanted was always in use by somebody
else, and we had to wait for it. Tony came round on 'Anti-litter' campaign and
everyone rushed round removing bits of rag & spare parts and making
everything tidy and inconvenient for work. We were told that distinguished
visitors were coming and expected Churchill or the Little Princesses [*Elizabeth
and Margaret*] at least, but nobody arrived.

Nelly Vivian began her test, and was as sulky as a spoilt child about it. She
hardly made any attempt to do it herself, and gaped about while
Mr Williams did the first part and Bert did the second. She said she had messed
it up. But we don't know whether this was really true.

Friday 24 April
Not a very good day for us as we seemed to get on very slowly. Nelly Vivian
completed her test, most of which was Mr Williams's own unaided work, but as it
neared completion Nelly seemed to get more proud of it! She is a queer one!

Gloom and indignation reign once more with us, because this afternoon our
test marking papers came into the section and we found on prying into them
that E had 80 per cent, Lil 80 per cent (and we feared she was a certain failure)
and K only 75 per cent. This was a staggerer as K had been pretty well pleased
with her effort and Els had thought hers dire, so the marking seemed a little
odd. On prying further we discovered that there was no sort of resemblance
between the measurements done by the trainee inspectors & our own measuring
of them. Furthermore, K had been debited with an enormous error in a part of
the work which was supposed to have been left untouched. We were fogged by
this, and as K had heard Mr Williams say that 75 per cent was bad she was cast
into gloom and told Mr Williams that the report wasn't accurate. He said that the
tests are a farce anyway and nobody bothers about them. K, flushed with rage,
continued to bother about it all the rest of the time, and finally went over to her
darling Mr Evans for sympathy. He was astonished at her 75 per cent and said he
would enquire into it if she liked, but she said no. He says all the marking is

chaotic at present, and it is because the trainees do it. The teachers have given up complaining and only make a blaze if somebody actually fails. The other day a dud piece of work came back marked 100 per cent – he says. One more unsatisfactory feature of the Training Course!

Saturday 25 April
Another slow morning, everything we looked for disappearing, but it was a rather amusing morning nevertheless, because Mr Williams found that our work on our lathe would be an illustration of the arithmetical problem he had discussed in a lecture, so we all went off together with paper and pencil to work it out for ourselves, and Mr Williams suddenly found that though he could arrive at the answer he couldn't make out or explain how he had come by it, and even then it was wrong, so he departed by himself to puzzle it all out again. We joined him every now and again and poured over his work and made bright suggestions and finally poor old Els was able to hit on a solution.

This is the end of our tenth week, and we are more cheerful and can survey the scene again. The chief event of the week is our dear little teacher, Mr Williams. He is a tiny little man, 36 years old, with a sarcastic tongue tempered by an endearing smile. He drifts round the place and sees how everyone is getting on, which is more than old Powney ever did. 'Well, ducks, what do you want?' he said to K the other day when she approached him with a questing look. He looks ill, tired and exhausted. We are getting fond of Mr Willlams and dearly love his explanation 'Like So' which interlards his demonstrations. Today when he came round to our lathe, K said she wanted to move a certain screw. He paused and said wearily, 'That, dear, is a nut!' We have said goodbye today to Eileen, Reenie and Lil who are returning to their own factory.

Monday 27 April
Night shift this week, and we got on somewhat slowly.

Mr Williams told us he had been to see a factory where they do not like trainees. He took umbrage at this, and says that the quality of the work at the factory was bad, and no trainee would be allowed to pass such work in a training centre.

Tuesday 28 April
The book on trigonometry arrived. Felt very 'unworkish' when we arrived. Mr Williams showed us a letter criticizing the Training Centres which he had had published in an Engineering paper. We thought it was a very good effort and said so. Then ensued a long discussion on the impossibility of getting anything altered in the Government Scheme. Any suggestions had to be made through the next man senior to you and so on, and by the time they reached anyone high enough up to make any alterations, the matter was too small-beer for him to concern himself with it. So it all started all over again. A terrible indictment of the Civil Service. 'Now you come for a walk with me and I'll show you some-thing,' said Mr Williams, and we trotted off after him into the gloom of a distant part of the shop where he showed us six milling machines partially constructed.

These had been made by Mr Williams and his then section, and were the successors to six more which he had also made and sent out into production.

The whole scheme had caused a row amongst the other instructors who said it was not possible to 'produce' and train students at the same time. Hence, these machines had sat there for 6 months getting dustier and dustier & some of the parts broken and practically nothing more done to them. All very disheartening to Mr Williams in view of the scarcity of machine tools. We fully agreed with Mr Williams, that the Training Centre should go on production as it would do away with the feeling so many of the trainees have that they are simply wasting time & material. It would also make the instructors feel they were doing a more worthwhile job. So many of them seem bored & dispirited.

K and E started their second test but didn't get very far with it, as Mr Williams arrived with another gas-pipe to be repaired which interrupted us badly. Nelly was full of tales of Mr Williams' highly-coloured past most of which we don't believe.

Wednesday 29 April
Sleeping very badly this week. We get to bed about 8 a.m., but usually wake up about 10 a.m. and lie tossing for the rest of the time, so we are now getting more and more exhausted as the week goes on. A questionnaire came round the machine operators asking if they would prefer to do night shift for 4 weeks at a stretch. Most people emphatically negatived this suggestion, so we don't expect there will be any change.

We both did a little more to our tests with many interruptions and delays. The main excitement of the evening was over poor Nelly who had failed her first test owing to taking too long over it! She was hauled up before the CI and Assistant Manager. There was a lot of head-shaking and fuss and she came back very red and flustered. We had considered that Nelly had behaved very badly over her test, like a sulky child and we think perhaps it is just as well that she hasn't got away with this perverse behaviour. The actual work was well done and she had got 85 per cent, which was not surprising, as Mr Williams had done most of it for her.

Thursday 30 April
Again slept fitfully and went to the centre very tired. K got on with her test, very slowly and making every possible miscalculation due to tiredness. She finally gave up an hour before the end, as she could neither see nor think and thought she would be certain to 'bugger it all up' if she continued. So we drifted about the section for the rest of the time doing nothing. Little Williams gave us no help at all, in spite of the stories that he does all your test for you and spent all his time with Fat Fred, who was in a way about a rather difficult job. At the end Williams announced that we should both have to finish our tests tomorrow. Els was so tired that she was contemplating absenteeism for Friday night, but supposes she will have to go through with her test now.

Little Mr Williams had an outburst at the end of the lecture. He felt he was stuck and that no one in the section was progressing at all. He felt thoroughly disheartened both with himself and with us! We felt awfully sorry for him, but thought it was a pity he told us all this as it made everyone feel a dud and most unloved.

Friday 1 May
Slept slightly better today and went off full of nervous anticipation about the tests. K hadn't much more to do to hers, but E had a lot and was in a nervous flutter. She had to keep on reminding herself that it was vanity alone which made her nervous and fear of being proved the fool she doesn't like to think she is. This produced a state of calm which helped to keep the head clear for calculation and the hand steady, the former never a strong point with poor Els. K got on well with her test, with the aid of Mr Williams' moral support, and Tubby Davey hanging over her all the time and making her frightfully nervous. However, he got so despairing at the way she 'nibbled off' in thou's that he finally removed himself. He told K that the test marking was incredible. He finished his test 1½ hours under the time allowed and Powney measured it all up for him and pronounced it accurate in every measurement to a 'thou'. He therefore expected to get 100 per cent. But no – only 85 per cent was given. K then told her sad story and also how E had, to her certain knowledge, taken off .015 too much in one measurement, as she misread the gauge in the bad light, but though the error was detected by the inspector-trainees they were unable to do the necessary subtraction sum so she was credited with more marks than she was entitled to. However, in common with everyone else, we no longer have any conscience about tests. E got on steadily with her test, slowly, but with extreme accuracy. At the crucial moment Mr Williams came to help, as she too had sunk to nibbling nervously.

Our tests having had to be spread over more than one shift – owing to the shortage of machines, much calculation was necessary to discover how long we really had taken. Mr Williams said he was going to cut down the actual hours owing to waste of time waiting for tools etc. He said he didn't want a repetition of the Nelly Vivian fiasco. He said, very bitterly, that she certainly had taken 9 hours for her test, and had agreed to this when he signed her paper and in fact said she didn't care if he put down '3 weeks'. However, as soon as any questions were asked, she rounded on him and it was 'all his fault.' He is obviously as sick as mud over it all. K told him she thought N had behaved like a child over the whole test. Williams certainly credited E with a shorter time than she really took and as we consider the whole test system a farce we accept this without demur. Someone rather amusingly said that they thought E had better start her third test now so as to be quite sure of finishing it before she went out 5 weeks hence.

This being the end of the week we take stock of our new situation. We like our section immensely and the whole lot of them are extraordinarily friendly. We also like Mr Williams very much in spite of his moody temperament. We have watched this little man with interest ever since we came into his section for a couple of days at the beginning of our Waddon training. He seems to us to look more & more miserable and he stares into space with a look of utter dejection. When teaching he presents his subject in a sarcastic manner and then suddenly his face lights up with an impish smile and he says something completely disconcerting – irrelevant and amusing. In the lectures he fixes his beady blue eye on the one sitting immediately in front of him and delivers the entire lecture, questions and answers, to him or her. For about 3 days this was poor K, & as she became exhausted by the strain and hypnotised by the eye; she has changed her seat and finds it much more restful. We now take it in turns to occupy the central seat.

Bert says that all the lectures seem to be aimed at some error of his during the shift, but we tell him that this is just a guilty conscience which we all share. Bert we hope to retain as a good friend after we leave as we like him immensely. He is the sunniest, best-tempered little man we have ever met – looks 25 and is 43. He showed us a picture of his charming daughter aged 3.

Fred looks 18 and is 27. He is a thick-necked lout and a hard swearer. He appears to be having an affair with a hard faced little bitch in the section opposite. We gather she has left her husband on Fred's account, although they have only known one another about 2 months; she shocks dear Bert with her too intimate conversation with Fred. This pair is the only evidence of 'lubadubs' amongst the trainees that we have seen – although we were told darkly that there were 'goings on' amongst the trainees 'something shocking'. On night shift one bumps into Fred and his girl locked in a bear-like hug just outside the back door. As there is always a stream of trainees going out to the cloakrooms in the interval, they must be considerably bumped, but it seems to make no difference to them.

Ronny Davey (Tubby) is the Prize Boy of the section. He is 18 and weighs about a ton and looks 25. Is enormous, like Dickens' Fat Boy. He is extremely good at the work and Mr Williams thinks the world of him. Then there is Bob – a dear little man aged 57 – with a lovely Cockney humour. We think that our Nelly is in a bad way with her swollen legs. Her Mum swept down like a wolf on the fold last week and said she must return home. Nelly seems in holy terror of her Mum and she certainly sounds a tartar. It amuses us frightfully that anyone aged 29 could be so scared of their parents.

Our section is imbued with a very simple humour. One night last week we were very tired & dragged ourselves wearily home. Our shopping bags seemed to weigh a ton. When we emptied them we discovered odd lengths of scrap metal, – so no wonder! We suspected Nelly of this simple little joke so presented her with the metal as a birthday present. She was astonished at the gift – as it was nothing to do with her – but told us it had been done by our dear little cockney Bob. So today I persuaded Tubby to fill Bob's overcoat pockets with metal. But we have since discovered that Bert was the culprit – so await retribution from Bob.

Monday 4 May

Very stuffy today as the main doors were not open. We got on with a job of work set by Mr Williams to make some bolts and nuts to fit to some of the lathes. Quite a nice job though we felt rather tired and disinclined for work.

Our poor Nelly leaves us today for good. She saw a specialist on Saturday, and has got something wrong internally and will probably have to have an operation. The poor girl was in an awful way about it and evidently felt the indignity of the examination very acutely. We have urged her to get another opinion before having any vital organ removed and have promised to get a name from Uncle Buzzard. She is so illiterate and so 'het up' anyway that we think she may not have completely understood the doctor's advice. We shall miss Nelly very much as we like her immensely. She is a most extraordinary mixture, looking like a tart, but with a tremendously puritanical upbringing and outlook. She is shocked by so many things that we think nothing of at all. She was horrified today at over-hearing some low comment by Mr Williams (to another man) about the bulging contours of some female visitor who passed down the shop. The only thing that shocks us about Mr Williams is when he spits on the floor.

We said 'goodbye' to Nelly with fond farewells, and promised to keep in touch.

Tuesday 5 May
A quiet day. We got a lathe each and K was set to cut the screws while E got on with turning the pins. Mr Williams looked gloomier than gloomy. Everybody got on steadily, and two of our late Powney companions came up to the section, and Bob went to the Placing Officer and off to look for a job. In the lunch interval we ate a succulent lettuce at 1 o'c looking out over the aerodrome and the ruins of Bourjois scent factory and watching the soldiers drill.

Wednesday 6 May
Everyone felt idle and hung about talking at first. E had a dud day and everything that could slow up her naturally slow methods happened. K did one screw entirely unaided and was taken off the job and given something else to do, so Els will have to do the screws for the next few months, if ever she gets the work set up in time to begin. K got quietly on with the job. We lay out on the concrete top of an air raid shelter again for our lunch break. Wednesday is the day for the long lecture and Mr Williams' lecture was more discursive than technical. He answered the complaints that trainees make (ourselves amongst them) that we spend a lot of the time learning things we shall probably never have to use afterwards, by saying that nobody ever knew what we might be called upon to do as in an examination where one acquires masses of information and can only be questioned upon a very small part of it.

He said he would never really expect a trainee to have to do trig., but the other day a trainee went to a job, and it was the first thing they asked. Similarly, with logarithms and screw cutting on which last so much time is spent.

The rest of the lecture was given up to telling us the sort of work we might have to do – the problems involved in going on production at the centre (which both teachers and trainees would think was more worth while), and the troubles that highly-skilled men had had until the armaments programme began – less than £3.0.0 p.w being the usual and you had to go for that 'cap in hand, and carrying your own bag of tools to do the employer's work, or you don't get the job and there were many others ready to step into it if you complained.' His own father and many of his friends suffered in this way after the last war and he doesn't think that 'They' will dare let it happen again. Even now, he says skilled men are working on capstan lathes, which any fool girl could work, because the basic wage of the expert setter cannot be increased, whereas a skilled, quick man on a capstan lathe can make quite a lot of money with production bonus. He says you can't blame them for sticking to those well-paid jobs when you know what they have been through in the past, though the country is crying out for skilled men.

Muriel Hansford told us that she overheard her instructor going for Powney because the trainees who come up to him from Powney's section know nothing.

We see old Powney roaming round the place looking very happy, presumably because his back is towards his section. He seems to have a herd of men at the moment. We actually heard a good word for him today. Tubby says it hurts him to hear Powney so much criticised as he liked his section very much. Of course Tubby is a very good trainee, and so is no test of teaching at all and can safely be left to teach himself.

Thursday 7 May

When we arrived today we found that our section, together with 3 other MO sections, had to go to the ARP lecture and incendiary bomb practice. K & E and one other woman were the only females among a horde of men and we had a lecture and demonstration with the usual air of unreality of these things. The many war reserve police were exchanging anecdotes of the real thing. The firemen who instructed us rather appalled us by telling us that all the fire extinguishing appliances in the centre were unfit for use by now. But within the week they are being put ship-shape and an ARP officer is being appointed.

We have been astonished that we never have any air raid practice here as at Croydon. We stood out in the blazing sun for 1½ hours and then went in for a cup of tea or yellow crystal lemonade which we now drink to our astonishment.

Tony had come round fussing on his cleanliness campaign and Williams said bitingly that if he wanted the lathe cleaned he might get the lubricating pump repaired at the same time. So this was done and Els' lathe was put out of action for the rest of the shift and she drooped over K's lathe for the rest of the session and had time to gape round the workshop which was quite interesting, though her yesterday's depression continues. K got on happily with her job. Mr Williams had a frightful day preparing to set up Fred's test. Instructions coming in from other sections with odd jobs for 'George' to do at once. Bert's lathe going out of action and a general fradge [*confusion*].

In the lecture George made another mistake which K was happy to point out to him and he apologised most magnificently as this, strangely, had not been one of his 'creative mistakes.'

Tonight an air raid alert, but the all clear followed in about an hour without incident.

Friday 8 May

Three more ex-policemen trainees came up from Powney's section. Els had to move onto another lathe and spent ages getting filthy changing the gear wheels for screw cutting. However, all was satisfactorily done at last and she spent a quiet day cutting screws, which she found very fascinating. K had a policeman mate put to work with her and they together had a fairly successful day. He has had 3 awful weeks with Powney and came up full of black despair and ready to hate the whole thing. He found a very sympathetic audience in K and they then happily exchanged gloomy anecdotes of the wickedness of the Lazy Old Bugger and Life in the Depressed Area. The policeman then went off for a chow with his friends and K who was wrought-up by these tales of Powney's iniquities, spat it all out on Mr Williams who received it in astonishment, though he said he always thought there was something wrong with that section, as all the trainees who come up from Powney are 'so dashed miserable and take about a fortnight to raise a smile'. When K told him Powney had only lectured to the policeman on gardening and the right time to plant potatoes, he received it with astonished comments of 'Naow! Go on!'. When K had spilt a good bibful she had a sudden excess of school-girl *esprit-de-corps* and said 'Oh! Mr Williams, I oughtn't to be saying all this to you.' But 'Gawge' said 'That's all right, ducks, I shan't let it go any further'.

Today we also had visitors, a lady and gentleman who hung over K's lathe. K was so surprised not to be treated as part of the machinery (which is the usual industry manner) that she immediately became 'Mrs Church-Bliss' daughter' and did the honours of the house with charm and society smiles.

Today we had a reply from Uncle Buzzard and sent his letter and advice on to Nelly. We think that the notepaper 'From Sir Farquhar Buzzard' will give Nelly great cause for gossip that 'we are related to a Lord'!!

Poor 'Gawge' had to go on fire watch tonight. He said it wasn't too bad, but depended who you were on with. If on with the office staff they wanted you to spend all your time filling in forms; if you went with 'the Boss' he expected you to walk round the buildings; and if you were on with the instructors they just wanted you to go along to the Propellor [*local pub*]. Els wondered 'if you were in with Gawge' what he wanted you to do but forebore to ask.

Saturday 9 May

K and her policeman got on with their job. K finding she was somewhat edged out by him. Williams spent the greater part of his time doing a job on the best lathe, overseeing the nice middle-aged policeman who has joined our section.

Els spent her usual hours preparing the lathe for a job, only to be given a completely different job, which necessitated more hours altering the machine. Mr Williams actually did the turning for her, so she set to work again to set the machine up once more for her original job. At last she got the necessary tool and after some reflection about how to fit it to the work, she set off, but it was not altogether successful as she had not really set it correctly in the tool post. Another black day for poor old Els. However, she found a friend in Bert, whose usual amiability had gone sour on him. He had only drilled 'one lousy little hole' in his test all the morning. He couldn't get Gawge to take any interest in him and had wasted his day. He thinks the lot of the gentle is hard – 'If you are as common as mud, and blaze around like Fred, everybody attends to you'. The little man has never seemed despairing before.

When K's screw had a shocking finish Gawge buttonholed her, and had a big confab. He said he could teach her a better way of setting the tool to get a good finish, but that the last time he had tried to explain this was in the brief 3 nights when K first came to Waddon and she had said she didn't understand what he was talking about, and forthwith left the section. He has evidently been bearing malice at the loss of his Golden Girl for 8 weeks!

Tubby today was dressed up to the nines in a slate-grey lounge suit, too much cut-in at the waist, oiled hair and the self-conscious smirk which goes with new clothes. He was teased a good deal and asked what 'her' name was, but replied that he wouldn't know till he met her! Tubby has been 'placed' this week and goes off to the job next Thursday.

Monday 11 May
We all hung around waiting for work as Williams was late, and looked grey and weary when he did arrive. He gave Els a job of work and said it was 'important' so she was all nervous, especially as she had to start it on the big electric lathe. Everything went slowly, and finally there was no tool for her job when she got back on the small lathe, so Williams, after much vain searching, said he would make her one tomorrow.

K learned a better method of screw cutting, and set up another job entirely by herself to her delight, most successfully, but while her eyes were elsewhere, her policeman partner, Fred Feeley, managed to break the tool and spoil the work. They tidied this up and set to work on a repeat, though Gawge said she had better let well alone as she had done it successfully once. Again her policeman mate, whose style is dashing and careless, spoilt it and broke the tool, and as time was late and Gawge was occupied they decided to let it stand over till tomorrow.

Fat Fred was kindly, and looked after Els when things went ill with her. He is the hardest swearer ever, and every sentence is interlarded with foul words. However he is a nice boy and is always ready to help a 'maite' as he calls everybody.

There was the deuce to pay today. Bert had made out a matey little sweeper's rota with all our Christian names only. But he had unfortunately written it on the back of a small Requisition Form and this awful offence caused a frightful stir. The CI came down and there was an inquest, and Bert answered back, and the CI took himself off leaving an indignant section wondering whether he couldn't justify his salary better than by his futile paper chase.

Tuesday 12 May
K and her policeman made a bolt and a nut quite successfully and unaided by Gawge. Thereafter K's mate did his test and so she was out of a job.

Els required a tool, and when she had laboriously set everything up Gawge said he'd make her one, though he shouldn't have to really as his own had been stolen. So he and Els trailed off to the grinding depot and he made a lovely 'forming' tool, & so back, and he put it in and did the work for her, having previously borrowed a 'hard centre' from a mate, who lent it with threats of dire penalties if it were not returned as good as new. By this time, poor Els was trembling like a jelly, and when she tried to set the work up found there was no 'stop' of satisfactory size, so she and K started improvising one till Williams saw what was going on, and said 'Naow. Where are all the screwed pins you made last week?' We said brightly they were all too long, and he said we could saw them off to the required length – that was why we made them too long.

Els was delighted at this opportunity of 'avoiding action' and dashed off with her bit of metal, and sawed at it merrily for half an hour, thoroughly happy to find something perhaps she could do and enjoying the rhythm of it, also delighted to give Powney a poke in the back with her elbow when he drifted into the section.

Then came 'knurling', but Mr Williams couldn't bear the thought of spoiling his friend's 'hard centre' so did this himself, and gave Els a parting tool with which she nervously nibbled an eighth of an inch off, and as it was nearly time to stop she cleared up the mess and so home.

Poor Gawge got a mote or a beam in his eye, and K and E waxed all motherly and insisted on his seeing Miss O'Brien. She told K she wasn't allowed to do the men, but later came popping into the section to explain in person. When Gawge came back Miss O'B pounced on him and led him away to the Ladies' Cloaks, leaving a flutter of excitement in the section with Fred 'smacking his lips' over such a pretty little piece as Miss O'B. However, even Miss O'B couldn't dare touch poor Gawge's bad eye, so he will have to go to hospital if it doesn't get better.

Wednesday 13 May
K spent a wasted day, walking about and talking, as her policeman had the lathe for a test. Finally, in despair, he sat down with the trig. book & did some sums.
Williams finished Elsie's thing for her all but one bit, and took it off to be vetted. Declared accurate he set her to make another with different dimensions and a lovely little tool specially made for the purpose.

Just before lunch, Gawge, who was all covered in bandages around the head, had to go off to hospital again and left us.

Lecture time, we had no teacher, and sat chatting until the Gestapo Hyde, as he is called even here, hove in view. Bert was about to pose a problem in 'naughts & crosses', but at frantic signs from the class he substituted a triangle with A's & B's & TANS, & Tony passed by unaware of high jinks proceeding. Dear Bert then gave a lesson in arithmetic with a life-like imitation of 'the Guvnor' in his most typical mood. At this point Gawge hove in view, and there was a long argument between him & Arthur and Bardolph Caldecourt about their method in the test, while K and Bert and Fred and Tubby kept up an animated flow of gay chatter at the other end of the bench.

Thursday 14 May
Els got on with job only to find the metal was unsuitable, and she had to start all over again, but she had a satisfactory day all the same.

All the lathes being occupied with tests and other jobs K had nothing to do – she did a little trigonometry and just before the end got the promise of a job for

tomorrow. We have a new-comer, a large suave ex-War Rescue policeman –
'Drummond Sutherland' – very Scotch and brawny, also consumed with a sense
of his own charm. He evidently thinks he has a way with the ladies, and he tried
to spend a little time in dalliance with Elsie who is far too much occupied to
respond. He also had a go at K, and taught her to roll cigarettes, and as she had
licked the sticky, he murmured in her ear that it was a kiss by proxy. We have not
met this particular type of heavy charm at all so far in Industry.

Friday 15 May
K was set to cut a square thread, and a tool had to be made for it, and a
requisition form had to be filled in by the CI and Gawge. K thought she might as
well try for a broom at the same time, as our section broom is caked with oil and
swarf and has few bristles. This was successful, though the old broom had to be
handed in before the new one could be taken out.

K and Gawge went off to make a tool, and then he taught her the square screw-
cutting. This went successfully for a time, till the point went off the tool, so after
repairing it he finished it himself. K then set to work to practise on her own, but
hadn't been at it long before Gawge came and said he had a job for her. This was
to 'part off' a long steel rod into 6" lengths. This involved a chapter of accidents.
First, Fred Feeley broke a screw into the precious holder then the long rod stuck
out into the capstan section, and hit one of the machines every time the rod
revolved. Then the tool broke several times, and finally the capstan teacher
explained the difficulty and all went well after that, though Gawge was irritable
and nervous all the time and seemed to fear some frightful accident. 'Parting off'
seems to cause nervous apprehension in all the teachers which is very queer.
Finally, when Gawge had departed K thought she would be helpful in
dismantling the machine, but when altering the belt, it suddenly slipped out of
her hands and soared up to the moving shafting and fell in a limp coil at her
feet. The millwright having gone, poor Gawge had to climb up on the lathe to
repair it while K apologised abjectly below.

Els set to work, and had just got everything nicely down to size when Williams
came up and said that particular size wasn't wanted and gave her some different
dimensions and she set to work on this. However, just at the end she found the
tool had 'dug in' through no apparent action of hers – so the work is spoiled,
and as she can't imagine the reason for this she fears another wasted week draws
to a close.

Saturday 16 May
K spent the day 'facing' up her 'production' job. As Gawge looked occupied Els
got herself a piece of metal and tried to discover by elimination and deduction
why her work had gone wrong the day before. However, she hadn't been at it
long before Gawge came up and said 'Well, ducks, and what are we making this
morning?' as he gazed in astonishment at the odd looking affair on E's lathe.
E explained, but he wouldn't have it, 'Naow you can't discover what's wrong
after, it must be at the time and anyway I can tell you everything that could go
wrong'. So evidently Gawge doesn't like it if one tries to elucidate one's own

problems, which K has already fancied, as he always stops her when she practices on odd bits of metal.

The morning passed without incident and at the end we discovered from Gawge that we are down to do our 3rd test next week which is a hateful thought, particularly on nights. He also gave us some dreadful stories of the official mind in action. The following is an example. There were twelve fitter's benches supplied to [*the*] centre and duly inventoried. Time passed and one was broken and tossed out on the scrap heap. At the next inventory it appeared as 11 benches and 1 broken. Time passed again and a rush order received caused a bright boy to go out & scrounge the broken bench, bring it in and repair it satisfactorily, fit V. Lees onto it, and bring it in to help with the rush order. When another inventory has to be taken, instead of 11 benches & 1 broken, there appeared to be twelve benches and this wouldn't do at all. There appeared to be no satisfactory way of accounting for this extra bench, and so it was broken up once more and returned to the scrap heap.

Monday 18 May

Els has acquired a cold at the weekend and so took aspirin and retired to bed for the rest of the day in readiness for work on nights.

Gawge seemed in unusually high spirits and we talked about the country and bluebell woods.

K got on with her job, a steady, unexciting turning job. Els got on with feeling very sorry for herself with her cold, but otherwise all going well.

Poor Bert had a streaming cold too, and as he had nothing to do he had to drift round for 8½ hours feeling rather wretched & shivery.

There was one awful moment when 'Mr' Drummond Sutherland, our large conceited policeman ('a man of action' as he calls himself) did something incorrect with a lathe and there was an awful noise of bumping metal. Gawge leapt at him, roaring to him to turn off the machine – purple in the face and with a string of what must have been frightful oaths judging by the outstanding veins on his purple, agonised face.

Tuesday 19 May

We slept for hours and woke refreshed and went off eager to get on with jobs – but Gawge announced that we must do our tests. We both said we didn't fancy the look of the test at all, but Gawge said he would help us, and he did. Between us we worked the lathe about 5 minutes each, and Gawge did the rest. It was a most instructive and helpful evening with private demonstration and '*Tu*' [*French, familiar form of you*] from Gawge for the whole eight hours – and we certainly learned much more than we should have done fumbling by ourselves. Gawge says it is a beast of a test, and that a lad apprenticed to an engineers in normal times would take five years before he could do this job satisfactorily alone.

Gawge told a story about K's Mr Evans, who after having a disagreement with the management on the subject of these ridiculous tests made one of his trainees attempt it without any help, with the result that the man never even got started! There was an appalling row. The trainee was passed out on a production job and

Evans was put down to a lower class and Gawge took over the senior section, which all seems very absurd, though we are very much pleased to have had dear Gawge ourselves.

Today was a black day for poor 'Mr' Drummond Sutherland. He got on with his test very slowly without much help from Gawge, who was tremendously occupied with us, and after hours he messed it up and had to start all over again. This is the second time he has spoiled it and he was naturally very down and depressed. Gawge says you can't teach Sutherland anything. He always says he knows before he starts and doesn't like being told. E said that it might just be nervousness and Gawge agreed and said he wouldn't let him spoil it in the end, but we all agreed that Mr Drummond Sutherland was a very conceited man. We were really very proud of our tests when finished, & they looked most professional!

Gawge was born in the Gower peninsula so no wonder K loves him, and he is very fond of Swaledale, so no wonder Els loves him.

Wednesday 20 May

Nothing doing for Els and K this evening and a very long night in consequence. Gawge helped Mr D. Sutherland with his test, and never strayed far enough away from the lathe for any mishap to occur, and so it was finished & taken safely off to the office. Fred did a job today and had several catastrophes, possibly nervous apprehension because he is going out on a job – possibly distrait [*distraught*] because his Phyl has proved false to him and he has 'packed her up'. Everyone else is very much pleased about this, as she is, what Bert calls a 'thing'.

We and Bert trailed off after George to harden the centres which K had been making this week. When we got there, there were no tongs to hold them with, so Gawge got a rod of metal, and forged a pair while we watched fascinated. He then showed us how to harden the centres and we two and Bert had a lovely half hour in gloom, lit by the furnace, supporting ourselves on seats for the operation. A most unorthodox method and chatting of this and that.

On our return we tried to get a job from Gawge, but he took no notice so we continued to sit about & chat.

Then suddenly he remembered our tests hadn't gone in, so he had to stamp them with our numbers. We looked at the marking of our 2nd test papers, which had come back, and as we might have expected K was glorified with 90 per cent, though her test was not remarkably accurate. While E's, which was accurate in every particular, only got 75 per cent. Gawge pointed at her low marks and said it was very peculiar as her test was accurate. However, we are no longer impressed by these things. Exactly the same thing has happened with Muriel and Violet in Mr Tooley's section.

Thursday 21 May

We set to work to make a scribing block for our own use and had a pleasant evening. Bert, who had no work to do, joined us on the lathe, so there were three hands to the pumps and Fred often joined us bawling teasing comments at Bert's old-maidish slowness. Towards the end of the session, Gawge, who had given us this job hoping he would not have to come and supervise us, paid us a visit, and though the work looked rather good he soon saw that it was not quite as it should be, and had to spend half an hour covering up our mistakes. Altogether, rather an evening of high jinks and frivolity round our lathe.

Friday 22 May

Today we had to do the fiddling bits of our scribing block and it was a frightful evening. Everything we had to do was completely new to us, and we were exceedingly stupid about how to set to work, doing everything in the wrong order and having to ask poor Gawge for assistance repeatedly. All the bits were so small that we had no sooner asked him for information than the operation was finished and we had to ask for more help. He was driven nearly dotty with this, and we got stupider and stupider as the evening wore on, till in the end we hardly dared touch the lathe. However, Gawge made a marvellous job of it and it looked grand when finished. We offered Gawge some plants from the Benacre garden and he said, Gawge-like, that he'd like them very much if they were nice ones!

Saturday 23 May–Tuesday 26

Retired to bed but got up early to prepare for our weekend at Hindhead. . . . On Tuesday 24 May E & Auntie dug up all sorts of plants from the garden, and a few from Benacre and we set off for Croydon.

Lunch at the Civic and so to the centre feeling very unworkish. We took the car with George's floral tributes in two whacking great bicycle baskets brimful.

The day was mainly devoted to finishing off our scribing block. It was nearly all fitters' work with a file and Gawge did it, while we watched fascinated by his skill and speed. It occupied him pretty completely and we think the rest of the section will be glad when the scribing block is finished.

This was the evening when we had decided to celebrate Bert's imminent departure from us by a party at the Jubilee Fish Saloon. We got him to ask Gawge to come too, but Gawge said it all depended what the atmosphere was like at home. He gladly accepted our offer to drive him and his plants home, but reserved judgement on whether he could return with us to the Fish Fry. [*They delivered the plants to Gawge's. He could not join them for supper. Kathleen and Elsie had a 'lovely supper' with Bert, then drove him home and met 'Mrs Bert' who was 'charming and friendly'. Bert proudly showed them his beautifully kept garden.*]

Wednesday 27 May

Got to the centre and foregathered with Bert about our pleasant evening last night. Gawge joined the group and said wistfully that he would have liked to have been at the party. He seems to have spent the morning putting in the plants and is obviously very pleased with them. We then asked his advice about seeing the Placing Officer about being sent out to a job together. Thereupon he wrote a note, and before we knew where we were, we were interviewing the Placing Officer. He turned out to be quite a pleasant little man and referred to us as the 'two ladies with the love letter'! He mentioned jobs here and there for 2 women and then suddenly said 'Croydon' at which we jumped. We then immediately found ourselves committed to interviewing the Morrisons Engineering Works, Purley Way, just by our old training centre. So we came home and washed and clothed ourselves, so that we looked like Leisure Girls, and went off quaking. Bert was also going out after a job at Ewell and in his fatherly way was most insistent that we should not accept the offered wage.

When we arrived we had to fill up a long form stating our ages and previous work etc. After the usual Industry wait a very nice man came out and said he thought it was all right. They have already had 3 girls from the Training Centre – and they have turned out very well (rather to his surprise, he said!) – so now we are 'placed' at Morrisons and start next Wednesday at 8 a.m. The hours are 8–5.30, Saturdays 8 – 4 p.m. No Sunday work, no night shift. One hour off at lunchtime. The pay is not at all good – 1/1 – 1/3 per hour and bonus, which we doubt we shall ever be quick enough to earn. The atmosphere of the place seems very nice and friendly. The factory makes aircraft, which has rather a glamour for us, and it seems fairly small, so perhaps it will be human. We have to provide our own overalls and expend coupons on them which seems to us very hard.

Thursday 28 May
We went to the Placing Officer and told him we had accepted the job. K saying she was very much aggrieved at having to buy our own overalls with precious coupons. Gawge gave us a nice screw-cutting job to do, and the time passed quickly enough. Bert came in to say he'd been on a wild goose chase the day before as there were no vacancies in the job so he went out after another. Els asked Gawge whether he would do her bag repair which he had promised, but he forgot.

Friday 29 May
Spent a long time with the Placing Officer and various departments returning books and tools and Els's overall, K having 'lost' hers and buying tool kit. Much amused and slightly annoyed at the imperious beckoning hands which summoned us hither and thither about the general office. The more we see of the 'Black Coated Worker' in Industry the less we like him.

Returned somewhat late to the section and had got nicely started with helping on one of the production jobs when Gawge asked us to make him a couple of gauges. As it was getting somewhat late in the evening and this was to be our last night we were somewhat surprised, but started off, only to find that every tool in the section had disappeared and the only things we could find to use were very makeshift. Rather a dire last evening as everything that could go wrong did. When the time came to stop and the work was not nearly finished Gawge said 'You're coming in tomorrow and can finish it then.' We said the Placing Officer had told us to come in the morning on Saturday and be paid and 'terminate' then. However, if there was still something for us to do we were quite ready to come in on Saturday [to] finish it. Gawge was rather pleased, so K rushed off to the CI to see whether this would be 'agin the regulations'. And so it was all OK by him. It had been a melancholy evening & we should have been rather sorry for it to have been our last.

Bert and Gawge had a long heart-to-heart on Gawge's unhappy home life. He told us Gawge was coming up with him to the Propellor for a farewell drink, and invited us to join them, but we thought tongues would be looser without us, so declined. We walked along with Bert and were regaled with Gawge's home misery and were just telling Bert that he must advise Gawge to leave his wife, when a voice behind us said 'Well & where are we all going?' – & there was Gawge looking very smart in a light tweed overcoat and Prince of Wales green hat. A deathly hush fell on us on account of our embarrassing conversation, everyone wondering how loudly they had been talking. They went off to the Propellor we to the Fish Restaurant.

Saturday 30 May
Found Bert waiting for us at the bottom of the road and we all went off together to collect our money. We were told to get there at 9 & we should be away at half past, but by 11. o'c. we were still there.

We had a long gossip with Bert and various other trainees who were going out – Marlene, among others, looking like a dummy out of a shop window, in clothes of the smartest & worst possible taste, but nothing can take away her sweet and gentle face.

Bert told us more stories of himself and Gawge at the Propellor the night before, and Bert apparently made quite a pretty speech about how much he and 'the Girls' (as we seem to be even here) had enjoyed our time with Gawge. Gawge told him, rather touchingly we think, that he would like to keep up with us and not lose sight of us altogether.

We rushed back to a hurried lunch and then back to the centre for our last shift, somewhat late owing to more office delays. It was nice to have our heads free of the horrid little Industry headhankies, now that we had terminated and were free to break rules with impunity.

We had a much better afternoon, getting on quite well with our gauges and finishing them early with Gawge's help. Then we made a round of good-byes – farewell to old fat 'Stores' who is very sorry to lose us. He says you don't get many of our sort in Industry. Perhaps he says this because we take the trouble to say please and thank you when asking for tools from the store. Gawge, quite unasked, stalked off with Els' bag and repaired the broken handle, which we think was very touching and thoughtful of him.

K had a long farewell with her dear Mr Evans and then we said goodbye to John Bailey and some of the other trainees we know and were wished 'All the best' innumerable times. Els met the CI at the stores and chose that moment to say thank you very much for a pleasant course at which he seemed surprised and pleased. The session ended with terrific handshakes from all the section, and dear Gawge said he hoped we'd keep up with him. Gawge has really added very considerably to our life at the centre. We shall miss him and his unexpected ways and his clever brain & diverse interests. His little catchword 'Well, and how're we doing?' has become a household phrase.

On the way out K went up to say goodbye to the CI and get Mr Hyde's initial so that we can write and say goodbye to him as he has been away this week. The CI was quite overcome by Mrs Church-Bliss's daughter and there was handshaking and smiling going on all round. K said we had so much enjoyed the course, particularly the last seven weeks when we had such an inspiring instructor! Els was watching all this going on, and the manager, whom we have never met, simply goggling. We think perhaps that nobody has ever thanked them before! 'Quite a termination' as Gawge said sardonically.

[*Kathleen and Elsie now have three days off before starting at Morrisons.*]

CHAPTER TWO

Morrisons

1942
Wednesday 3 June
An alert in the middle of the night, but with no incident and soon over. Set off in good time to walk to Morrisons where we waited some little time in the front hall for the Foreman, Mr Rapley. We were put through the usual office paraphernalia of Health Cards etc. and taken off to the store and doled out with a dozen metal checks, and a brooch with our clock numbers on it, and enamelled with the title 'Morrisons Aircraft' and this we are, most absurdly, rather proud of! We were then taken along to the workshop and introduced to our setter 'Stan' a pleasant-looking, delicate, youngish man. The workshop is a huge place (though not nearly as big as the Waddon centre) and machine operators and fitters and inspectors are all working under the same very low roof so that the noise is absolutely deafening. There is artificial light in all the centre part of the shop away from the windows and we think it must be neon. Anyway it bathes all the workers in a ghastly green light which makes them look at death's door and turns all blue garments to a deep violet hue.

The first thing we saw was a bench full of 'viewers' or inspectors who looked bored to death although it was only 8.30 a.m. We thanked our stars that we were to make the stuff and not 'view' it.

Arrived at our section. Stan told us that we were to watch two girls for today and pick up what we could by watching. These two, Muriel and Hilda, are also Waddon trainees and have been at Morrisons 14 weeks. To our nervous inexpert eyes, they looked highly skilled! Muriel was engaged on making 1,500 brass unions and as each one takes about 20 minutes to do, she has been engaged on it for some time. It looked an interesting job – with a good many different operations and she seemed very quick and good at it. She is a very nice girl, pleasant, chatty and friendly. She worked in a flowers, fruit and vegetable shop before the war. Hilda, to whom K attached herself, was engaged on a less finicking job, and seemed to work more slowly. She is not such a taking personality, but they were both very pleasant to us and looked after us in all the 'breaks'. We watched them and watched them and watched them till our eyes bulged, the bones of our feet came through our soles and our backs ached. The first break came at 9.30 when we had ¼ hour for tea and a bun, but by the time we had stood in a long queue to be served most of the break was over and there was little time left to sit down. Back again to our watching brief till the lunch interval at 12.30. We again joined a long queue and had quite a decent lunch of liver and bacon, quite well cooked. As we had one hour for lunch we were able to have a short sit. Unfortunately, there is nowhere nice to sit, so in common with many others we sat on the grass verge by the side of the road, facing the gasworks, a very pleasant outlook and baked with the hot sun! Back at 1.30 once more with 7 p.m. stretching interminably away into the dim distance. We continued our watching for the remaining 6½ hours, getting more and more exhausted as the day dragged on and longing for anywhere to rest our weary feet. Everyone seemed to wilt as the sun got hotter and hotter and our entry into Industry proper seems to be coinciding with a heat wave. We looked at the clock anxiously, but it never seemed to advance more than 10 minutes at a time and Muriel and Hilda seemed equally exhausted. At 4.20 we had another ¼ hour off and so back for the remaining 2 hours. At 7 p.m. Stan told us to clock off, but the poor man remains on till 8 p.m.

Thursday 4 June
Another exhausting day. Very hot once more and no lathes will be available for us until two men go on night shift, so we spent the day watching once more. The tedium was a little alleviated by our taking it in turns to pull the belt round for Muriel during one of her many operations. This we found needed quite a physical effort and Muriel, we think, must be an Amazon, as she manages easily with one hand. The main improvement on the day was that we took sandwiches and sat out of doors for our breaks. This was very much more restful than standing in the interminable queues and having to sit in the canteen where the wireless blares raucously all the time. The snag of today was that we found out that we are really expected to do Sunday work more often than not. This is a great blow to us as we had not expected it and are not at all sure we shall be able for it. Of course it is not compulsory, but when everyone else is doing it, it is a little difficult to refuse without appearing less public spirited than the others. We think it is a very short-sighted policy, as we consider people would produce just as much with shorter hours. Towards the end of the day everyone is going more slowly, they can't help themselves. The wretched men work 12 hours every day – and are only expected to take one Saturday afternoon and one Sunday each month. This seems to us simply terrible. One boy told us that recently, on the occasion of a rush order, the men were asked to work all day Friday, all night Friday and all day Saturday, followed by all day Sunday. They said that at the end they were working quite automatically and had no idea what they were doing. We bicycled to work today and found it quicker and less exhausting in the heat.

Friday 5 June
Still no machine available for us so another exhausting watching day with the hours dragging by. However, we hear we are to have machines tomorrow so we live in hope. We think that Muriel and Hilda, good as they are, are very spotty workers and spend a lot of time having chats and pokes with their fellow-workers and are always back to work late after the breaks. They say it is impossible to earn any production bonus, as if you hurry you get inaccurate. We are told that the whole factory is closing for one week on 20 June and that everyone is to have a

holiday. This seems to us almost too good to be true. We hear that our setter is to be Fred whom we understand is pleasant enough and knows his work. We shall be sorry not to be with Stan whom we like very much. He has a gentle, quiet manner and a pale green face and looks very ill and delicate and no wonder, with the long hours he works. All the men in Morrisons give one a great wink as they pass down the shop, where obviously one would just smile amiably. K has got eye-ache by trying to respond in kind. Els retains her smile which served her very well at Waddon. The 5 p.m. exit on Fridays is not quite so roseate as it sounds as it is then followed by 'pay' (which produced nothing for us this week) and more endless queues. We almost feel it is hardly worth waiting for our charwoman's wage!

Saturday 6 June

Set off in high hopes this morning, expecting to have a production job given us, but we were doomed to disappointment once more and started our endless watching and waiting. When we arrive first thing in the morning, the night shift is still there as they don't leave till 8. o'c. so the place seems very full with both shifts. Then a whistle is blown down the different sections and the night shift take themselves off. Apparently when clocking on in the morning three minutes grace is allowed, after that a quarter of an hour's pay is docked as it is assumed that you arrived at 8.15. If after 8.15 and before 8.30 half an hour's pay is docked and so on.

In addition to Muriel and Hilda and the dreary Mrs Peggy Hazelgrove, who is a 'biddy' of the worst type, there are in our part of the machine operating section two other women, middle-aged both. One is a nice-looking little woman called Nancy Deacon. K had a long crack with her today. She came into Morrisons the first week of the war. She told K that after Dunkirk they all worked 13½ hours a day, Saturdays and Sundays included, for 2 months. She doesn't know how they did it. Her eyes filled with tears at the recollection.

By dinner time we had decided that this was going to be another blank day, when Fred Lundy, who is to be our 'chargehand', came up to Els and said she was to start a job. There was a tremendous paraphernalia of getting tools from the store and exchanging checks and then Els was shown the blueprint of her job, which put the fear of God into her. It looks far more complicated than anything we did at the centre & Els quailed at the thought. Fred took her off to a lathe and started setting up the work, but there were various interruptions which took him away and he had one or two mishaps with tools and appliances which didn't function quite as they should. This took most of the afternoon, and at about quarter to four he left Els to start the work. She spent the time getting conversant with the lathe, which was unlike any she had used at Waddon, so when the whistle went for stopping she hadn't taken any cuts at all. Fred and Stan both said it was too difficult a job to give anyone for a first attempt – as the limits were very fine. They advised Els not to break her heart over it. Frightfully hot again and we were thankful to have the prospect of Sunday off. We have decided that we are going to stick out for our free Sundays, at any rate for the first few weeks, until we get used to the work.

Sunday 7 June

Quiet domestic morning and lunch at the Civic. Back and changed into our smartest clothes and off to visit dear Bert and his wife.

[*K and E enjoyed themselves at Bert's house in North Cheam, where they were joined by George. Due to transport problems they did not arrive home until after midnight.*]

Monday 8 June

Very exhausted after our short night – but Els got on very slowly with her job, frightfully nervous but accurate and scratching about after the thous like an old hen. However, the Inspector pronounced it a 'good' job so she feels slightly better in spite of having taken so long over it. K had another watching day getting angrier and angrier, but just before teatime she too was put on a job and proceeded to rush at it and spoil several bits of metal. After this the job was somewhat simplified and she got along like a house-afire piling up the production.

Tuesday 9 June

K finished her job, rattling away as fast as she could & when she'd done at 11.30 a.m. she was told there was nothing more for her to do for that day, so she hung about again looking bored and miserable. Towards the end of the day, however, she was fetched by Hilda who showed her the job she is to do tomorrow on a lathe right at the opposite end of the section from Els. Els never straightened her back or raised her eyes from her work all day, and accomplished very little, but that accurately. There was one awful moment when she had a mishap and it looked as though hours of work was spoiled, but Fred Lundy took over and did a marvellous make and mend and it was passed. We have had only one chat with a fellow worker, a nice truculent-looking Home Guard man whom we have always liked the look of. For the rest we don't find the inmates particularly friendly. In the canteen when all the women go to the ¼ hr break, if one sits down at an odd seat, someone is sure to say 'Oh! that seat is taken' & one moves miserably off wishing one had the assertion to say 'Bums bags seats in 'uddersfield' – but it is, after all, only like the permanent resident at the hotel taking the best chair by the fire.

We think that our chargehand, Fred Lundy, must think that we are quite bats, as when working we never notice the passage of time and every day he has to hound us off for elevenses, for dinner, for tea, and finally to go home.

Wednesday 10 June

K was terribly disappointed to find that Hilda didn't get her new job, so she, K, had to watch Hilda most of the day instead of being in charge of the lathe herself. She is now getting so nervous with all this watching and being, like Mr Drummond Sutherland, 'a man of action', she thinks she will never be able to 'turn' again.

Els worked practically unaided by Fred all day and was unconscionably slow and very accurate. She had the misfortune to spoil one piece of work (she thinks due to the vagaries of her beastly lathe) so that her production was a very small quantity. By the end of the day she was trembling with exhaustion from so much concentration and would be feeling very despairing only she is too tired to care.

K had a little chat with dear Stan and learns that he has worked seven days a week, and only one day off a month for three years so no wonder he looks so desperately ill.

Thursday 11 June

K's day began with 'words' with Mrs Peggy Hazelgrove, the biddy in our section. She accused K of having put her tools in her own private locked box! K said she hadn't done so and said she had given all her tools to Stan. Peggy watched K remove her paraphernalia from the precious box, with suspicious glances, as if she suspected K of taking something she was not entitled to. K was in a rage over this, and recounting the story to Hilda, was told that Peggy was a terror and was always known as Old Mother Riley at Waddon! Stan also came up – and said – 'don't take any notice of her!' Altogether quite an amusing little breeze, with the whole section laughing and joking at Old Mother Riley's expense. Els had a quiet day and continued her job slowly. Not quite so tired as yesterday. K & Hilda continued their job and at lunchtime Hilda was removed to another job and K was left in charge of the lathe which she was delighted with. Both K & E were given Job Cards today and formally 'clocked in' on these jobs. So now the authorities will know how slow we are and only hope they will consider us worth our wages.

Friday 12 June

Today E had a word of praise. As she is very conscious of her slowness, this was meat and drink to her. One of the inspectors, 'Godfrey Tearle' [*British film and stage actor*], came up to her lathe and examined her latest effort. When he pronounced it correct he added 'When are you going to do one wrong?!'. So perhaps if accuracy is so all-important, E's slowness may be forgiven her. K got on with her job, which everyone says is a hateful one as the result cannot be satisfactory as the necessary tools are not available. However, the chargehand said the reamer had already made about a thousand of the wretched little bits so it was about time they had a new one. This is now in the process of being made. As K's job is very mechanical and has to be done extremely slowly she has time to let the mind wander. Today she had a little day-dream, an imaginary conversation with Mr Rapley, the foreman, who came up to her and said 'How are you enjoying your new work?' K then replied 'Enjoying it? I don't see how anyone could enjoy standing at a lathe for 11 hours a day with their feet aching and in this hellish noise and all for a charwoman's wage. However, I never expected to enjoy it. I am doing it for war work.' She tossed her head at him and then woke up! All this is so particularly absurd as Mr Rapley never speaks to us at all and treats one as if one is part of the machine. Pay day today and we are lucky this week and are paid first of anyone so got away quickly. Next week the numbers are reversed so we shall be the last. If you aren't nippy you miss your turn and have to wait till the bitter end. However, we were nippy and got away on record time. The first wet day so were unable to eat our lunch out of doors. We collected two hard wooden stools from the millers and sat perched up in the machine shop eating our sandwiches very unrestfully in the hellish noise. We should have mentioned that E is making a small part of a Spitfire and K a small part of the aileron of a Wellington Bomber. This gives a zest. From lunch time onwards today we became conscious of an atmosphere of rising spirits due, we think, to its being pay day. Everyone clocks on early after lunch and examines their cards to see what they have earned with bonus: We earned £3.7.2 each – made up of 46½ hours at ordinary time (1/1*d* or 1/3*d*), 6 hours overtime at 1/6, and 1½ hours at special overtime at 1/8½ (Saturday afternoon from 2.30) and 5/- War bonus.

Saturday 13 June
Els' Spitfire has now reached its next operation, just as she was beginning to get slightly quicker at the first part. The present job is to take part of her work down to a 'push fit' and fit one of them into each end of a number of rods which she has been doled out with. It is again very accurate work and Els was slow at it and very tired. K had more fun and games with her reamer and spent a long, boring day messing about with her job. However, at the end of the afternoon, the new reamer was pronounced correct at last so she will now be able to get along. Today Fred asked us if we were going to work this Sunday. We said that on account of the prospective week's holiday, we would work this Sunday, but that we didn't intend to come usually, as Mr Rapley when engaging us, told us there was no Sunday work. Fred said 'Well then I should keep him up to it and not work Sundays'. However, he had a word with Stan and came back a few minutes later and said that if we would work this Sunday they would be very grateful. So there it is and our lovely peaceful recuperative Sunday has gone west.

We have now been in Morrisons for ten days: we review the situation. We learn that before the war Morrisons employed about 150. Now they have nearly 500 and the cloakroom and canteen accommodation has not been enlarged to match. This means that it is pretty comfortless for the workers. There is a great squash in the canteen and if you eat sandwiches in the workshop there is nowhere at all to sit, not even a chair, and everyone has to perch on odd stools and pieces of machinery. If the day is fine a good many people like to take their lunch outside, but again there is nowhere to sit except on an ARP bucket with a piece of asbestos put over the top. We have been lucky enough to find an old sack of wood shavings which is quite soft and pleasant to sit on. Somebody is Digging for Victory like mad in the odd little bits of dirt, about the size of a pocket handkerchief, between the air-raid shelters. All manner of delicious vegetables being tenderly cared for in this appalling soil.

The factory is really a very fascinating place to look at. In our huge workshop there is the eternal clatter & bang of the machinery, which is deafening, and above the green lighting bathes us in its ghastly hue. Leading out of this is another enormous workshop looking like a giant Meccano playroom, where the large parts of the aeroplane are rivetted together. This shop, for some reason is deathly cold, even in the heat wave. Erect lorries wait outside and bear away the fruits of our labours to Vickers of Weybridge to whom Morrisons are sub-contractors.

We don't think that the inmates are particularly friendly. Hilda and Muriel say that they are jealous of the trainees who of course get slightly higher pay. We were quite entertained today at the tea break by the chatter at our table. One very common little thing with flashing eye – much dolled up and extremely 'wolatile' was yappering away about the daily newspapers. 'I like The Telegraph' she said 'But at home they take The Times – but that's just snobbery'. Her draggled friend said 'I take The Express', 'Ooh! Lil,' said the little wolatile 'and you call yourself class!' 'Well yes,' said Lil doubtfully, 'but not very good class.'

Sunday 14 June
Our first, and we sincerely hope, our last Sunday working overtime! We rose at 6 a.m. regretfully, having been more or less asleep since 6 p.m. the night before, so we ought to have been rested, but evidently weren't, as we were appallingly tired when we came home at 3 p.m. Els had an eye-straining job which wore her out and accomplished very little. K had a fairly cheering day, as the final stage of her 42 little rods was reached, and to the eye, they looked fairly correct. However, time will show, when the inspectors examine them tomorrow.

Monday 15 June
Today, for the first time since entering Morrisons, K found she was not looking at her watch every ten minutes. On previous days she has almost taken the face off her watch by looking at it so much and can't even believe that it hadn't stopped. So far as she knows she has never done this before in her life! Els continued with her job, very tired and incredibly slow. Finally in the afternoon Fred offered her a change of job and she presumes this was because some of the Spitfire sockets were wanted at once. He finished them all off in record time, and E was given another tricky job which she was rather stupid over. She is relieved to learn that she is to return to her sockets tomorrow and gathers that the nerve-wracking interlude was merely something to keep her occupied while Fred finished her Spitfires.

K had a fairly successful day and seems to have taught herself the art of drilling. She has been engaged on this operation for days and was never able to get a bright shiny hole. Neither Fred nor Stan could tell her why this was and Hilda was no more successful than K. However, by trial and error K has found out the secret for herself and now makes absolutely prize holes. So much so, that Godfrey Tearle squinting down one of them at the Inspection Table, said 'that's a marvellous hole'. So perhaps that accounts for why K has not looked at her watch so much today.

Tuesday 16 June
Nothing happened to Els today and she worked on very slowly. K had a new job, a real turning job this time, and she had Fred's undivided attention for a

considerable period. She was so nervous that she had to tell him to go away which he did rather amused.

Came home and dolled ourselves up like 'Class' to go and visit the Waddon centre. Had supper at the Fish Fry. [*K and E chatted amiably with old friends, including Gawge, in their old section at Waddon, then visited other people in the training centre exchanging news.*] Then back to Gawge . . . he asked us if we would go out and have supper with him. We were rather taken aback at this, knowing that wifey keeps him on a short leash. However, it transpired that wifey has taken a job as Assistant Matron at a Nursing Home at Godstone, and taken herself off there with the baby, leaving Gawge as a grass widower, so off we went again to the Fish Fry for a second supper and after that Gawge asked us to go to the Propellor for a drink. He remembered that K didn't care for pubs and plied her with lemonade and Els had sherry. The Propellor was packed and full of smoke. We sat some time, over drinks, while Gawge entertained us with stories of centre ineptitude. During the evening Els had been assailed with visions of what 'Mum' would think of her darling Kat sitting in a pub drinking in that smokey atmosphere with such a comic little man.

Wednesday 17 June
Els got on slightly quicker today and feels much cheered by this and thinks she is getting her second wind. She is certainly not so tired and actually washed a couple of pairs of stockings when she got in, which she wouldn't have been capable of last week. K had a wonderful day being praised by Godfrey Tearle, and told her that her work was good and also by Fred who told her she was getting on nicely, so she feels rather conceited. She could hardly endure the last couple of hours of work today. The sight of Old Mother Riley going off at 5.30 filled her with envy.

Friday 19 June
K got on fast & clocked off on her first fifty bits and started on the second. Els had a slow day, accurate and laborious. At lunch time in the yard she saw some assembled bits of aeroplane, painted and already to go out, and was delighted to find her bits of work protruding from either end of a crossbar.

We had a conversation with the man on the night shift who works on K's lathe and always leaves it in a filthy condition for her to clean up when she comes to work because he will work up to the very last second. He says Morrisons is appallingly equipped, and he asked for his release as he is fed up with working on such bad machines, but of course he is not allowed to go. Fred, our chargehand, chatting to K said that this man was a proper 'bonus merchant' and a well known grumbler. Fred, too, says that it is not a good firm to work for – the worst equipped place he has ever known – and they'll twist you on the financial side if they can. Pay day today & we had £4.1.11 each, plus 10/- holiday bonus, which we think is not quite as it should be as they engaged us without telling us there was a holiday without pay in the offing, and for all they know we have several little bastards to provide for. However, we are delighted at the prospect of a holiday.

Saturday 20 June
The morning passed quickly and the latter part was spent in spring cleaning the lathes in readiness for the holiday and getting grease up to the eyebrows. Everyone clocked off on the dot of 12.30 and so to our week's holiday.
[*K and E spent the weekend together, then separated. Both came back feeling rested and well.*]

Monday 29 June
K's birthday passed without incident, except that she had a long boring day on her job which didn't go at all well and drove her nearly dotty. Even the precious new reamer went wrong (after it had been borrowed by Mr Rapley for an hour) and she and Fred spent a hot afternoon trying to discover the fault by trial and error. However, one good thing was that everyone went home at 5.30 for some unknown reason. As it was extremely hot we were not sorry, though we shan't like it too much when we have to stay late tomorrow to make up. Els got on with her second operation of her job and had quite a good day. K had a sad conversation with Fred. He would like to get out of Industry and go in the Air Force, but he is not allowed to leave.

Tuesday 30 June
Frightfully hot and thundery. In the afternoon the sun pours through the windows onto us, and only ¼ of the window space opens, so it is like working in a greenhouse. Everyone gets hotter & dirtier and crosser as the afternoon progresses. Els was chatted up by a new capstan woman who has come on from Waddon. K had a long talk with 'The Lizard', one of the inspectors. He told her that he has been an instructor of fitting and inspection at both Croydon and Waddon. He liked Croydon very much but didn't care for Waddon. He thought the place was unfriendly and stiff and he was glad to go into industry proper. He said, that as we are no longer trainees, there would be no harm in telling us that the instructors were told not to fraternise with the trainees, not to walk home with them, or if going by the same train, not to get in the same carriage with them. He thought it was absolute rot, and has frequently been out with his trainees and had drinks with them.

Wednesday 1 July
We learnt on arrival at the factory that they had had quite a flood during the thunderstorm last night and the water was about 2" deep in the centre of the shop. Everyone had to rush about with brooms to sweep it away. Els had a bad day with the screws, as her lathe was full of vagaries. She has started off with another batch of her tricky Spitfire sockets. However, by 7 p.m. she had just done a screw in record time and came home more cheerful than she has been for some days. But she is pining for inspector Godfrey Tearle. His place has been taken by the Lizard who came round today and questioned every blinking measurement she made and tried to say they were wrong. However, Fred stuck him out and he went away in the end. But Els felt furious at having her careful, accurate work questioned. K, while talking to Fred today, told him that the Lizard had been a

Waddon instructor. At first Fred simply wouldn't believe it and said 'Who on earth told you that?' When K said the Lizard himself told her, he said 'Well I can't imagine what he could be instructor of!' He is certainly not liked among the machine operators, who consider him pernickety over inessentials. We learn his name is Holliday – so we must ask George about him. K began her day very well and got on fast, in spite of several altercations with the Lizard over measurements, and had planned that if she hurried along she would finish her job by the end of the day. However, about 4 p.m. the machine suddenly developed a terrific taper and it took Fred nearly 2 hours to get the thing right. However, the time was not quite so boring as it might have been, as Fred was a bit more human today and inclined to be chatty. He seemed rather amused when K said that she thought she wasn't worth her overtime wages after 5.30 as she was always too tired and stupid by then to do any good work. Apparently, no one is concerned as to how the employer should make the best use of his money. Muriel has sprained her wrist while pulling the belt round for her job and was absent today. K and E invited Hilda to have her picnic lunch with them out-of-doors, but she saw Stan in the offing and had other fish to fry so decided to go her own way. We were not particularly sorry, as she is almost too refined to speak at all and is not faintly interesting, though she has a pretty if discontented face. She and Stan certainly have a slight interest in each other and Hilda particularly enjoys herself when Muriel is absent.

Thursday 2 July
We learn that Muriel's arm is in plaster of Paris from her strain and she will be away a fortnight at least. We are told she will only get ⅕ of her wages during her absence. This seems very hard as she was engaged on the firm's work, and doing a job which is really too heavy for a woman.

Els progressed a bit better today and the lathe behaved alright with the screws. By lunch time, however, she was feeling far from well, with a blinding headache and seeing double. The sickening Lizard, after having a slight 'argufy' [*dispute*] with Kathleen, went off and Ivy took his place, a nice bright little thing whom everybody seems to like. She even has smacks and pokes with the saturnine Fred. She measured up everything and was satisfied with everything, just like Godfrey Tearle, so of course we like her. K finished her job and clocked on for a new one. If only her machine hadn't gone wrong she would have got a bonus. To her great fury her new job has not been roughed out on the capstans, so she has to do it all with no extra time allowed on the job-timing.

Towards the end of that day Els was wilting and wondering how she could last out till 7. When Mr Rapley came up to K & said with an amused grin that 'Mr Williams would be waiting for us outside Morrisons at 7. o'c. – 'Mr Williams!' K screamed incredulously, thinking she couldn't have heard aright. But sure enough it was so. Els' headache departed in a flash, and we slipped out like all the other girls do (but not usually us) to wash and clean up before clocking off time and feeling rather giggly at this amazing visitation. At 7. o'c. there was George, looking very well and gay and smart on his old bicycle. We invited him back home to supper with us and he accepted though protesting that he had already had a meal. We had a pleasant evening entertained by George's volubility. We felt rather amused at having a boyfriend waiting outside for us to beau us home. It seems to lend colour to K's often expressed fear that we shall land as joint corespondents in the Williams divorce case. We very much enjoyed our first male visitor to Duppas Hill and he departed just before 10 and we think he was probably nearly late for night shift. However, before he went we had arranged that he should visit his wife on Saturday and picnic with us on Sunday.

Friday 3 July
K had an awful day sawing off lengths of metal and was as cross as two sticks as she felt it was wasted energy as the job should have been done on the capstans. We were also very much annoyed to find that in spite of having received no wages for the holiday week we were docked off the insurance money, which we think very mean as they only gave us a 10/- bonus. They really are a cheese-paring firm and the workers' comfort and welfare is never considered in any way. We learnt today that the men's cloakroom has hot water while the women's is never more than tepid and generally quite cold. Another petty tyranny is that the cloakroom mirrors are removed at 8 a.m. and not returned until lunch time. Again removed in the afternoon and only put back at clocking off time. So if you want to tidy up during the ¼ hour breaks you can't do it. K is sorry to find that she seemed to be turning into the traditional grumbling British working man and is now bright red in political views. She finds herself thinking the most awful things about the capitalist employers. Els is far too humble to let her mind turn to grousing and is always wondering when she will be called up before a tribunal for holding up the war production because she is so slow! She goes on in her dog-like way, nibbling off the thous, with never a thought of grumbling.

Saturday 4 July
Els worked slightly quicker – K spent another day sawing miserably and thinks that most of her work will be wasted as the reamer is going wrong again. After work we bicycled home in a high wind and bought things for tomorrow's picnic.

Sunday 5 July
Today was a very peculiar day. We packed delicious food with salad and fruit and tongue and cakes and all sorts and departed at 11.30 to pick up Gawge in the car. [*They picked up Gawge as arranged and drove to beyond Caterham for their picnic.*]

We lay in a lovely clearing in the wood, and told Gawge tales of Morrisons and K's red leanings which amused him and poor Els' slow accuracy. We plied him with questions about shop stewards and works committees and K was appalled to hear that stools, by law, are provided for all machines save only the lathes, so she can't have the law on Mr Rapley as she hoped. In the middle of lunch Gawge said if our rooms weren't very comfortable why didn't we come and live with him? We were non-plussed at this suggestion which he protested was serious.

[*After lunch Gawge decided to walk the four miles to Godstone, where his wife and child were staying, telling K and E that he might not return. He didn't and the two women came back at 8.45 p.m. without him.*]

Monday 6 July
Terribly tired today though we can't think why as we had such a peaceful effortless day yesterday. Els clocked onto a new job which took Fred ages to set up. But it looks quite interesting and not too difficult. K was in a rage all day as neither the reamer nor the drill chuck would work properly, and she fears that all her day's labour is wasted. She felt she would have done better to stay at home as at any rate she wouldn't have wasted metal. At 5.30 K felt slightly better as Old Mother Riley took herself and her spinstery ways off home. 'Grannie', as she is called derisively, does not seem to be at all liked. She is so pounceful on her own interests. Very nice letter from Bert arrived today, inviting us to meet them again and saying that he had heard of our reckless evening in the Propellor with George!

Tuesday 7 July
A long boring day sawing for K but she is getting a bit quicker at it and anyhow the day was an improvement on yesterday with its infuriating slipping reamer. Els had a very bad day being unconversant with her new job and felt she would really have to 'terminate'. K had rather an amusing conversation with Ivy, the jolly little inspector. K had enquired where the Lizard was as no one has laid eyes on him for days and Ivy said he was away ill. 'At least,' she added conversionally, 'I think he has "job diarrhoea" as he slipped up on a job so badly last week and £50 worth of stuff has had to be scrapped.' Fred wants to keep bees and asked if, 'when we had our hotel' we kept bees. Said we would write to M. Barker [*friend/acquaintance?*] for a book for him to study. He could make his own hive he thinks.

Wednesday 8 July
Els got on better today & did quite a number of her little horrors. K was given a new chuck key, so she was as happy as a sandboy.

   In the evening we went to the Fish Fry and then on to meet Gawge outside the centre in order to fetch back the key which K had lent him as pattern for the chuck key he is kindly making her. Gawge appeared and we brought him back to Duppas Hill and cooked him a nice supper. It appears that he had to spend the night at Godstone on Sunday as he couldn't get into the buses. After a little mixed conversation at the beginning Gawge held forth for the rest of the evening telling us of various inventions which he has made from time to time. He is the direct lineal descendant of Stephenson of the Rocket fame and time was when he used to use his inventiveness for the benefit of the firm he worked with, but he gave it up in the end. Generally nobody even says 'Thank you Gawge' or 'You have a day off Gawge' so in the end he just 'acts daft' when they ask him questions. He talked and talked until eleven o'clock and then like a flash he was away out.

Thursday 9 July
Elsie had a frightful day as she hadn't the physical strength to move one of the handles on her lathe. Fred stuck her out that it was all OK, and finally after a long time of struggling in vain she gave up altogether. Fred then altered the height of the tool and it immediately worked quite satisfactorily for the rest of

the day. K got on all right and enjoyed her new chuck key, but was appalled to find that 2 of the teeth were broken off already. She wonders what metal it could have been made of. She is getting quite friendly with Fred and they exchanged 'intelligence test' problems. K regretted to find that she fell into one trap and was not so intelligent 'after all', but anyhow she caught Fred out too so was quits. Old Mother Riley has at last finished her 1,000 rods, and has embarked on a new job. It's funny how everyone seems to dislike this woman. Everyone makes game of her and we haven't heard one good word about her.

Friday 10 July
Fred had said during the week that he would like to see over the training centre as he had once contemplated applying for an instructor's job. We had asked George if this could be arranged and he had agreed to show him over the centre himself. This was all fixed for tonight. K has been on the warpath today. Her eyes are set towards ameliorating the lot of the workers and today she pounced on Pussy Bradford, the assistant foreman, and asked who was responsible for the welfare of the women workers. He said that no one was really, but that the Red Cross nurse was a self-appointed supervisor. K said the water was never hot in the women's cloakrooms though she understood that the men always had boiling hot water. He was surprised at this and said he would look into the matter. Later he returned and said K must make her complaint to the nurse and she would attend to it. So after lunch K went off quaking to the nurse who agreed to speak [to] Mr Hurst about it, and it now remains to be seen if anything will be done. K told E nothing about this until all was done as she was so afraid E would try to dissuade her from getting on the wrong side of the authorities. E denies this hotly as she says she would never do anything to prevent K's masterful ego from finding its self-expression. E's plans for the improvement of industry are long-range visions. She wants to alter the system by which a skilled man is encouraged to waste his talents by doing unskilled jobs because he can earn a better production bonus on these than he can on a job requiring skill and knowledge. Also, the system by which a skilled worker will idle after producing a given amount of work because if he produces more than a given amount in a certain time the rate of pay for that job will be lowered. This is due both to the meanness of the employers and the greed of the worker and seems to be a vicious circle. Tonight on our way home we called in at a low eating-house labelled 'SNACKS' and had wonderful cheese and salad sandwiches and tea. A great air of camaraderie filled the tiny place and customers and proprietors are all on Christian-name terms. It was filled with the Home Guard and loutish lads, but we shall go there often as it is clean and the food good and cheap.

Saturday 11 July
K now keeps a camp stool under her lathe and intends to sit on it if she has any idle moments waiting for equipment. Today we found a kitten bedded down [on] it, wrapped in oily rags and tended lovingly by one of the men on night shift. This is one of a recent family of the factory tortoiseshell cat. Hilda is so

pleased with K's camp stool that she is going to get her Dad to make her one too, as Mr Rapley has refused to supply them to the women. After 4 K went off to register with the 1900s [*compulsory registration for war work, called up in batches according to year and month of birth*] and found a horde of women, a few of them looking much like herself, but the majority of them large working-class women looking like 'The March of Time' at Benacre. K couldn't believe they were less than 55 or 60.

We learnt from Fred that when he presented himself at the centre last night he couldn't get past the door keeper. Infuriating for him and we shall have all the arrangements to make again. Els heard one of the women in the cloakroom say that the water was quite warm for a change and reported this with glee to K.

Monday 13 July
This seemed an interminable day. We survived all right till 5.30 – but the last 1½ hours really seemed too much. K's efforts about the hot water have not done any good as today the water was completely cold all day.

Tuesday 14 July
Free France took the name of the Fighting French. Els finished her tapered socket job and presumes she will return to screw-cutting tomorrow. K had a long Bolshie talk with Fred. He thinks Morrisons are an appalling firm to work for and told her that a lot of the men joined the Amalgamated Engineering Union some months ago to get their rights. The office had them all up and called them Communists for this! He was amazed to hear that Bert is earning 1/9 per hour at his firm although he is only a trainee and no better than us. Jim Moore told us he only earned 1/7 an hour (2/1½ on night shift) and he is a skilled man with 12 years experience.

K, in her cynical contemptuous feelings for the delinquencies of Morrisons, is much annoyed by the smug texts which adorn the walls, and hang from the overhead shafting. 'One minute wasted may cost a brave man his life' and K thinks of many moments wasted because of inadequate tools provided by the firm. 'The accuracy of your work may save a man's life', 'When in doubt ASK' etc. 'Mill & Turn for Victory.' Els is simpler minded than K, and as she slowly works away she thinks of another little text 'If it's scrapped – it's Hitler's' and she cheers herself with this thought as she plods accurately along.

Wednesday 15 July
Another late night tonight. Els did not do her screw cutting but the next operation of the queer job she has been on up to the present. She got on slowly with this. K thinks very little of the manners of the industry-inspector type. There was an altercation about some tool K had been using which was not suitable for the job and a young man from the AID came to examine it. He took no notice of K and carried on a conversation with Fred and the Pierrot as though K were not alive at all. The Pierrot has not been mentioned before. He is an inspector and has an air rather much dressed and boundery. Maroon silk shirts and the whole manner and look in the eyes of the young man in the Seaside Pierrot troupe. He

is married, but 'carrying on' with a Pierette, a girl in the tool making dept. She is very pleased with selfie and Fred describes her as a wax doll. On one occasion the manager told her that she was not a 'glamour girl' (more gossip from Fred.)

Thursday 16 July
Another late night. K is intrigued with a story Fred tells her, that the women are to have a bonus on the hours of work they take over their jobs. The present bonus based on men's speed is too unfair for the women. It remains to be seen whether this comes to anything.

Friday 17 July
K started the day by getting a bit of metal in her eye, and while it was being attended to in the FAP the nurse asked K if the hot water was now all right. K said indeed no – it is absolutely frightful. She then explained that she thought the gas boiler was out of order as the gas is full on – but no hot water comes. Everyone in the FAP joined in on the subject and was very eloquent and the nurse said she would see Mr Hurst the manager herself and try to get it repaired. K said we shouldn't be half so miserable if we could be cleaner! K finished her next batch of 'bits', having had a frightful time getting a 'mirror finish' on them as instructed by the AID, but all the same she has to admit they look much nicer when shining silver and much more worth while doing. She only wonders why she was allowed to make 150 of them with a rough finish with no one making any comment. Pay day today and we were delighted to find that we were paid a bonus on our first original jobs which we clocked onto on 11 June. E earned 22½ hours @ 25/4d and K earned 16½ hrs @ 18/7.

Saturday 18 July
No particular incidents today, but for once K's job progressed fast and well. Els had a frightful time with a slipping drill and got completely fed up. Fred had a job which he seemed very pleased with as he could make a good bonus on it. He said it was 'money for old rope'. Jock, the funny old Scottish sweeper, told K today that all the old oily rags are now collected and sent to be laundered, instead of going to salvage. He sends about 7 sackfuls a week. The oil is extracted from them and used again.

This afternoon K was delighted to find that the water was boiling hot, so she hopes her reforming zeal is bearing fruit. The girls were delighted with the change. The expression 'Roll on 7. o'c.' is the Industry phrase. As one clocks on at 8 a.m. someone is sure to say 'Roll on 7. o'c.', and at all times during the day it is the universal comment. We take a long view and are thinking 'Roll on Sunday' from first thing Monday morning.

K is delighted that sawing is now no longer the labour that it was to be. It is like slapping up the cakes, and she seems to have developed the right muscles and knack of it. When her arm wearies a little she is pleased to be entertained by Hilda who comes up to her for a moan for no one 'grumbles' in Industry they just have a 'moan'.

The mystery of Gawge deepens. Not since he left us at the double at 11. o'c. at night, saying he'd bring the chuck keys round, and fixing up to take Fred over the centre have we set eyes on him.

Monday 20 July
Els finished her job and to her horror clocked onto a hundred more of the little beasts. Fred took a very long time setting up the work, and she only had time to do one before 7. o'c. had rolled on.

We were not very pleased to see that the Lizard has returned. He spent the day fussing round as usual and arguing over ¼ thous. K was furious to find that someone had taken her reamer and in an attempt to mend it had spoilt it completely so she had a fiddling morning bodging along with various make-shift appliances. The water was beautifully hot today, and Mrs Church-Bliss's daughter thanked the nurse very charmingly. However, this was somewhat premature, as at 7. o'c. it was stone cold and the gas out.

We had a little chat with Pussy Bradford, the assistant foreman, as we sat on our camp-stools by the lathes eating our picnic lunch. He certainly is a very nice gentle creature and most friendly. Everyone seems to like him. Mr Rapley is on nights and we find the atmosphere pleasanter with Pussy Bradford in charge.

Tuesday 21 July
Els had a strange conversation with a fellow worker today. Just behind her at a milling machine works an elderly man of 60 with whom E occasionally has a word when waiting for Fred. He looks like a dissolute hippopotamus with his dark grey clothes bagging round his seat and legs and belongs to the fraternity who solemnly wink one eye in greeting without any change of facial expression. Today he suddenly said to Els 'Don't you want a husband?' Els was taken rather aback by this, and said 'Not particularly,' with a foolish smile. The hippo said 'You're a long time making up your mind', and as Els departed back to her lathe he added, 'I expect your head has always been too full to bother with it.' Whether the hippo is a widower and wants a nice housekeeper and thinks that Els works pretty continuously without any let up, and would therefore do, remains to be seen.

K finished her job and clocked on to a repeat. She has got so sick of the Lizard coming round and questioning the accuracy of her work that today she had a little ruse to keep him quiet and not worry her. Every time he came to see a specimen of her work, she showed him the first one of the day (which incidentally had been made by Fred) and each time he pronounced it satisfactory and told her everything was now better. Fred was greatly amused when she recounted this story to him and said it was a good way of keeping him quiet. All the bits are checked up afterwards by inspectors and the Lizard only does his complaining to justify his existence.

We finished at 5.30 today and all the workers go off together with no overtime. There are only two clocking off machines and 170 clock off on one, and more than 300 clock off on ours, so that the queue of unnecessarily wearied workers is terrific. Tonight Els couldn't face it, and so got out a book and her camp stool and had a quiet sit and read for 10 minutes behind her lathe while waiting for the queue to dissolve. Some bigwig from the firm walked down the shop and looked aghast at the strange sight.

Wednesday 22 July
Els got on very quickly in the morning and was just planning to do a record day's work when she was taken off her job and put onto the second operation. As the lathe was going very badly, most of the afternoon was spent by Fred in dismantling it and getting black oil right up to the eyes. However, at the end, the machine worked considerably better. K had a long boring day, roughing down her 60 bits. The only incident was a row which she overheard between Mrs Peggy Hazelgrove and the Lizard who was questioning some of Mrs Hazelgrove's measurements. They went at it hammer and tongs and in the end the Lizard retired worsted. He certainly is an amazing man and spends his whole day bustling up and down the machine shop, with the air of one who hasn't a moment to lose, whereas, in reality, he has very little to do as 4 of the lathes are idle today. K, being on a 'roughing down' job, told him flatly it was no good measuring any of her bits, but he insisted all the same and spent some time 'milking' her rods with an earnest expression on his reptilian face. As all K's work has been left ⅛th of an inch too big on every measurement intentionally this was all labour lost.

Thursday 23 July
Elsie had a bad day as the Lizard persecuted her over fiddling measurements. Then to crown all, Ivy came down from inspection with E's sockets and complained to Fred that the lengths were wrong. This was Fred's fault and not Elsie's, but it made a black day even blacker. E was slightly sorry for the Lizard yesterday as no one seems to like him and all the machine operators exchange weary glances as he comes along. But today Elsie has no kindly feelings for him at all and thinks him unutterably loathsome. We think he must live in an imaginary world where he is shop overseer. His consequential purposeful air, as he bustles down the shop, is infuriating and one can feel him exude pleasure when he is able, occasionally, to make a complaint. The amazing thing is that no one has the faintest respect for his opinion and everyone is near rude to him.

Friday 24 July
Another bad day for Els. The lathe was going badly and the reamers were skimming around in the chuck and she had no confidence in the gauge which Fred had given her, as she found it inaccurate. Altogether she felt she had almost better terminate. We were glad to find that the Lizard had been removed to the Tin-Basher's Shop [*as the sheet-metal workers are called*], and we had Ivy prowling up and down today which was a nice change. She told Els that she had already had a quarrel with Jim the Pierrot, and enlarged on how badly he behaves with Pierrette, the Wax Doll Glamour Girl. Ivy says they ought to be ashamed of themselves behaving so badly in the factory. They are both married & he has a very nice wife & a little boy of 10. K today had a lovely silhouette of the two of them. The Wax Doll came up to the Pierrot & hung over him with her hair

caressing his forehead while she ostensibly showed him her work. The 11 hours must pass more rapidly for them than it does for us.

Saturday 25 July
On a Saturday morning, there is apparent a difference among the men. All the week they have looked grimed & fubsy [*poor*] as to clothes, but on Saturday morning smart lounge suits appear and double-breasted waistcoats with lapels and highly polished shoes. They are evidently out to kill at the weekend. Saturday makes no difference to the girls who spend all their spare time, and some of the firm's time too, everyday prinking & dolling themselves up.

During the morning break we were horrified at being charged 1½d for a tiddly little piece of swiss roll. From our Benacre experiences we knew that this was a gross overcharge, so when Pussy Bradford prowled round the shop K confronted him with our purchases, and told him that having been in the business we knew that this was profiteering. He said it wasn't the first complaint he'd heard, and as he's on the Canteen Committee he went off and spoke to the manageress who made a not very good excuse and said it shouldn't happen again.

When we were at Waddon the trainee girls all seemed little dots, and we towered above them and were conspicuous for this reason. Here, at Morrisons, we find this is not so at all. There are quantities of 'Little Women' as before, but also a large number of giantesses who make us feel quite petite. There is an odd assortment of women at Morrisons. A bunch of nice middle-aged grannies with kindly worn faces and amiable manners. Then there is a horde of ghastly looking wantons with long golden locks and buffon erections on top and enamelled faces. Sometimes they bulge out of trousers, at others they sprout out of skintight jumpers. Always they are conscious of one thing only – their exceeding beauty, charm and glamour. Quite a bit of their time is spent hidden away in the Women's Cloaks making up their faces at Morrisons' expense.

Down in the machine shop, behind where we work, there are about ½ doz lads – the Dead End Kids and very engaging boys they are too – friendly and easy to get on with. Next door to Els works a diminutive boy who looks about twelve (but must be fourteen) and is said to be seventeen. This we can hardly believe. He has a round, chubby face and baby hands and his head isn't much above the lathe. He was brought up in Czechoslovakia. He is a very solemn little boy & works with fierce concentration – never letting up like some of the Dead End Kids do, to beat a tattoo with spanners and tools on some available box lid. The lads in Industry let out from time to time, strange animal raucous cries which wail above the noise of the machinery. We suppose this relieves pent up feelings in some way, but it is very odd.

Three trainee girls have come to Duppas Hill and live in one room. They are in inspection.

Sunday 26 July
A quiet domestic morning & in the afternoon we set out in the teeth of a high wind to cycle about 8 miles to North Cheam to visit Bert and family. We had a girlish gossip with Bert and he told us all his tales of the factory where he works.

He has had a rise and now earns 1/10 an hour, rather a contrast to our mangy 1/1½ especially as Bert is no more experienced than we are.

We told him that we think Gawge has passed out of our lives, as we have heard nothing from him for nearly 2 weeks and no chuck key has arrived. We are deeply distressed at the loss of Gawge.

Mrs Bert produced a most marvellous tea, and we took a little offering of Benacre bottled damsons & some sugar.

Monday 27 July

Elsie was very pleased as she did a record number of her 'bits' and felt that she is slowly getting quicker. But every afternoon for the past few days she has been overcome with sleep about 2 p.m. – which is so acute that it is absolutely painful. She almost contemplated asking for an hour off to have a little lay down! As K's reamer was still not correct she had to start on another 50 rods and spent the day sawing through an inch rod 27 times – and roughing down her jobs. The book on bees arrived from Margery Barker and we presented it to Fred who was very pleased to read it during all spare moments. We find that Ivy also keeps bees so they had a good chatter about them.

We were woken by gun-fire at 2.45 a.m. this morning and the alert went later and we got up and went down to the cellar when the firing seemed to be getting rather near. We thought we heard one German plane and the guns opened up on it instantly but no bombs fell anywhere near here.

Gawge has come back into our lives again! Feeling somewhat tired on our return from work we made supper and then curled up on the divan under a blanket and had a lovely sleep. Suddenly Els felt as though an earthquake were happening and discovered that K had leapt up from sleep to answer a thunderous knocking on the door and there was Gawge looking frightfully spruce and shaved and hair cut. We were still asleep [*and*] we didn't know whether it was yesterday or tomorrow, but we did recognise Gawge and were able to entertain him with great ease and charm in spite of bedroom slippers and tousled hair. He produced four lovely chuck keys, which will save poor Els' sprained thumbs and also make K's life much easier. We cooked Gawge some supper and he stayed talking for an hour in very good form. He has promised to arrange for Fred to see over the centre again as the manager and Mr Simpson had both given permission for him to come, and only the time keeper barred his way. Gawge will see that this shall not occur again. Gawge told us they had had a trainees' dance at the centre and Gawge, as a committee member, had insisted on having the piano tuned and moved from the girls' Rest Room to the canteen where it now remains for the trainees to play upon.

Wednesday 29 July

The chuck keys taken to Morrisons created quite a stir. Fred goggled at them and kept on bringing up people to look at them as such a number of chuck keys had evidently never been seen before. Even Mr Rapley had to be dragged up to look at them. Els used hers and found it v. good.

We had another little talk with the Gaudy Image, the new trainee at Morrisons. Her name is Marley and we still don't care for her at all. She had the effrontery to tell us that she was very good at her job and 'They' were pleased with her. We had asked Gawge if he remembered this woman at the centre and he said he did indeed and that she was a terror. However, he said she was also evidently intrepid. She was the first English Woman to make a parachute jump.

Thursday 30 July
Nearly the whole of Els' morning was spent watching Fred repair the chuck on her lathe, so by the time the lathe was ready for her to work she was feeling she had had enough for today and would like to go home.

Hilda has got a week's holiday, as her husband is on leave, and Old Mother Riley was put on to Hilda's job much to her disgust. She had quite a row with Stan for taking a tool she wanted and he told her off for being very selfish and out for everything for herself. She was quite humbled by this and at clocking off was still hard at work because Stan had told her she must get her job finished. He was giggling and exchanging glances with Els and K over all this.

One of the trainee women in the capstan section rushed up to Els at lunch time and asked if our chargehands were as beastly rude as theirs were. E said 'no' they were charming to us and the capstan woman said their setters were almost more than the women could endure. They are young lads of seventeen who bark at them and are always disagreeable. She said she thought she'd hit her one if he spoke to her again like that. She'd got a son of his age and she wouldn't stand it. Another alert at 2.15 a.m. – with guns going. Didn't last very long.

Friday 31 July
Pay day again and K got a mysterious bonus of 11½ hours. As she couldn't understand this she asked Mr Rapley to explain the principle of the women's bonus. But he was quite unable to do this and said he didn't know how they were worked. He promised to enquire why E had only had one bonus since she came. He said it certainly was not correct.

The last two days the water has been quite cold again. We shall have to stir them up once more. We have made ourselves moderately comfortable now at Morrisons. We each have a camp stool (tho' Elsie's is now broken) and K has taken a board which she puts in the lathe tray and can get a few minutes sit in it occasionally. As she felt sure an old board would be instantly removed by someone – she has wrapped it up in brown paper and string to look like a parcel and has so far retained it safely. We have also produced a hanging mirror, large enough to see the whole head in, which we have put on a nail behind E's lathe. This mirror is much appreciated by the whole machine shop and we have a continuous procession of men and girls coming to pat their hair and make up their faces. Godfrey always makes a face at himself in it as he goes down the shop to E's great amusement. It's now getting quite like home as we also hang a roller towel on a nail in the shop and we each have scrap boxes.

Tuesday 4 August
Unwilling to go back to work. The day passed without much incident. K wasted 2 hours while Fred repaired her reamer. The day dragged slowly at 5.30 and we

were thankful to come home early, though Els did a good day's work and got on fairly quickly.

Wednesday 5 August
Fred set Elsie's job at a quicker speed with the result that she got a record number done. K spent 3 more wasted hours waiting for her reamers and sat about looking very melancholy. Even when the reamers were finally ready it was not altogether satisfactory, so K had a sad, disheartening day. She had a little talk with Jean, the most radiantly attractive little thing we have met in Industry. A beautiful, neat little figure, a charming face full of character & fair wavy hair parted in the centre. She is one of the young marrieds and is on the best of terms with everyone. She told K she had been in Morrisons for 15 months and had before been 7 years at another factory on capstan work. As she can only be about 22 or 23 she must have started young. For the last few days she has been working on the centre lathe and wants to get a transfer from the capstans as she likes the work better. We hope she will succeed as we enjoy her cheerful presence and she even makes Fred smile.

Friday 7 August
Today was a day of catastrophe. First of all there was no Fred. No one was very surprised as he had complained of not feeling well yesterday. Els was sunk without Fred as her job is tricky to set up, and needs an expert. K was able, with a little help, to start herself off, and after he had done with his own girls, Stan came to Els and spent some time tinkering. He then found that the thread of a bolt was stripped so that he couldn't set up the job, so Els clocked on to her other operation and got on with this instead, while a new bolt was being made. Els hadn't been long at this job when K came up to her having nipped the tip of her thumb in her lathe and bent it backwards, and most peculiar it looked and we thought that perhaps the top was dislocated. Off K went to the nurse who made light of it and bathed it and bandaged it up, telling K to return to her for her to have a look at it after lunch. She was quite kind to K & gave her sal volatile for shock. After some time, Els feeling interfering, walked off to the FAP to have a look-see herself, but was snubbed for her pains and banished. However, after lunch K returned to the nurse, the thumb still exceedingly painful, and the nurse no longer liking the look of it (Els never had liked the look of it!) sent K off to hospital where it was X-rayed and diagnosed as a fractured tip of thumb. K came back to Morrisons as nobody was free to plaster it till 5. o'c. at the hospital. This time the nice Nurse Burgess was on duty and came & fetched Els to see K & arrange about her money and clothes, the fussy Nurse Webster now off duty K had various visits from Mr Rapley and the office and Els had a succession of enquiries for bulletins of her girlfriend.

The capstan woman who besieged Els with complaints of the rudeness of the boy setters had another explosion while we were having lunch today. Her bonus is too tiddly for anything and she can't see where that munition-makers fur coat [*joke from First World War*] is coming from. She told us long stories of other arguments with Mr Rapley and others, all accompanied with poking and expressive gestures. She too is an Els – short, fat, blowsy & henna'd hair. High spirited and with a voluble clack. We think that we shall hear more of 'capstan Els' as she is a character. She told Mr Rapley that as things stood she 'bloody well wasn't satisfied' and when he said in a shocked voice 'What did you say?' she repeated it.

We had a further example of Industry broadness during the tea interval this morning. 'Lou' (the Fat Cooky) was being rallied by little Wolatile for presenting her back to her. 'Well, never mind,' said Wolatile, 'but I'd rather have your front.' 'You can't have that,' said Lou, 'I keep that for my husband'. This absolutely finished our table and Wolatile Eileen squealed 'Oo, & I thought you were pu-er!' Els, who has been reading an earthy farm novel, thinks that you pay £2.0.0 a year subscription at Harrods to read this sort of thing and it is really cheaper to go to Morrisons.

K is to go again to hospital at 9 a.m. tomorrow morning and hopes after that to be allowed back at her job.

Saturday 8 August
K went to the hospital and sat in a mixed casualty dept with men, women and children showing their suppurating sores. K didn't like it at all as everyone wanted to display their injuries to her. The doctor decided against reducing the fracture and told her she could have a fortnight off if she liked, but K, smug-like, said she would return to work at once. However, when she got back to Morrisons, Mr Hurst, the manager, was not so keen on this returning at once and said she must go off today and come back if she liked on Monday. K was very sharp with him.

And so K was segregated in the front hall while Mr Rapley fetched Els out to have a word with her. No worker in a hat or coat is allowed into the workshops during working hours as it creates a diversion.

Monday 10 August
Fred back to work again – saying that he had been suffering from National Loaf poisoning and that his doctor had had 500 patients suffering from this. It was caused by the bread being undercooked. Hilda also returned having taken 10 days off, although her husband only had 7 days leave. As Stan had no lathe to work on he took charge of us as well as his usual 3 and Fred had a peaceful day to pile up the bonus. However, we didn't cause Stan much bother and he didn't go near Els until 5.30 p.m. when he went down for a chat. K had a long chat with Pussy Bradford and he is going to concern himself in the mystery of our non-existent bonus. He thinks it scandalous that we have only had about 25/- in 2 months. He will try to put the matter right. K also had a talk with Stan who told her that Mr Rapley was a weak and timid man and that it is quite useless to ask him to do anything for you. He says he will do it, but never bothers. Pussy Bradford is quite a different story and takes endless trouble to have the shop going well. Unfortunately, we learn that Mr Rapley may be going permanently on nights too to be with him, as the atmosphere of the shop is so much nicer with him in charge.

another perfect metal ruler from Mum. This is an absolute prize as E was in desperate need of a small flexible metal rule and life will now be much easier. Moreover, Mum has also found an address where other rulers can be bought. We are passing this information on to Morrisons and many workers will have reason to bless Mum for her good offices as these rulers seem quite unprocurable.

We have now been with Stan for a week and like it very much. We hear that 2 more women turners are joining us next week from the Polytechnic. We wonder in our cynical way if Morrisons can get the Polytechnic girls cheaper than those from the centre!

Monday 17 August

K finished her Wellington bombers and was given a much easier and pleasanter job – part of a Spitfire. She also had a slight passage of arms with Nurse Webster who said very tartly that she hadn't reported to her on her return from the hospital on Monday. K said that Nurse Burgess was on duty and she had reported to her. Nurse Webster said that she was the Senior Nurse and K should have come again to the FAP and reported to her. K said very crossly that she didn't require anything to be done to her thumb and thought she had done all the reporting necessary. In any case she has no intention of wasting any more time fussing around after the stupid woman. If she'd wanted K she could easily have found her in the m/c shop. Very hot day and we were terribly tired at the end of it.

Tuesday 18 August

K got on nicely with her new job and Els had a quiet day with hers. 5.30 came as a welcome respite. We learn that Hilda has 4 brothers & 3 sisters. We can't imagine why she is so spoilt and self-centred when she is one of a large family. We have seldom met anyone so provocative – and she has a good time with all the Industry men. We find her pleasant enough to talk to, but very selfish to work with, as she never returns any tools or equipment she borrows.

Wednesday 19 August

A new woman turner joined Morrisons today. She is also an ex-nurse who has been a Sister at Warlingham Mental Hospital for 16 years. Now she has been told she is mobile, and as she has a disabled husband and cannot leave him, she is forced to leave the nursing profession and go into munitions. She has done 8 weeks training at the Croydon Polytechnic, but seems very nervous of the big machines at Morrisons as they only had the small Atlas lathes at the Polytechnic. She seems a nice woman and will be an addition to the m/c shop. The poor wretch spent the whole day watching and we felt desperately sorry for her as we so well remember the endless exhausting days we spent when we first came to Morrisons.

Thursday 20 August

K had a very good day & made more bits than on any day since she joined Morrisons. We learn that the new turner's name is Mrs Laurie Charman. She did a bit of drilling on K's work to relieve the monotony of the day – but apart from that she spent the whole time endlessly hanging about. She told her husband she would never stick the week out! E had a quiet day and finished the job. She couldn't start another, as there was only an hour of the day left and the job takes too long to set up. So she had a grand spring-clean of her lathe and general surroundings and got herself decently clean before going home, for once. Stan cut his finger rather badly, and on his return from the FAP he gave K an amusing sideline on the awful Nurse Webster. K said 'That nurse is a horror isn't she?' But Stan said with a grin 'She's all right with the men'. Apparently she had just said to Stan 'You don't often come over here,' and when he replied 'No – I've only been over twice in 4 years I think,' Nurse Webster then said very archly 'You don't have to wait until you cut yourself before you come over to pay me a visit!' Stan told K that there are always several of the chargehands over there having tea etc. with her. And this is the woman who is 'self-appointed' Women's Welfare Supervisor! She takes no interest whatsoever in the women and her only thoughts are for the men.

Friday 21 August
Els clocked on to another 100 of her tapered sockets, which should keep her employed for another month, and Stan spent a very long time setting up the job for her, and after that she got on quietly by herself. Hilda and Old Mother Riley looked rather sick at Stan being so busily engaged elsewhere and the horrible OMR kept Stan away from his tea interval while he ground her up a tool.

We have been pained to see, the last few days, that the slices of cake & swiss roll have been getting smaller and smaller again. In the tea interval Parachute Marley and Little Kilby had a minute slice of yellow egg-powder cake for 1½d. They were indignant, and we encouraged them to complain. So off went Parachute Marley to Pussy Bradford and together they bearded the manageress who made the same lean excuse as before. Other onlookers backed up Marley, who told the manageress that there would be complaints to the Food Office if she did not do something about the prices and then there would be a thumping great fine to pay. We shall look with interest at the cake tomorrow.

Saturday 22 August
The very small slices of cake were priced at 1*d* today, so Marley's efforts have borne fruit, at any rate for a short time. K went off to hospital and had her plaster off, and her thumb, exposed to public view, looks bulbous and brown and peculiar and she preferred it as it was in its little plaster case. Stan had a talk with Els and told her that OMR complains to the foreman if even she is kept waiting by him when he is busy helping somebody else. Els said that surely the foreman would snub OMR and tell her that Stan had other people to look after besides herself, but he said 'oh no! He was ignorant'. Old Mother Riley told us she was so tired yesterday that she couldn't even go to the cupboard to get the bottle of wine, which she usually has a nip from as a pick me up. Stan's comment on repeating the story to Els was that he'd be sorry to be anywhere near her after she's had a nip!

Els' tapered socket job used to be timed for 68 minutes and the time has now been lengthened to nearly double (2 hours). This is a much fairer timing. The original worker, Everett (an unpleasant man) complained that it was impossible to do the work in the time and asked for an increase in hours. This was refused and he went off the job. It was then taken over by a very pleasant-mannered boy called Catford. He also found that it was quite impossible to make any bonus on the job. So he 'went slow' for a fortnight, earning no bonus at all and then the office agreed that the timing was unfair and nearly doubled it. This sounds an appalling story, in wartime when everything is so urgently needed, but there is another side to the picture which also explains the scandalous-sounding accepted fact in the factory that a worker mustn't do more than 'double time'. [*This means getting the work done in half the allotted hours, i.e. earning double money.*] If a quick worker completes a job in less than half the allotted hours, the management immediately lowers the timing which is then very hard on the average steady slow worker who can then never earn a bonus. This 'go slow' story one hears so often in tales of Industry, and it is a shocking thing, but at the same, time the meanness of the management is partially responsible.

This boy Catford is a very nice lad, exceptionally clean and spruce & well mannered. He takes over Els' lathe on nights, and always leaves it spotlessly clean, and the apparatus all ready for what she wants next day. While we were quietly working this morning and 4. o'c. seemed to be a long way off, someone said that we finished at 12.30! and so it was – it seemed too good to be true and having the whole of Saturday afternoon free makes the weekend a real rest.

Monday 24 August
K found her lathe taken over by Ken Thoroughgood, who has gone off nights, so she had to move off to another machine and start a new job. However, it was quite a nice one and progressed fast. She was annoyed to have to wait nearly an hour in the afternoon while changing over to the second operation, as Stan hadn't had the forethought to organise her work. E got on well with her tapered sockets and did a record number. In the middle of the afternoon an amazing moaning noise suddenly started. And when we saw the shops emptying and everyone streaming quietly towards the exits, we realised it was an alert. We all went to the shelters where we remained for about ¼ hour and then we all returned. We learn that the factory has a control room connected with the Air Ministry and when planes are near, the workers go to the shelters. Otherwise, no notice is taken of ordinary public alerts. No planes were heard on this occasion so we think the management was using the general alert as an air raid practice for the factory. K and E are not in the same shelter and think they must take steps to get united.

Tuesday 25 August
K clocked off one job and on to another & hopes the bonus is piling up. Els had rather a wasted day because she hadn't enough bits to keep her busy all day and the next operation takes too long to prepare for it to be worthwhile to set up late in the day, so the latter part of the day was spent in idling and trying to discover

how to set the work up for herself. However, she got some more praise from Stan who said it was a great help to him that she could get on by herself so much. Another warning in the afternoon and we all trooped down to the shelters and heard distant gunfire. It only lasted about ¼ hour and we returned just in time to tidy up. Mrs Hazelgrove caused great annoyance by refusing to go down to the shelter and spent her time ranging about the factory with everyone arguing with her.

Wednesday 26 August
We were shocked to hear on the 7 a.m. news that the Duke of Kent [*the fourth son of King George V*] has been killed in an air crash.

At the factory Els partly set up her job for herself and Stan finished it, so she saved a certain amount of time by doing this and got on quite well through the day.

Having had to go down to the shelters twice in the last two days, K was determined to get transferred into E's shelter and talked to a Shelter Marshall who seemed quite amenable and said he would arrange it with the ARP officer. However, he came back a few minutes later and said the ARP officer had flatly refused to do anything about it. This resulted in an emotional scene. K went off to interview the ARP officer herself and asked him politely to transfer her to the same shelter as her 'cousin' thinking he would be more likely to put relations together. He talked her down, in the usual Industry way, & she held her ground, & finally after telling him he was utterly unreasonable and very cruel she burst into tears and walked out saying she was a law-abiding woman normally, but was not going to put up with this. K then returned to her lathe where delayed shock from her injured thumb and overtiredness from the factory life, plus not being able to get her own way, caused her to dissolve weakly into tears. When she had somewhat recovered she had a word with Stan who said he wouldn't take any notice of the ARP officer but go where she liked, in fact the Shelter Marshal said he wouldn't have any objection to her coming into E's shelter. All this caused such a flow of adrenalin through K's system that production soared and she finished her job in double time and in fact was told to go slow at the end of the day or the price of the job would come down.

Thursday 27 August
A frightful 'to-do' in the machine shop today as the Home Guard of the district are having manoeuvres on Sunday and these will take away the men Sunday workers at the factory, so Stan came round explaining this & asking for volunteers from the women for Sunday work. We listened to all this and were very reluctant, but said we'd think about it, though we think we only survive the week having one day to recuperate in. We thought it over and decided that the whole thing was 'Eye-Wash'. The slogan 'The factory Home Guard must not interfere with production' which we have read in the papers was being interpreted by the management as keeping the machines going, and so four inexperienced women were to work on Sunday so that four machines should not be idle and appear to replace all the machine shop men. The production of the poor girls would be negligible in comparison with what all the men would have

turned out, and so we decided that it was pointless to wear ourselves out to no purpose. We were annoyed at being asked as we always do our agreed overtime and have never taken a minute off, although many of the women go early when they feel like it. The firm closed last Saturday afternoon and could just as well have stayed open to get the production done.

A curious alert happened just before 7 p.m. We all went down to the shelters (K joining E in her shelter regardless of regulation), [*but*] it only lasted about 5 minutes and we trooped out again before clocking off time. No public warning was given, but a loud explosion was heard.

Friday 28 August
Another tiring week is drawing to its close, & today we came away with our mangy £3.0.0 which we feel we have well earned.

The heat is terrific. Where we are the sun pours on to us all day through frosted glass windows of which very little opens. Our clothes stick to us, blobs of sweat bead on our faces and drop onto the lathes.

Saturday 29 August
K went off to hospital again to show her thumb to the doctor and he seemed very much surprised at the strapping the hospital nurse had put on nowhere near the seat of injury. Another absolutely sweltering day and we dripped. In the afternoon the Home Guard went off, muffled up in khaki and hung round with equipment. They must have been dying of heat. There was practically no one left in the place after this and the 500 hp machines roared away all the afternoon while only about 8 or 9 girls were on production. K worked at fever pitch all the afternoon and just clocked off her job before closing time.

Monday 31 August
Pouring with rain but still steamy & stuffy. We had a kind present of runner beans from little Manchester Kilby. This little woman we have become very fond of. She is a little oddity – tiny – with the rolling gait of a sailor and she wears very long skirts. She is very plain but with a humorous expression and has an amusing turn of phrase – a great character. We generally have our afternoon tea interval with her and always enjoy her comments. The other day we were talking of Capstan Els, whose aggressive spirit rather amuses us. Mrs Kilby said she liked fairness & justice – but she thought it a pity Capstan Els used such bad language 'as it spoils a woman.'

Tuesday 1 September
We read in the papers that the Amalgamated Engineering Union are to admit women members so K & E will join if eligible.

We also read that it is the desire of the gov't that work should cease if practicable between 11 and 11.15 a.m. next Thursday for the Morning Service in the National Day of Prayer. We wonder what Morrisons will do about this.

The factory was very stuffy and hot again today although there was no sun. It stinks in the morning when we come into it after it has been blacked out for night shift.

After having had several alerts on recent afternoons we find that at the same time daily our eyes slew round to where the Raid Signal lights show just above our 'clock'. We never used to be conscious of this before. A white bulb glows all the time when all is clear, this changes to blue when a public alert is given, and when enemy aircraft are dangerously near a red light shows and we all move down to the factory shelters.

Wednesday 2 September
Elsie did an absolute record number of 'bits' and hoped she will finish her job tomorrow. K also had a good day and finished her job and clocked onto another one. During the afternoon K was struggling with a lever she couldn't move and asked Stan to help her as she said the strain of it made her feel 'gone in the head'. Stan laughed & replied that it was lucky that K was only gone in the head sometimes as Mrs 'Islegrove' is gone in the head all the time!

Thursday 3 September
The National Day of Prayer and Morrisons rigged up a portable wireless down one end of the shop and at 11 o'clock the machines went off and everyone stopped working to listen to the service. Unfortunately, the reception was not very good and no one asked the workers to come up near the microphone so everyone stayed at their bench or machine. We didn't think it was a very impressive service, but this may have been because we couldn't hear it very well. However, the congregation of workers behaved excellently, there was no shuffling or coughing, and no fags were lighted up by the irreligious. The only interruption was the deafening crash of a crowbar which the Hippo hurled off his table onto the stone floor during the service. Today was a fevering day as Stan was fully occupied on a rush job for Vickers, and the lorry was waiting at the door for his work while he was still engaged on it. This meant that he couldn't attend to any of his harem and Els had a considerable amount of idle time as a result, as the nightworker had damaged her tool. After lunch she went over to her second operation and got on well with this, but it was infuriating to have wasted so much time during the morning. K did a record day's work and got on well. During the afternoon Mr Rapley asked Muriel and Hilda if they would go on night shift next Sunday for a fortnight. They agreed to do this. We wondered why we had not been asked too and on enquiry, learnt from Stan that they hadn't liked to ask us, as they thought we should refuse. We said we didn't like night shift, but were willing to take our turn at it like everyone else. Stan said we need not do it this next fortnight, but we should probably be asked to in about 6 weeks time.

Friday 4 September
The day began with Muriel and Hilda saying they had decided that they would not go on night shift after all as they thought they were much better off as they were! However, they finally decided to try it for a week and see how their tummies stood it, so perhaps our 6 weeks respite won't happen. Pay day again today and K got a big bonus. The usual argument ensued about sharing it. E refuses to take half of it. [*At Benacre K and E pooled their income from the café*] It was

a record day for Els who did her job in well under time and K is also getting so quick that with a job which used to take her 25 minutes she can now do 5 an hour. After work we tidied ourselves up and took some Milford shallots round to George. [*He was out.*]

Mrs Marley returned to Morrisons today after a week's holiday while her husband was on leave. She gave Els another specimen of her swank. She said that either she or Mrs Kilby would become the 3rd Red Cross nurse in the FAP. She added that Mr Rapley didn't wish her to take the job as she was too valuable in the m/c shop. We think that with being away from our influence for a week she has become conceited and aggressive again.

Saturday 5 September
K, on visiting the FAP to get a pass to take her thumb to hospital, had a gossip with the big nice Nurse Burgess who told her that there is a row in progress over the appointment of the 3rd nurse. It was offered to Mrs Manchester Kilby who is an SRN, but Mrs Marley applied for it on her own and the nurse fears Mrs M. will get it as she has more push than Kilby, though Kilby is the senior nurse. Kilby, we hear, is very upset about the whole thing, as she and Marley were friends before they came. Marley followed her here and Kilby thinks that Marley should not try to pinch the job that has fallen at Kilby's feet. She says she will leave the place altogether if Marley gets the job. We are very sorry for Kilby as we like her very much. None of this quarrel has been told us by Kilby or Marley. We think it amazing that the nurse should gossip like this to K, whom she hardly knows at all. She criticised Nurse Webster to K on previous occasions and there seems to be no old school tie *esprit de corps* among those in authority in Industry.

K came back from the hospital very early as the doctor wasn't there and there was no one to attend to her. There is a rumour that Rapley is going to provide us with stools. Nancy Deacon has kindly asked him on our behalf. In the afternoon K and E were the only two women in the machine shop and we went round giving great pleasure by doling out beautiful Victoria plums among the men.

A new girl has been transferred to the machine shop (to the drilling machines) from the big Meccano fitting room. She is a startler and K thinks she has never seen anything that looks so bad. Els thinks that it is worth while coming to Morrisons just to see her. The Peccadillo is very young, about twenty we should think, and looks like the frightful painted kewpie dolls which are seen lying about in some girls' bedrooms. She is small and rounded with a little enamelled heart-shaped face and large scarlet bowed lips. Long blonde hair hangs to her shoulders and her eyebrows are plucked into a thin arch, much above their normal position. Her face is so thick in make-up, that in repose no expression can break through. When she smiles, however, it becomes a rather taking little face, and we expect we shall like her when we get to know her. Her rounded form is usually encased in trousers (above scarlet toe-nailed sandalled feet) and her bosom sprouts out of a very tight jumper. When she came to work this morning and the day shift and night shift overlap, she created a stir among the men. They couldn't keep their faces straight with amusement and they obviously all think her a 'thing' (as Bert would say), but wasn't the atmosphere electric!

Monday 7 September
We met Stan going off from nights and looking very bleary and tired. Back to Fred as our chargehand, but Els got on all day without reference to him, so it made no difference. K got on quite happily with her job and then suddenly Fred & George Bradford arrived and said she must 'break down' on that job as they urgently needed some cast steel levers. K has watched this job with aversion, being done by various men, all of whom loathe it, so the rest of the day she was miserable as the job is boring and mechanical and physically hard work.

Els visited the FAP, having had a piece of metal in her eye which has left her eye bloodshot and a little painful, in fact she wondered whether she had pink-eye. It was bathed twice and seemed better by the end of the day.

Bradford got hold of us both and said they wanted us to go on nights in a fortnight's time with Fred as our chargehand. We are very disappointed as we so much prefer Stan as a chargehand, and don't also like the news (which we weren't told before) that it would be a fortnight on & a fortnight off.

During our dinner interval Els thought up that if we were to do 6 nights a week of the longer hours of night shift we should be working 61 hours a week instead of 54, and we both thought this was most undesirable, and E suggested that we should ask to take off one extra night in every fortnight of night shift in order to bring the total hours more nearly to what we normally do on days. K put this to Pussy Bradford who said he thought it could be arranged, so if this happens every month we should get one really decent weekend, consisting of two completely free days.

Tuesday 8 September
A long boring day. K hated her job and watched the clock creep forward in the same way as she used to do when she first came to Morrisons. Els also got on drearily with her job and we both hate having Fred as our chargehand – as he is so saturnine and unfriendly. We had a surprise present of runner beans from Old Mother Riley. Really very nice of her as we are never in the least bit friendly to her. Nancy Deacon seems to have taken us under her wing. She has been on the warpath for several days past, on our behalf. She has a friend who is a bigwig in the Trades Union Congress and has been putting her wise about the Factory Act and how to improve the conditions of our factory. Last week she asked Mr Rapley if we might have stools, and he agreed and said he would get the carpenter to make them for us. However, some days have passed and nothing has been done and so Nancy has interviewed both Rapley & Bradford today and is going to return to the charge every day if she finds that the carpenter has never received the order. We are delighted to see today that they have reorganised the paying-out system and there will now be 4 different pay desks for the 500 workers. Heretofore, we have suffered an appalling arrangement in which a seething mass of 300 men and girls crowd like a football scrum round a man who calls out the numbers and hands out the clocking out cards. Everyone has to press close to the speaker or they may miss hearing their number, and when they have at last obtained their card they have to fight their way out of the crowd and leg it into the other factory to the pay desk, to get paid in numerical order and if they

arrive late they have to wait until the very end of the queue. This Friday scrimmage has always been a nightmare and adds quite unnecessarily to the normal fatigue of the week.

Wednesday 9 September
Another long day. K still on her boring mechanical job, but feels that the end may be in sight, as Pussy Bradford told her that the job is shortly being transferred to the capstans, so she lives in hopes. Fred slightly more amiable today, largely because he had a job he didn't want to do so stayed as long as possible with his 'charges' to fill in the time. Elsie had another piece of burning metal in her other eye today, but rushed off to the FAP for treatment and it seems none the worse.

We think Parachute Marley is a scab of the first water. She told us today quite brazenly that when she heard that Kilby had been put forward for the job of 3rd nurse, she, Marley went off to Mr Overton and said she would like to put in for the job herself. She then proceeded to tell us a lot of uncomplimentary things about little Kilby, which unfortunately we were not in a position to refute, but we think it is extremely disloyal and unfriendly of her. She is sure to have tried to spike Kilby's guns with Overton too. Considering that these two women worked together for 3 years at the May Day Hospital and entered the Waddon Training Centre together we think it is very unfriendly of Marley to put in for this job over Kilby's head – especially as Kilby came to Morrisons first and Marley followed her here. Little Kilby looks rather miserable, but she has never uttered a word to us about the whole affair. We heard today that we can have our one night off a fortnight while we are on night shift and we have chosen the second Friday of each fortnight.

We fear we shall never see the Peccadillo again as she has gone on nights and will probably come on days when we change over.

Thursday 10 September
An incredibly wearing day for Els – it went on and on and she didn't know how to endure it. K was delighted to see this morning that there was only one of her horrible levers left to be done. She completed this and was put to an entirely new job, a release pin for a hurri-bomber, a fiddling job and she doesn't much like it yet. As several were required immediately K got Fred to do them as she knew she would be slow. We both felt exhausted today. Miss Corney, one of the Office Staff, came round to Els this morning, and gave her the fright of her life. She asked 'Did you register last Saturday?' Els gaped in horror and said 'no' and unable to think of a disarming explanation of why she hadn't registered among the 43s she merely said gruffly 'I am older than that'. Miss Corney looked surprised (as E had filled in her Morrisons papers as 43) and went away looking slightly embarrassed as Els made no attempt to amplify her statement.

Friday 11 September
Els had a dreary day and got on slowly, but at lunch time she had a surprise packet £9.5.1 bonus on her horrible tapered sockets plus her ordinary week's wages. This

was a staggerer and we both think there is a mistake somewhere, but we are not bothering about it, as we have both lost bonus earlier through ignorance, and we don't think it will hurt them to make it up to us a bit. In the evening we felt like the traditional munition workers, dividing out the £18 which has come into the house. Of course it represents weeks of work, as E hasn't had any bonus for a long time. As the bonuses seem to be equalising out fairly well we have now gone back to the system of pooling our total wage packets.

K had a frightful day with her new job which is very fiddling and the machine kept on behaving 'contrariwise'.

We hear that Hilda fainted on night shift last night, but wouldn't transfer to days as Mr Rapley wanted her to. We presume she prefers nights and Stan to no Stan and days.

We have been developing the agitation for stools and today wrote out a suggestion and got the machine operator women to sign it – as follows:

> The women operators on the centre lathes & capstan would very much appreciate it if they could have stools or chairs by their machine. The long hours of standing are very tiring, & there is often opportunity for a few moments rest, but there is nowhere to sit. – signed – etc.

Nancy Deacon asked us if she might show the note to the shop steward as he would like to vet it. He pronounced it ideal, so we shall get Hilda and Muriel to sign it and then send it in. The new paying-out system today was an unqualified success. Instead of the usual hurly-burly, everyone went to their 4 pay queues and we were out of the place in 5 minutes.

Saturday 12 September
Els was horrified to find that the charming Peter Catford, who works at the same job on nights, had substituted a failure socket of his own for one of Elsie's perfectly good ones which he had put in his own pile. This was a bitter blow as she has always thought him such a nice boy, and so helpful in putting the lathe ready for her to take over. There is a peculiar casting on his job which made Els sure she was not mistaken, also the fact that she knew she had no failures, and when Els told Fred about it – he thought it was more than likely Catford had taken it, and exchanged them back again so we are as we were. At the end of the day Els hid the rest of her pieces in K's box down the other end of the shop, so hopes it won't happen again.

K had a better day today and struggled on with her pins without too much strain. We heard from Stan that Muriel doesn't want to continue night shift and will probably return to days. We saw a possibility of joining Hilda with Stan, and K asked Mr Rapley if he thought it could be arranged and he said he would try.

We circulated some plums in the machine shop in the afternoon to everybody's delight. At least 90 per cent of the women in Morrisons are married, and their husbands in the Forces and they simply live for the 7 days respite from the factory which they get when their husbands come on leave. This they get four times a year and it seems to enable them to support the long hours and trying conditions of Industry. We poor old spinsters have just the same conditions – but no relief except the one week's holiday a year.

Monday 14 September
Surprised to hear on arrival that we are not going to be required to do night shift after all. Pussy Bradford told us this and said also that there was probably a new rota plan coming into operation shortly by which everyone works on Sundays and has one other day off a week instead, in turn. This would mean that K and E would never have a day off together. They are in a state of mind about this. So also are all the other women in the machine shop. The married women say they won't stand for working on Sundays and there was an absolute fradge all day, everyone threatening to ask for their cards. If this plan goes through there will be an outcry. To add to the confusion a new girl arrived for the centre lathes and caused a general post of jobs. Els had to go back onto her wretched screws on a new machine and she was in a state of nerves all day. Laurie Charman, who took over E's job, was also in a way and was last heard threatening not to come in at all tomorrow as no one had helped her with her new job nor shown her how to work the new machine.

Tuesday 15 September
Another awful day. Fred had 5 women to look after today, 5 of whom were unfamiliar with their jobs so he was kept busy all day running from one to the other. Mrs Hazelgrove insisted on having his attention whenever she wanted it to the detriment of everyone else. When asked by Ivy how he liked his harem he was heard to mutter that he'd like to shoot the lot! Els was nearly sick by the end of the day, watching the movement of the screws, and feels a nervous wreck. We hear that the Production Committee meets tonight and will discuss the new 7-day rota plan. K got hold of Pussy Bradford and told him that there was great feeling among the women about the proposal, and that if it went through there would be an outcry. He seemed interested and rather surprised to hear this and we hope he will pass it on to the meeting. The atmosphere in the m/c shop is still electric and everywhere there were knots of furious women grumbling at Morrisons' bad equipment. Laurie Charman did turn up after all today, but spent all day raging and finally went off saying she was going to ask for a transfer. Muriel has come back on days looking a wreck after her week's night shift. She has got a doctor's certificate to say she must not do any more night shift. She says the heat and lack of ventilation is dreadful, though she liked working quietly on without any interference from any one. Stan tells us that Mr Rapley, the foreman, isn't seen much on nights, so we suppose he goes off somewhere for a little lay-down. We had 2 kind presents of runner beans today from Mrs Hazelgrove and Mrs Marley. Els went over to the FAP with a cut finger and saw the hateful Nurse Webster who was surprised to find that E was not K's sister – but her cousin! She said that K had informed the ARP officer when she interviewed him about changing her shelter that K and E were sisters! Els said very firmly that K couldn't possibly have said this as she had no sisters. The nurse then held forth about the impossibility of changing people's shelters as once they started that, they would

be doing it all the time. E said gently but firmly that once they took to satisfy people, no one would ever want to change again. Els forebore to mention that K had taken the law into her own hands and now goes to E's shelter, and the shelter marshall winks at it. The nurse even said that mothers and daughters working in the factory go to separate shelters, which we think is pretty inhuman.

Wednesday 16 September
What a week of awful days. Rows and rumours of rows, but anyhow all these excitements do make the days pass quicker. No one could say that factory life is dull! During the course of the day K enquired from Bradford how the Production meeting had gone and what was the result of the new rota suggestion. Pussy said, rather ruefully, that he had been on the carpet at the meeting and when he had said that the women were up in arms at the idea he had been told by the management that he was more 'for' the women than 'for' the firm; he doesn't think the plan will materialise. K passed all this on to Ivy, who said that when a chargehand was being appointed he was always asked whether he was 'for' the firm or 'for' the workers! We can hardly believe this but Ivy swears it's true. And it would certainly account for the way [in] which our nice Stan diddles the women into doing extra time, by telling each woman, quite untruthfully, that all the other women have agreed to do it. We have always thought this most peculiar behaviour on his part, but perhaps it's his idea of being 'for' the firm.

The next excitement of the day was a fearful upset when K handed in her last 3 days work and it was found that the whole of yesterday's production would have to be scrapped owing to K having been given a wrong tool to work with. Pierrot, the Chief Inspector, came rushing down the shop and rounded on K and then on Fred who is responsible for setting up K's work. Ivy was purple in the face as she was to blame for not having noticed the error while the work was being done. Fred was to blame for having given K the wrong tool and K was guilty of not having recognised it was the wrong tool! Altogether everyone was pretty well in trouble and K was absolutely furious at having wasted a day's work. Ivy was so browned off that she went home at 5.30. Luckily the wasted bits were not large pieces so the waste of metal will not be very great. After all this excitement Fred suddenly became extremely amiable and cut 2 screws for Els and made K a special gauge. We think he feels contrite that he has neglected us very much in the last few days and was trying to patch.

Laurie Charman has regaled us with an appalling story of Catford. It appears that he has been placed on probation for robbery with violence, stealing silk stockings and holding up a policeman with a revolver. We can hardly credit this story as he always seems such a superior boy, but it would account for his crooked behaviour with Els' bits. His record seems well-known in the shop, and George Bradford told Laurie to lock up all her tools and equipment carefully as she was sharing a lathe with a man who couldn't be trusted. K also got a scandalous story about the Peccadillo. She is returning to day shift next week, as she has arrived late every night this week smelling of whiskey and part-sozzled. Her further misdemeanour was to be caught canoodling in an air-raid shelter with one of the fellows during working hours. The girl is only nineteen so it's a poor look-out for her. We learnt today that Miss Corney has been appointed Women's Welfare Supervisor. As every factory with over 40 women has to have a WWS – we think it is about time Morrisons had one for its 300 women.

Thursday 17 September
Els' cold, which has been threatening for the past few days, is now in full blast and she is streaming and feels wretched. A quiet day in the factory, everyone suffering from reaction at the alarms and excursions of the last few days and the atmosphere felt dull and lifeless. We learn that the Peccadillo's boyfriend, who was caught misbehaving in the shelter with her, is none other than 'stick-em-up' Catford, as he is called. He does seem to be a one! We are delighted to learn today that little Mrs Kilby has been appointed the 3rd nurse after all and starts work on Monday. Marley has tried to indicate that she has withdrawn her application as the hours were not good and the money less than she is now earning, but that, of course, it would be a step-up for Kilby! We take all this with a grain of salt.

Friday 18 September
E's cold frightful and her eyes filling with tears every minute so that she couldn't see her work. The main excitement of the day was a personal visit from Mr Overton and George Bradford to each woman machine operator to explain the new rota system and to ask our co-operation. He started on K and E where he got a mouthful. He tried all the gambits from King and Country and personal sacrifices via soft soap to compulsion. But we stood him out on all grounds and pointed out that if we couldn't have our time-off together we should have no life at all. He then tried a lot of soft stuff about the sacrifices he had to make and how little he saw his wife and daughter so we told him of our own sacrifices in giving up our home and business to do war work. He kept on saying that of course he realised that the happy worker was the best worker and he asked our willing cooperation. We told him that of course if the scheme was adopted we should have to do it, but that we certainly should not be 'happy workers' but utterly wretched. And, moreover, that we should prefer to go to the Midlands than abide by it. This appeared to finish him off somewhat and he went on to the other women. Here he found that Muriel and the new girl were quite willing, but that Laurie Charman was adamant and told him off fiercely like a tigress. Mrs Hazelgrove also flatly refused to cooperate and finally Mr Overton was heard to say that he didn't think the scheme would work. The poor man looked quite worn out after dealing with all these overbearing women. Though we flatly refuse to welcome his scheme we felt rather sorry for him, as he had obviously spent hours working out this complicated plan with charts & graphs. By the end of the day E's cold was worse than ever & she found she had a temperature so retired to bed, having warned Bradford and Fred that she was not coming in on Saturday which we learn is to be half-day.

Saturday 19 September
E stayed in bed all day gently sweating from time to time. K went to work alone and gathered that the rota scheme had fallen through. K had a frightful

morning as she couldn't get Fred to help her and nearly had a row with him. Everyone delighted to go off at 12.30. The last half hour was devoted to throwing onto the floor any pieces of scrap metal which were not needed and the resulting chaos was frightful. We learn that the place is to have a spring-clean over the weekend.

Monday 21 September
Els remained in bed but moved into the sitting room, as being more cheerful than the bedroom. K went off to Morrisons alone. Hilda has returned on days and the morning passed in an 'atmosphere' between her and Muriel, both of whom said the other one 'cut' her, so they tossed their heads at each other and took no notice. Ivy says that 'Moaning Minnie' (Hilda) has been carrying on a flirtation with Rapley and they go out together. Muriel doesn't hold with this behaviour, and in the past has taxed Hilda with it and stopped it. Nights with Rapley in charge has apparently caused it to flare up again and Hilda and Rapley arrive together very late most evenings – so Muriel is up in arms again. They scrapped all through the dinner hour, to Laurie Charman's annoyance, until she told them they were behaving like children and they'd better have it out elsewhere, so this they did and are evidently now friends again. Ivy says that everything said to Hilda goes straight back to Rapley so we must beware. The Peccadillo was there today, looking awful, her yellow mane in a red string bag with a coquettish red bow perched on the top. She seems to be on good terms with Hilda. Many kind enquiries after poor Els whose temperature is alas up again.

Tuesday 22 September
K had a long boring day . . . only enlivened by a gossip with Ivy, who told K that her husband left her 5 years ago and she has since divorced him. Ivy had a nice home then and everything she could wish for. Now she has to live in rooms. She has contrived to keep herself and her charming little daughter Pamela, aged 15, by her own efforts. There is a man who would like to marry her now, but she can't make up her mind. He is the exact antithesis of her first husband, steady, reliable, quiet and rather dull, we gather. She rather dreads the thought of loneliness now that her daughter is growing up. We feel very sorry for Ivy Barney, as she is such a game little thing and always friendly and cheerful. She has the very difficult position of being 'Floor Inspector' of the machine shop, which means that she has to roam from machine to machine, inspecting the work as it is produced, and if necessary tell off skilled men if their work becomes inaccurate. Not at all an easy task and needs great tact. The fact that all the men and girls like and respect her shows that she is an unusual person. We have always liked her, and admired her neat, gimp appearance and her hair always beautifully kept in rows and rows of little curls. She always seems in good spirits and will stand up to anyone. The only thing that makes her rabid are the little bitches who go chasing after the more presentable married men! Since we have heard her life story, we see the reason for her rage.

Wednesday 23 September
An interminable day for Kathleen who did a record day for her present job which she learns is the release pin of the bombs for the Hurri-bombers. Els had another boring day at home.

K went to visit little Kilby, Nurse Kilby of the FAP now. She certainly looks more presentable in her white uniform than she did in her dreadful rubber apron, all spattered with grease at the capstans, with a cigarette protruding from her mouth. She seems quite settled in at the FAP and is very nice to the girls.

Thursday 24 September
K thought the day would never end, though she got on all right with her work and had a long talk with Stan. Apparently, he has been ticked off in the office because some of Hilda and Muriel's work was wrong and he was told he didn't look after his girls enough and was too slack with them. He feels rather aggrieved about this, as he doesn't believe in bullying people, though he does think Muriel takes advantage of his easy discipline. Rapley came out rather well in this row as he went to the office and said he was equally to blame for any work in the machine shop. Rapley, by the way, is reported to have said *à propos* of Hilda that if anyone talked scandal about him they could come to the office & he would pitch 'em out on their ear. This must be a guilty conscience because he was seen out with Hilda on Saturday, by various members of the firm. Scandal rushes round the factory like a wind.

Friday 25 September
Elsie's first day back at work but the lathe she was to work on had been broken, and Stan was busy helping the others, so Els stood about all the morning, her back aching, and wishing she had stayed in bed or gone for a nice walk in the sunshine. However, in the afternoon, after another delay, Stan set her to work on a new job in aluminium, which was a pleasant change for her. K didn't have a very good day, and nothing seemed to go right. When we came to our pay packets E was surprised and pained to find that the repeat of the job which had produced a £9.0.0 bonus, this week produced a bonus of 3/5. Though we think the £9.0.0 was a mistake the 3/5 is equally absurd, and Els told Stan about it and he agreed it was wrong and Rapley would enquire into it tomorrow. K thinks the week seems endless partly due to absence of little Sunshine Elsie and partly due to K's having returned each day at lunchtime which makes it seem like two days in having to go back in the afternoon again.

One of the millwrights welcomed Elsie back saying she had had all the luck being at home a week. Els, anxious to disclaim having enjoyed herself – narrowly stopped herself from saying: 'It's not much fun being in bed alone!'

Saturday 26 September
A quiet morning, both of us getting on happily with our jobs. At 12.30, however, we departed to see *Gone with the Wind*, as with the alterations with night shift we had expected to be free in the day time this Saturday and could not now alter the arrangements. Mr Rapley wasn't very pleased with us for going, but as the whole

affair was his fault for chopping and changing so much we didn't feel very contrite. We enjoyed the film exceedingly.

We were delighted to observe today that a new tin hut is being erected in the yard outside the factory and learn it is to house 4 clocking on machines. This will be a tremendous improvement as at the moment there are only 2 clocking on machines and 175 workers use one and about 350 the other. Unfortunately, we are in the latter and the queue is terrific – especially on Tuesdays when the whole factory empties together at 5.30. We have frequently had to wait 10 or 12 minutes to clock off, which has made us feel more [*than*] usually red, and hating the bloated capitalist who can walk out of the main entrance!

Tuesday 29 September
Uneventful day, full of hard work. There seemed to be petty women's quarrels going on most of the day between Hilda and Mrs Hazelgrove, the latter having 'passed remarks' about Rapley's favouritism of Hilda. Each in turn told their version of the story to all and sundry – which was very boring, but it revealed that Mrs Hazelgrove though rather deaf, can lip read, so we shall have to be careful. In the middle of the afternoon Rapley went the round of the machine shop and asked us all our ages. We wonder what this portends, perhaps fire watching? We learn that Ivy also knocked 5 years off her age when she entered Morrisons and had to confess to it later on.

Wednesday 30 September
Nothing of interest today, with the exception of the news that the awful Mrs Parachute Marley has had two husbands, the first a squadron leader, the present one a soldier. We don't know if no. 1 died or has left her. No. 2 is a 'paratroop'. We also learn that he is shortly due for a week's leave again and gets 4 of these weeks in the year and Mrs Marley gets the 4 weeks out of the factory to be with him. We really think that we shall both have to marry into the Forces so that we can also occasionally get a week's holiday! These married women just hang on with these holidays to look forward to and we do feel a little envious.

K had a gossip with Jim Moore today. He told her he had been a turner for 12 years and thought Morrisons was the most awful place he'd ever struck. Go-as-you-please discipline in the work shops but the powers-that-be an absolute collection of duds. No one sufficiently expert at the job to be able to help the hands when a problem arises. Even the experienced turners get jobs which baffle them sometimes and he says there is no one in authority from whom you can get any help. He particularly loathes the foreman Mr Rapley and he once told Els that when he (Jim) is called up for the army he is going to celebrate the occasion by knocking Rapley down before he leaves!

Friday 2 October
Hilda said today that she had egg on toast nearly every morning for breakfast, and when we said enviously 'Oh! Do you keep hens?' – she said almost as one hiding a skeleton-in-the-cupboard 'Well, just down in the kitchen garden part'

and then as though in extenuation 'We never used to, of course.' Hilda evidently likes to consider herself a cut above those who keep backyard fowls.

We much regret to record that we are getting Industrial Dirt on the face. We can bear our hands becoming spoiled with the honourable scars of our labours, but somehow blackheads on the face are degrading and we have realised that something must be done about it. [*Through a friend they arrange to have 'facials' in town.*]

Saturday 3 October
A busy day – when women of all ages up to 45 had to register for fire watching. As we were going up to London it was impossible for K to register and poor old Els is too old and decrepit to be compelled. We worked busily all day and Els finished her job just before the end, and then we rushed off to London with very little time to spare before the theatre, *The Man who Came to Dinner*, which we very much enjoyed.

Sunday 4 October
[*Visit to the 'complexion lady' in Maida Vale then home.*] K went off to register for fire watching at 6 p.m., but found a queue nearly 100 yards long, so came home again.

Monday 5 October
Under Fred this coming fortnight – however he seems less irritable than last time. K got in touch with the women's shop steward for the Municipal Workers' Union which the women can belong to. She told K to keep quiet about it as it is a non-union firm and members of the union are regarded with disfavour by the authorities. The whole conversation was carried on *sotto voce*. Lou (the Fat Cooky miller) told K that she only earns 10½d an hour, though she has been there a year. However, the union officials visited the factory the other day and she understands the pay will shortly be raised. She says this is why they took all our ages the other day. K went off at lunchtime to register and got done quickly and no waiting about.

Tuesday 6 October
Industry seems to have settled into a rather dull routine and there is nothing much to write about. K had another to-do over her bomb-release pins. She sent in 85 all correct and completed only to learn from Pierrot, the Chief Inspector, that the drawing had been altered and the pin now had a slight addition which neither K nor Fred nor Stan nor Ivy knew anything about. This took K the best part of 2 hours to rectify and she felt annoyed about it. Fred was also in a rage as he was ticked off by Pierrot for 'not working to the drawing'. He very reasonably replied that he had never been informed that the drawing was altered and also that he had been on night shift until yesterday. Elsie had a quiet day and got on steadily without requiring any help from anyone. This was just as well, as Fred had 'got the rats', as Ivy said, and was immersed in a job of his own. K had a bad afternoon and when she spoilt 3 consecutive pins she felt she would really do

better to stop. However, Fred came to help, very disagreeably, so she continued, though in a frightful rage, as Ivy had told her that Fred's comment on her appeal for help was 'Oh! She's always in trouble!' K is furious, as she is a very independent worker and seldom calls for help, and in any case fiddles about by herself for ages sooner than appeal to Fred, who is always so bad tempered and saturnine. Oh dear! How can we endure another 10 days of Fred. We get on so much better with our nice friendly Stan and nothing ever seems to go wrong when he is there.

Wednesday 7 October

We learn, to our horror, that Fred has been asked to do a month on days! We think we shall be in an asylum by the end of this time, as the 3 days we have already had with the ill-conditioned, saturnine brute has seemed like 3 weeks. K struggled for 3 hours today trying to get her work set up correctly – pride not allowing her to ask Fred for help, and he never came near her all day to see how she was getting on. Laurie is also in a rage with him as he wouldn't help her, and when she said, in fury, that she felt like going home at 5.30, his only reply was that she could for all he cared! We can't see why the wretched boy should be paid 2/4 an hour as our chargehand and then be so abominably disagreeable. He certainly takes away any pleasure there is in our work, and factory life is quite bad enough on its own merits without a bad-tempered boy to add to it.

Thursday 8 October

On arrival this morning we found the men of the night shift in a state of excitement over the delinquencies of Catford, who had only worked for three and a half hours. He was missing the greater part of the night and was not to be found anywhere. Ultimately, he was found sleeping in the canteen behind a pile of chairs and the men pitched him out of the shop. While he was asleep they decorated his lathe with Iron Crosses and placards saying 'While brave men die, rats sleep' and Stan placed upon the lathe a wire spider's web (complete with colossal wire spider) spun during his absence. He was told finally to come back this afternoon on day shift but never turned up.

Fred started this morning just as disagreeable as yesterday and everybody hates it. K has sworn a vow that she won't speak to him, and won't ask for help however long it takes her to fiddle about on her own. Laurie had a frightful day, everything going wrong and Fred wouldn't help at all. Finally Pussy Bradford helped her. K nearly had high blood pressure with rage when Ivy repeated that when she asked Fred to touch up K's tool, he refused and said that if the surface was bad it was pure carelessness. K was so furious that she went on with her awful tool for hours until it was so blunt it would not have sharpened a pencil. Finally, the belt of her lathe broke and she went off for some time to get it repaired, & we think, perhaps, Fred feared that she had gone to complain to the manager (as Mrs Hazelgrove once did), because while she was away he sharpened up her tool and put it back again. Els had a successful day, fortunately not requiring much assistance from Fred.

A new young girl has come to the drilling machines about a week ago. She is very pretty, though a hard face, and well dressed. We have all tried to smile amiably at her, but she responds with a stony stare. Today she told Fat Cookie Lou that she didn't like it here and was going to ask for a transfer, as all the girls were 'ignorant'! We don't quite understand what this word means as we have heard it used before in rather strange contexts. We suspect it means 'low class'.

Friday 9 October
K continued her policy of self-help and no words passed between her and Fred all day. K had a chat with the old sweeper Jock. He said he couldn't bear going about hearing people saying they were 'browned off'. If they did not like a thing they'd got to stick it, so they had much better get a philosophy. All this said with the broadest of Scotch accents, and his cheerful outlook ill consorts with his lugubrious blood-hound's face.

Catford arrived on days today. May Nolan, one of the millers, took a morning off to do her household shopping and chores. We think this sounds a darling idea for those who have to do their own work and we feel very self-righteous.

Marley tells us that we could have got exemption from fire watching on the grounds that our hours, plus travelling, add up to more than 55 hours a week, but we don't like to get exemption unless we have to.

Els very disappointed to find that her promised bonus still hasn't arrived and K also has some queer muddles on her bonus card, so we must send in a query form tomorrow.

Laurie entertained Stan first thing this morning when we met him coming off nights with graphic descriptions of K's rage with Fred and flinging about of rags and what not.

Monday 12 October
Back at the old drudgery again. [*They had been away for the weekend.*] Fred in more amiable mood. The only incident, which caused fury, is that the machine shop girls were told to go to their tea interval at 3. o'c. instead of 4.30. This gives us nearly 4 hours without a break for food, followed by getting home and then having to cook one's meal. This new arrangement appears to be due to the jealousy of the girls who go at three in a crowd and don't like us going in comfort with the men later. Making things more uncomfortable for us doesn't improve matters for them and we can't see what they complained for, especially as many of them go off at 5.30 and don't stay till 7. o'c. overtime as we do. Parachute Marley is furious and has complained to the man supervisor who has said he will look into it.

Tuesday 13 October
No news about the tea alteration, but as everyone leaves at 5.30 today we don't mind when the interval is.

K had a wasted day as Fred took the whole morning setting her up in a new job, and when she had got on happily in the afternoon and the day was drawing to a close, it was suddenly discovered that the micrometer was registering .005

small, so that her whole day's work was scrapped. Fred even tried to imply that it was K's fault. Little twerp!

Wednesday 14 October
The battle of the three o'clock tea continues. We interviewed Miss Corney and Bradford again and they said they would see what could be done and Marley went for Mr Payne (the Man Welfare Officer) again. However, by teatime nothing had happened so off we had to go at 3. o'c. and were pretty nearly dead by 7.

We had a visit from Mr Peckham (the ARP Officer with whom K had her row about the shelters). He was having a whip-round for the Merchant Navy which everyone subscribed to gladly. K handed her money over with a stony stare, remembering the last interview with him when *à propos* of shelters. She had roared at him that she didn't care if he was separated from his wife! However, as he departed from her he said, with a beaming smile, 'I haven't forgotten about your shelter, Miss Bliss and will alter it for you shortly.'

Thursday 15 October
We had rather a pleasant morning as Fred was on a rush job and we were in Dennis Ellis' charge. He is a very good looking and pleasant lad and was a nice change from the dour Fred.

A new dictum has gone forth about tea, as everyone again started prodding up the lethargic authorities. All the women are now to go to late tea in two batches and all the men are to go early. This starts next Monday. There is to be no tea interval at all on Saturday afternoon, which we think rather mean.

Friday 16 October
A nice letter from Auntie. She has sent some pink poppies to Gawge whom we now fear we have finally lost. We regret the dear departed very much.

We find the Industrial Day drags slowly, the only things which quicken the pace at all are Rumpuses or Love. Love seems to have passed out of our lives with Gawge, but Rumpuses crop up two or three times a week and do make a nice change.

We have had a strange conversation with May Nolan, the bright-faced little Irish miller who works near us. She ties her skirt with elastic to the knees when cycling as she is so modest that she would fall off her bicycle with shame if the wind blew her skirt up and showed her knickers. She has a frightful complex about going along to the lavatory when it involves going past the men who might know whither she was bound. This involves her in very complicated planning to time her visits with the men's tea intervals. She has also spent a period in hospital with kidney trouble entirely owing to her ridiculous prudery. We read her a lecture and hope we shall tease her out of this nonsense.

One of the capstan boys, Bill, is joining the Merchant Navy on Monday and we think it may be the making of him. He is an unsatisfactory boy of the lounge lizard dago type of good looks. He scrounges cigarettes and loans from fellow workers and never repays. Poor May Nolan has been stung for 10/- which she will never see again. Rumour has it that he has been in prison for stealing cigarette cases and jewellery, but his comment on it was that that was nothing. He is short of money because he won't do overtime and has lost (or sold!!) his Home Guard Respirator and Tin Hat and their value is being stopped out of his wages.

We returned to the question of stools when we saw Miss Corney today. She says we shall get them in time but there is no material. We said stools could be bought at Kennards and that it was stated in the Factory Act that women workers must be supplied with seating accommodation. We should like to know what our next step should be as we can see the war being over before we get them.

Monday 19 October
Darling Stan back with us once more and all the machine shop women were cheerful and contented. Three new girls came on the centre lathes, but all the machines were in use so they had to hang about all day – which exhausted them extremely. We felt very sorry for them. It was very hot and stuffy today and Mrs Hazelgrove fainted right off, falling backwards from her lathe onto the floor bumping her head. Stan rushed at her and picked her up and there was a general flap. Geoff rushed for the nurse and a stretcher, but by this time she had recovered and to Geoff's great disappointment the stretcher was not required and Old Mother Riley was led out by the nurses to the FAP. Later she returned and said she was going home to rest. We hear that 2 other women fainted today. Perhaps if this goes on they really will get us stools!

Tuesday 20 October
Another endless day, although everyone finished at 5.30. K is very much depressed at the thought of her 300 pins yet to do, as she has done this job so long that she has reached saturation point and to use the pet expression is completely 'browned off'. Hilda was overheard today to say that after the war she would take good care to get a job that hadn't any 'andles! Old Mother Riley did not come back so we hope she is being sensible and taking a rest after her collapse. Coming back from work in the dusk Els recognised Hilda's infuriating knock-kneed trousered walk and saw she was in company with a male civilian, whom Els believes was Rapley.

Wednesday 21 October
Two of the new girls got jobs, so they were happier. The third one still had to stand about. We find they all trained for 8 weeks at the Borough Polytechnic and seem to have had a good concentrated course. They are all young conscripted marrieds. The youngest is an enormous, stormy looking girl of 19 who used to work in a grocer's shop. She also is called Hilda (Carter). She is said to have a violent temper. This information comes from another of the Poly girls, Rachel Thurgood, who is a charming little thing whom we like very much. She is a Devonshire girl. The third Poly girl is a horror, and looks like a bad-tempered version of the Peccadillo, but without any of the Peccadillo's charm, and more inexpertly made-up. Her name is Israel and she hates the whole business and is plotting to get out of it. Her husband has already wangled himself out of the army. Mrs Israel is abominably made up. She has nut-brown eyes which show a

rim of white below the iris, mascara'd lashes and brows and two enormous blobs of peach colour on her cheeks. Her figure is slim and undernourished-looking and she is tiny. She makes up for this by tremendous self-assurance, and helps herself to anything she wants in the way of tools by rummaging about in everyone's boxes without so much as 'by your leave'. She is not liked by her Poly colleagues and she is already cordially disliked by all the old stagers of the machine shop.

The four clocking on machines are now in operation and will be an improvement. The only disadvantage is that they are outside so we shall get wet waiting to clock off. This infuriating firm has now ordained that our short rest after lunch is broken into for no good reason that we can see. However, the early morning tyranny has now been removed. They suddenly elected to lock the gates in the mornings until 7.45 am which meant that there were often between 40 and 50 people raging outside in the rain. However, after about 5 days of this things are as they were. Laurie Charman says that what with the barbed wire that has gone up all round the outside and the petty tyrannies inside, Morrisons is like living in a concentration camp. Hand in hand with the generosity of providing 4 clocks in place of the two which caused the enormous queues we have endured for months a new edict has gone forth. Any workers seen in their hats or coats before the time whistle goes will be docked off a quarter of an hour's pay.

Thursday 22 October
A quiet happy day under the aegis of Stan and everyone working quietly and well. Mrs 'Islegrove' is to have at least a week's holiday following her recent collapse. K did an absolutely record number of pins and can't imagine how she could increase her speed by about 300 per cent. She thinks perhaps it is because the end of her pin job is in sight.

Friday 23 October
As soon as work was over we dashed off to *The First of the Few*, a simply wonderful film, being the story of the designing of the Spitfire by Mitchell, all the opposition he encountered to his revolutionary design, finally working up to its being taken up by the Air Ministry, and wonderful pictures of air fights in the Battle of Britain. We were particularly thrilled being employed on Spitfire making ourselves.

Saturday 24 October
A collection was made for Nancy Deacon today. She has been away for some weeks having an operation and we hope she will get a good sum as she is such a dear little thing. We tried to get her also some peaches or grapes, but found the price was prohibitive so had to be content with some Cox's Orange Pippins.

Stan told K today that she and Els were less trouble to him than any of his other girls. K was so much moved by this that she immediately broke a parting tool.

Mrs Marley is again away as her husband is home on sick leave and he will get another week's ordinary leave next month. Really, life is quite bearable for these women married to men in the forces.

Yesterday Laurie complained to Miss Corney that the top ventilators really must be opened as the atmosphere in the morning was foul. After about two hours this was done and we were glad to say they were open again today.

Sunday 25 October
We went off on our bicycles at 11.30 to lunch with Bert & family at Cheam and enjoyed ourselves very much.

Monday 26 October
Laurie went off with a pain, thinks she may have eaten something that did not agree with her. The blue alert went on and off most of the morning and finally the factory siren went and we all trooped down to the shelters where we heard distant firing but nothing very near. We came up again in time for lunch and the public all clear went just as we clocked on again for afternoon work.

Tuesday 27 October
Laurie still away, also Muriel, so with Old Mother Hazelgrove still absent this made 3 lathes idle. Capstan Els has also gone to hospital again and Mrs Margetson is in bed with chronic cystitis. In fact most of the machine shop women seem to be fading out, so we think the need for stools is urgent and we intend badgering Miss Corney again about them. As Hilda's two cronies were away, she had her lunch with us and was quite pleasant & amiable. Her affair with Rapley is progressing. He is always popping along to have a word with her at her machine, especially while the other men are all in the canteen for their tea breaks. Tonight we saw them going off together after work, quite brazenly.

Wednesday 28 October
Rather a pleasant day today in spite of it being eleven hours long. There is always a contented atmosphere when dear Stan is in charge and today work went well and everything progressed smoothly. K finished her bomb pins and began her favourite job. Els had approbation from Stanley which warmed the cockles of her heart. He said he is very pleased with the job E is working on now and Els has made a very good job of it. He told K, earlier in the day, that E and she are less trouble than any of the others to him and that us older ones and 'Mrs Islegrove' are much more reliable than some of these young things who have 'off days' when they don't feel like it and don't do any work at all.

The awful little Mrs Israel was set to work on the small lathe next to Elsie, and E got heartily sick of her. She does very little work in a lethargic manner, at frequent intervals she lights a cigarette slowly and whenever Els catches her eyes she casts her own eyes up with looks of unutterable weariness. She frequently comes over to E & says in the manner of one saying something extraordinarily interesting 'I think-I'll-go-to-the-lav' drawled out with a whine.

Thursday 29 October
Today we had the factory inspectors round, male and female. The authorities were in a flap and Rapley insisted that E's lathe should have the guard put over the gear wheels. This was all very well, but the guard is so made that when a long rod of metal is being turned, it cannot be used! E pointed this out to Rapley and he simply said that the guard must be up while the inspectors were in the factory. He therefore gave orders for E's rod to have the end sawn off. After the inspectors had been & gone, E removed the guard and went on as usual! The woman inspector went up and had a word with Jimmy Dale, the shop steward. Apparently, he never told her that our stools had never been provided. Ivy was mad with him and said she only wished the inspector had spoken to her as she would have told her a thing or two. At tea this evening Mr Hurst and the commissionaire were up in the canteen watching the endless queue of girls patiently waiting for their tea in the meagre ¼ hour's break. Some of them only get 3 or 4 minutes to sit down after they have got their food and then the tea is too hot to drink. We hope that someone complained to the inspectors about these queues. It is a matter which does not affect us as we always bring our own food. The awful little Israel did practically no work today and the small amount she did do was all scrapped. Finally, Stan told Rapley she was doing no good and she was taken off the job and stood about idly gossiping for the last hour. She has been late every morning and is always ready dressed to go home before the whistle goes (completely against regulations). She is the only case we have so far come across of wilful, persistent idleness. Elsie, who works near her, is getting enraged about her and feels like taking her to task, but fears it would do no good. Neither Hilda nor Rapley stayed for overtime tonight, and we draw our own conclusions.

Friday 30 October
When Miss Corney came round K returned to the charge about the stools and hot water and Miss Corney said she would speak to Mr Payne about it. She said she couldn't move the authorities about the hot water, and when K said why didn't the inspectors do something about it she said that although they came about every 6 months nothing ever happened. K told sad stories of our facial maladies and the impossibility of getting clean in cold water and Miss Corney was sympathetic, but didn't know what she could do about it.

Mrs Israel spent another day doing nothing and told everyone she was not coming in tomorrow as she was going to the Labour Exchange to get out of Morrisons.

K also approached Mr Rapley to see if we can't go on night shift with Stan when he goes as she told him we couldn't get on with Fred. He said he knew Fred was temperamental and advised us not to sit down under it but have a good row with him. We don't feel very hopeful about going on night shift with Stan as we don't think Mr Rapley will do anything about it, and the thought of a month with Fred is more than we can bear.

Saturday 31 October
Mrs Israel appeared today after all but late as usual, so perhaps she has thought better of going to the Labour Exchange. Els is nearing the completion of her 300 sockets and Stan tells her he has got a brute of a job for her next: K's bomb

release pins. However, Els was smug and said she couldn't complain as she'd had a lovely job for a month.

Miss Corney said this morning that Mr Payne had not heard anything about stools and recommended us to write a note in and get all the girls to sign it. K said we'd already done this 2 months ago and that Miss Corney herself told us that 'the application had been favourably considered, but that there was delay owing to lack of material'. She looked non-plussed and said she would ask Mr Payne to see K. Later in the morning the fat and disgusting-looking Mr Payne arrived at K's lathe and told her that it was no good putting suggestions in the suggestion box as they never reached the proper quarters and we must hand them to him. So we have to start all over again with the 'Battle of the Stools'.

Sunday 1 November

As our Industrial diary book is filling up we once more survey the scene. First of all we are both quite convinced that in spite of the dirt of Morrisons, the long tiring hours, the noise and the annoyance of working for rather unhuman employers and the general austerity of our life, we are much happier than we should have been if we had remained at Benacre where we were continually wondering whether we were doing essential work. Now, at any rate, we are doing what the gov't has asked women to do and find the war doesn't get on our minds nearly as much as it did.

Looking back over the last five months we think that the training that we had at the centre was exactly right for the sort of work we are called upon to do. Mercifully, our chargehands show us how to set about each new job and come to our aid when we are in difficulties, but we find that our previous training makes us able to be fairly independent when jobs are repeated. We have very much enjoyed, both at the Training Centre and Morrisons, the opportunity we have had of mixing with working-class people on absolutely equal terms. We think that amongst the women workers it is the middle-aged who keep at it best. The young ones so often get 'browned off' and disappear to the Cloaks or need their chargehands to be after them to stop them from gossiping to their friends. The middle-aged seem to have their own standards of a good day's work and keep steadily on and on regardless of fatigue and boredom. This boredom is the bugbear of Industry. If something could be done about it, production would increase. Speaking for ourselves – we find that our jobs frequently are finicking and exacting and need all one's concentration and care to prevent making scrap, but on other operations of a job the work may be almost mechanical, and though it is a relief for a short time the novelty soon pales and we nearly die of boredom. The hours drag interminably, the clock never advances and Sunday seems a long way off. We often think that we might petition for a radio to relieve the tedium which must be much worse for those who are always doing the really mechanical jobs, but doubt whether a radio would make itself heard above the awful noise. Looking round the huge workshop it seems to us that the hundreds of workers, though only separated from each other by a few feet are each shut away in an impenetrable box of noise and live their separate lives for 11 hours a day hardly able to communicate with each other.

We now feel fairly 'old hands' and no longer suffer from the acute nervous dread we did when we first came to Morrisons. Els, during her first fortnight here, felt as though she were fielding bent double in the slips in a very important cricket match, poised on her toes ready for a movement in any direction and her hands darting from handle to handle. It was a very long cricket match and exhausting. Now she has long been able to straighten her back and relax and turn the handle with calm and detachment. In fact she is much put to it, in the mechanical jobs that crop up, to know how to while away the time. *A Midsummer Night's Dream*, which she learned by heart at the age of 16, has been a tremendous help to her. 'Now, fair Hippolyta' she declaims in a loud shout as she retracts the drill and so on scene after scene to the end. This talking aloud is evidently 'sound engineering practice' as it seems to be pretty general – for looking around the shop one sees everyone's mouth is moving, though no sound can be heard above the machines. K cannot amuse herself with these flights of memory so her mind turns to brooding on the wrongs of the workers – and she plans various reforms at Morrisons. Sometimes she holds imaginary conversations with the bosses out of which she always emerges triumphant.

We have got a most awful looking collection of bosses – foremen, managers and directors – and when occasionally they are all standing together in discussion they look like a group of vultures. Cruel mouths, hard eyes set too close together, altogether a grisly lot. Mr Hurst, the works manager is the King Vulture and is cordially disliked by everyone. Captain Lines is said to be more just and doesn't bear malice if he ticks anyone off. He is rather like Felix [*the Cat*], and keeps on walking, bent forward from the hips, hands clasped behind his back and eyes darting out in every direction. The managing director, Mr Proctor, has quite a genial air, but otherwise has the appearance of a well-scrubbed pig. He occasionally goes round chatting to the men, but we think he is really not much better than the rest. He seldom talks to the women; we think this is because he is afraid of what the women would tell him about our working conditions. The women, unlike the men, don't hesitate to answer back to their bosses. The factory building is really a disgrace. Broken windows let in the howling draught, the roof leaks and great puddles collect on the floor. The walls are splashed with oil and grease and the whole place is incredibly dirty and littered with filthy bits of equipment not at the moment in use. It is a frightful sight. These dirty conditions are made worse by the complete absence of hot water in the 8 washbasins and lavatories provided for 300 girls.

Morrisons has 3 other factories at Chester, Peterborough and Tadworth [*K and E did not know that this one did not exist*], besides its head one at Croydon. They recently issued a smug little monthly bulletin with news from all its branches. The foreword was by the Well Scrubbed Pig and was a pious plea to play up for the old side and to avoid kicking into our own goal, and much more in the same infuriating strain. The rest of the paper is given over to news of ex-workers and a collection of jokes and stories, some of them funny and most of them risky.

It is only 1 November but we have already begun to speculate on what holiday we shall get at Christmas. With only one week's holiday a year the Bank

Holidays shine like beacons and we are looking forward to at least a day off at Christmas.

Tuesday 3 November
Today was all one reads of Factory Life Whoopee. Mr McGiveney (the managing director, whom we have never seen before) gave a party in the lunch interval in honour of 'two famous pilots' who were coming to see the factory and talk to the workers. Rather, before 12.30 two enormous young men arrived and were taken round the factory by Mr Hurst and Mr Proctor. All the bigwigs had on their smartest clothes and looked very genial. At dinner time we all went into the New Factory (the Meccano room) where enormous queues waited for sandwiches, cakes, beer, port or blistering sherry, kindly provided by Mr McGiveney. We ate our food and perched on the benches, while relayed gramophone records were broadcast. Then Mr McGiveney . . . introduced the two pilots, Squadron Leader Bernard Meyer DFC of Bomber Command and Ft Lt Foulds of Coastal Command. Ft Lt Foulds spoke first and was very charming, slightly nervous, and apparently in the manner of all pilots, made very light of his achievements. He spoke very easily & colloquially with much 'damned' & 'damnably' cropping up. He was followed by Squadron Leader Meyer who was evidently much more used to this sort of public speaking. He explained that when pilots have done a given number of hours of operational flying they are put 'on rest' which means that they teach others at training schools. They also go round visiting factories, and he has been to factories all over England. He also told us that the common view that the 1,000 bomber raids had ceased because of heavy losses was a mistaken one, the reason really being that the Atlantic submarine menace was so bad at the time that a large number of Bomber Command planes had to be allocated to Coastal Command. He told us they had already built up a large reserve of planes again, and the quicker we could produce these planes the quicker the 1,000 bomber raids would start again. He said they hoped they would start them in a few weeks. There were then exciting stories of his night-bombing operations on Germany and he said that he and his observer had been together a long time & had now both come on rest. 'However, he is not with me now,' he said 'as he has just got married and I expect he is having more pleasant night operations now than he has had in the past.' This little sally was greeted with a delighted shriek from us factory girls.

Mr McGiveney then bounced up onto the bench again & announced that our local poet, old Jock the Sweeper, had written a poem specially for the occasion and he would now read it to us. Then scruffy old Jock clambered onto the bench, looking more than usually lugubrious and tousled, and read his poem in his glorious Scotch accent. It was quite a good little poem and he read it beautifully and he was greeted with thunderous applause. The proceedings then came to an end & the pilots were besieged by mobs of girls clasping dirty little bits of paper on which the pilots signed their autographs. It was really a very pleasant party and we were amazed and horrified that no one got up and thanked Mr McGiveney for entertaining us.

Wednesday 4 November
The Battle of the Stools has now entered its second phase. We rewrote our
request and got all the women to sign it & then K took it up to Mr Payne
personally. Later in the day a polite little note came down from him to say that
he had the matter well in hand.

E and K both clocked onto new jobs today. K has a glorious little aluminium
job and great fun to make, but poor E has a terrible fiddling job in steel with
tight limits everywhere & she feels very gloomy about it.

Thursday 5 November
At the 7 a.m. news we heard of the Eighth Army's great advance [*Battle of El
Alamein, North Africa*] and went off to work with a great feeling of elation.
Found everyone else very bucked when we got there. The morning began with
a catastrophe. Rachel Thurgood, one of our new turners, going behind one of
the lathes got her hair entangled with a revolving rod of metal which was
sticking out from Laurie Charman's lathe. Laurie, on hearing her shriek,
turned off her machine at once and Rapley, who was fortunately nearby, rushed
up and cut her hair free of the rod. But it had taken the greater part of the
hair off one side of her head and also left a completely bald patch about the
size of a 5/- piece just above her forehead. She was very much shaken and
Laurie took her off to the FAP. Here the beastly Nurse Webster took her in
charge and roared at Laurie to 'get out of here' and told poor Rachel to go
into the adjoining rest room and have a good cry. When Nurse Webster realised
that it was Laurie Charman she was speaking to (Late Sister at the Warlingham
Hospital) she apologised, but Laurie came back in a rage that the nurse should
dare to speak to any worker in that way. She forthwith sent a complaint in to
Mr Proctor and later she was summoned to the presence, where she told her
story. Mr Proctor then sent for Nurse Webster and Rapley and confronted
Nurse Webster with Laurie. There was a great to-do and the nurse was roundly
told off by Mr Proctor who said he didn't want his employees to be spoken to in
that way and it was never to occur again. The whole of the rest of the morning
the machine shop was visited by all the bigwigs viewing the scene of the
accident and conclaves were held all over the place. Actually, we are not very
surprised that there has been an accident as Rachel has obstinately refused to
tie her hair up in a scarf and only wore a stupid little chenille fishnet which was
no protection at all. She has now caused retribution to fall on all the machine
operators as the decree has gone forth that we are all to wear the hateful khaki
convict caps with a peak. And pretty good frights we all looked today, even the
young and pretty ones. Everyone's rage is quite amusing to watch. The
rudeness about no vote of thanks for Mr McGiveney's party has been weighing
on our minds, so today we wrote a polite little note thanking him for the
interesting interlude and for his kind hospitality and all the m/c shop and
inspection girls signed it.

Hilda and Rapley again went off early together and the affair seems to be
getting hotter as they go out together every night now. Stan had a long talk with
K about them and thinks they are very foolish, apart from the morals of the case.

Friday 6 November
Attempting to deliver the note for Mr McGiveney, K was warned not to give it to the office as it might never reach its destination. She was advised to give it to the commissionaire. This man is a horror, covered in medal ribbons and a sergeant major's crown. His function is to blow whistles to start and stop work at intervals all through the day and his greatest pleasure seems to be to find out what everybody's doing and stop them doing it. When E enquired whether Mr McGiveney was coming in today he said very rudely 'Why?', and when K said she had a note for him he looked very disapproving, but finally took it. Later he asked her name and whether she had signed it. He really is a most odious creature. Els had a frightful day with the job.

Saturday 7 November
We are getting very fond of the 19-year-old new girl, Hilda Carter. She talks a lot about her husband to us and obviously adores him. Rachel came in yesterday for a short visit with her head tied up in a pixie-cap. Beyond seeming rather voluble she seemed none the worse. She will return to work on Monday. Her main worry is that her husband is coming on leave shortly and she is afraid he will think she looks a fright.

Elsie met Hilda Greenwood and Rapley going off together after work. Hilda infuriates us by dolling herself up for her daily escapades with Rapley and edging her way in front of everyone at our mirror, which we provided for our own use, but from which we derive singularly little benefit! Hilda seems greatly flattered by the attentions of our Mr Rapley. We suppose he strikes her as frightfully gentlemanly with his light brown suits and snuff coloured shirts. We rather fancy his glorious waves are 'permed' as it is slightly growing out. Stan used to work with him at another factory and said he was always after one girl or another. We gather that Hilda is 'Rapley's latest'. Hilda 'packed him up' after her husband had been home on leave for a week, but she evidently suffered from pique when he immediately went off after another pretty girl, so she 'unpacked' him again and it is now hot and strong.

We are now members of a Trades Union. We are not quite certain of its name, but it's the Municipal and Something Workers. We joined in a most hole-and-corner way and pushed our subscription over to the assistant shop-steward who looked furtive & said she had to be careful! She evidently lives in fear of the firm's gestapo.

Sunday 8 November
At 9.o'c. this morning we heard the splendid news of the American landings in French North Africa. Poor K got nabbed for the local fire watch tonight, unexpectedly.

Monday 9 November
News still thrilling both from Egypt and Africa. K appeared in Industry in a taking little Dutch bonnet which she has substituted for the khaki cap. E's job is

taking all the vitality out of her and she comes back worn and white. K got on very well. She gave E's bonnet to Ivy who looked very nice in it. Life at Duppas Hill is rather beastly now. We go out in the cold dark, and three nights a week we drag ourselves back in the cold dark to an untidy room, and unmade bed, and a dead fire, because Mrs Hatton [*cleaner*] is still away and we doubt whether Mrs Bellwood will ever have her back or replace her.

Tuesday 10 November
Nothing much happened today. Els' job is getting her down. It takes ages to set up and generally two hours have passed before she gets to work at all on the job. Gone are the days of declaiming *A Midsummer Night's Dream*. Now Els concentrates all the time on a fiddling, tiddly job with very tight limits till she can't see and her back nearly breaks with aching. However, she feels slightly cheered, because when she told Stan how despairing she felt about it, he said it was a very difficult job and really only suitable for a skilled man, and she mustn't worry herself that she is so slow.

Wednesday 11 November
We now have our midday dinner at the canteen and find it very good & well cooked & the queue not too long. A plate of meat and 2 veg is 10*d.*

We heard this morning that Hitler has walked into unoccupied France and landed some Airborne troops in Tunisia.

Thursday 12 November
The whole of the centre lathe people are agog at the *affaire* Rapley and Hilda. Everyone is constantly meeting them after work, setting off together arm in arm. Gossip is rife about what will happen during the next fortnight when Hilda's husband returns from Northern Ireland.

E was much cheered today because she got on more quickly with her dreadful job. K's aluminium job looks lovely and clean and interesting.

The little horror, Mrs Israel, has departed. She went to the Labour Exchange for a transfer to a factory nearer her home. She had to get her release from Morrisons first, but as Stan said, she was so bad, he didn't think the firm would try and keep her.

Friday 13 November
With such a date we have had to be careful today as Jock warned us very gravely! We had a good lunch in the canteen and heard the grand news that Tobruk [*important Libyan port*] was ours once more. All our manoeuvres to go on nights with Stan next week have failed, in spite of all our pleas to Rapley. We don't think he has tried to oblige us at all. He simply hasn't bothered. We feel very gloomy, as a month of Fred is almost unbearable. However, K is fully determined not to stand much of Fred's bad temper. If there is any trouble she will report him to Mr Hurst. Stan seems really sorry to lose us and says we are no trouble at all. Hilda Carter is to go on nights next week. Perhaps Rapley thinks he can have a

go at her, while Hilda Greenwood is away. Hilda C. thinks it is a great scandal that all the nicest jobs are saved by Rapley for Hilda Greenwood. If she gets given anything she doesn't like, she pouts and wheedles until she gets taken off it and given something better. K very pleased today to get £2 bonus on her beastly bomb pins and also two other jobs bore fruit so she got £4 in all. Elsie's bonuses are absolutely abracadabra and crackers and Stan has promised to enquire into them for her.

This afternoon there was a fierce fight up behind E's lathe between Eddie, one of the chargehands in the 'automatics', and Reg, one of the boys under him. Reg was bumptious and uppish and finally said that Eddie was an old woman. This caused Eddie (who has a very fierce temper) to start blows, and there was an up-&-a-down-a- with handfuls of hair torn out and two other boys joined in to hold them apart. They both looked enraged and Els was quite frightened as she feared that one of them would seize a spanner and crack open the little one's skull. However, they calmed down, pulled apart, but nearly went for one another again a few minutes [*later*] like a couple of dogs.

Saturday 14 November
Our last morning with dear Stan. Els went up with him to one of the offices to enquire about the missing bonuses, and after much talk they said they would put it right. Els spent the rest of the morning learning how to do the next operation of her job, so as to be independent of Fred next week. K clocked on to a repeat job and so also hopes to be independent of him.

Monday 16 November
Fred in good temper for once. He started off by setting up E's job for her so she was well away early and did not need his help again.

Hilda Greenwood arrived to our surprise, [*as*] her husband had had his leave postponed for a few days. She had a very dull day as Rapley is on nights and Fred was determined to do nothing for her.

Mrs Israel also came back today, announcing that she had been out last week as her husband was not well. She said she is getting a transfer, & during the morning was sent for to see Mr Hurst. He said 'You can't get out of working altogether you know, but we shan't stand in your way in getting a transfer,' to which she replied 'You had better not – I shouldn't come in if you did!' The rest of the day there was no lathe free for her, so K gave her our library book, and she had a pleasant day reading a thriller.

Tuesday 17 November
K had an absolutely streaming cold and felt wretched. Her misery was greatly increased by the fact that the new job is the same awful pivot pins which have been causing E such tribulation for the past two days. After having had such a nice easy job for the past fortnight K is in a flat spin about this desperately fiddling job and fears she will make a lot of scrap. Fred now has Dennis Ellis to help him 'set up' the girls in the morning so E got started in record time. We

forgot to buy dinner checks so had to go out and have a very boring, tepid lunch at the Civic.

Wednesday 18 November
K's cold still streaming. The women have been told to band themselves into groups of 4 for fire watching and we have all had a form to fill in to claim exemption if we wish to, which we personally do not. A long day, E got on well with her job, [*and*] K got on quicker than quick in comparison. Fred went off early not feeling well. He seems quite amiable so far, though E has had no dealings with him at all except when he set her up on Monday.

Thursday 19 November
We were astonished to learn from Ivy that Fred had said to her that it was unnecessary for her to examine any of the centre lathe women's work as everyone except Mrs Israel and Bertie Symons was perfectly reliable. We feel that approbation from Sir Hubert Stanley is praise indeed. A very long day and we were exhausted when we got home. So far this week Fred has been quite amiable, though he never comes along to see how we are getting on.

Friday 20 November
Els disgusted to find that after all the trouble she and Stan took in the office last week over her missing bonuses they still were not paid this week. K also absolutely furious as she had expected 30/ on one job, but only received 5/1, all because she had 'co-operated' with the awful little Mrs Israel. Pussy Bradford spent the whole afternoon talking to all the centre lathe women and trying to pacify them. We all asked if we could go off the bonus system and have a definite increased basic wage instead. The bonuses are nearly always wrong and a great deal of time is wasted while we argue to try and get them put right. We hate all this quarrelling over money and would much rather have a fixed wage. K on fire watch from 2 – 4 a.m. last night. However, it is not taken very seriously in Duppas Hill and beyond sleeping more or less dressed and getting up at 2 a.m. to receive the duty book from a neighbour and getting up again at 4 a.m. to go down the road and deliver the book to another neighbour, she had quite a good night. Unless the siren goes, no one is expected to stay awake.

Saturday 21 November
We have gained nothing in our bonus arguments, except that now we are given 'setting up' cards for all our jobs and we clock on to them while our work is being prepared each morning. This will involve a great deal of rushing back and forth to the time office, and cause the clerks a headache trying to do the arithmetic, but anyhow it will be a little fairer for us. We each had a quite good day on our difficult job, but have decided we don't really dislike it very much now, in spite of the tight limits on all the measurements. The week has gone fast and we can't get over Fred's amiability. We wonder if someone has spoken to him and told him he must be better tempered. K had been fully determined to have a

blazing row with him at the first sign of 'the rats' but she has had no reason to complain in any way. Of course, he doesn't produce Stan's quietly pleasant atmosphere in the machine shop, but anyhow we aren't all in raging tempers as we were the last time we had Fred in charge.

Monday 23 November
Quite a good day for both of us, and E's pin job is drawing to a close. Fred continues to be amiable and even quite chatty and friendly. We learnt today that if any of the married women become pregnant they have to stay working in the factory until the seventh month. Certainly, they transfer them to a sitting job, but it seems to us rather dreadful for a woman in those circumstances to have to be in such a wearing noise and bad atmosphere, besides the general lack of comfort. Today there was a great to-do with officials coming round to make enquiries about Rachel's accident. They tried to cross-question Laurie Charman about it, but she vouchsafed nothing. Afterwards Bradford told me that he believes Rachel is giving trouble over it. Perhaps her husband has put her up to suing Morrisons for negligence. Certainly they were negligent to have the revolving rod exposed, but she was also to blame for not wearing a cap, as she had been told to do.

Tuesday 24 November
Elsie at last completed her 100 pivot pins and to her disgust was given another 100 to do. Actually, she has now mastered the job – but she doesn't like not being able to earn a bonus on it. Mrs Israel got her release today and has gone off in high fettle, hoping that she may evade service of any sort for some time to come. We learn from Pussy Bradford that if Mrs Israel hadn't asked for a transfer, Morrisons would have been forced to get rid of her as she was quite hopelessly bad and did nothing but waste material.

Wednesday 25 November
Elsie thoroughly enjoyed her day on the repeat job and got on fast. K nearly died of boredom during the afternoon and thought the day would never end. We learn from Pussy that Rachel is suing Morrisons for negligence and there will be a court case. A procession of officials came down the shop to view the scene of the accident and they questioned Laurie, but she very sensibly refused to know anything about it. The firm are worried about the case as this is the third or fourth accident they have had of a similar kind and they fear it will go badly with them. Bert Symons also got her release today – on account of her swollen feet. She also is a very poor operator and the firm is well rid of her. She hopes she may be allowed to return to her peacetime job in Harrods' accounts department. K feels most unsettled with all these departures and wonders whether the time will ever come when it will be our last day.

Thursday 26 November
Elsie had a frightful day as she had to share the large micrometer with one of the men and he seemed to want it nearly all the time. Dear old Fat Cooky Lou came

and sat at our table for tea today and entertained us all with her broad conversation.

Friday 27 November
Els disgusted to find she still has not been paid her bonuses on the jobs she has had so much controversy over. Pussy said he would speak to Mr Williams, the head accountant, about it. Continued excitement about Rachel's accident and many visits of the bigwigs to visit the scene. Everyone seems very worried about the court case pending. K delighted to learn that all her 100 pivot pins were OK and she had no scrap. She was not too pleased at being given a second 100 to turn. Have been without our wireless for a week which has been very irritating. We collected a battery tonight, and on putting it in for the 9 p.m. news were electrified to hear of the scuttling of the French Fleet at Toulon.

Saturday 28 November
We were the only women on the lathes in the machine shop today. Muriel, who was very piano and bad tempered yesterday didn't arrive at all. Mrs Hazelgrove wasn't well, so stayed out and Laurie never comes on Saturdays. All the new girls have either left or gone on nights. So we had the undivided attention of Dennis and Fred and got on well. At 12.15 the whole factory closed for the annual stock-taking and we were delighted to get a free half day.

Monday 30 November
Still no Muriel. She seems to be suffering from 'nerves', according to her doctor, which seems to us a very peculiar malady for a young bonny girl and the occasional days and weeks off is futile treatment. Another inquest on Rachel's accident was held and a woman factory inspector came round and interrogated various witnesses. Laurie had to sign a long written statement. We both nearly died of boredom today and Els has another cold, caught from standing so close to the wide open windows and a furious draught blows onto her. We never seem able to strike the happy medium in the temperature. Either we die of cold or we shut the windows and the men working a bit further away from the windows complain bitterly.

Tuesday 1 December
Fred out today as his wife is ill. Els' cold no worse – but she had the window shut. Both tired & bored by the end of the day, though mercifully it was a short one.

Wednesday 2 December
We have a new male inspector and he has been put to examine the work as it comes off the centre lathes. He is a middle-aged, pleasant & quiet little man and seems very nervous. He comes creeping up and down the shop and stands silently behind us fiddling nervously with all our 'bits' and taking so long to 'mike' each measurement, that we get anxious thinking he has discovered some awful mistake. But in the end he always moves quietly off. Laurie can't stand him and if she is to be believed, is excessively rude to him every time he questions any

of her work. It was a dreadfully long day. K felt absolutely desperate – & hardly knew how to endure it until 7 p.m. She thought it was almost the worst day she has had in industry.

Thursday 3 December
We heard from Pussy Bradford today that Rachel is suing the firm for a lump sum (amount not stated). We all think it is desperately mean of Rachel to make all this fuss, but Fred obviously thinks she is quite within her rights and that it is very wise of her to get anything she can out of Morrisons! Rumour has it that there is to be an increased rate of pay for all the women from tomorrow, but it remains to be seen whether we are included in this or not. Fred returned today after being absent for 2 days. He is still extremely amiable.

Friday 4 December
The milling women and others at benches, drills and taps have all had an increase of pay but not us at the centre lathes. We are enraged and to make matters worse no bonus arrived for E after all the talk she had with Bradford last Friday. E attacked him today again and will do so every day till something happens.

Saturday 5 December
Elsie had a visit from the little twerp from the bonus office. He could make no explanation as to why the money had not been paid and finally was extremely rude to her and said in any case nothing could be done for a fortnight until Mr King returned. His parting shot was 'and if you don't like the way the bonuses are worked you can come up into the office and have a go at it yourself'. Elsie was enraged with his rudeness and the final straw was when Pussy Bradford told her she wouldn't earn a bonus on her present job either. Various interviews ensued and E finally found herself, rather to her surprise, in Mr Overton's office asking for her release. He made it all rather difficult, but in the end said if he could obtain a substitute for her (which he perfectly well knows he can't, as they are short-handed already) she might leave or she could transfer to some other part of the factory if she liked, if she was not satisfied with her bonuses. When he heard that E had been waiting 6 or 7 weeks for 3 bonuses which she was entitled to, he said this should be looked into and was shocked to learn how very rude the bonus office clerk had been. Els is really delighted that she has reported this rudeness though is surprised at her lack of *esprit de corps*.

Monday 7 December
We both finished our pivot pin jobs and K went on to a job of metal spools with which Simon had littered the floor with scrap when Bertie had done it. Elsie's job looks much easier than anything she has had. Muriel came back having had a week off saying that she had been 'suffering from gastric'. We wonder whether the effect of Bertie and little Israel getting their release has unsettled her and that she is sub-consciously spelling up for a release on medical grounds.

Tuesday 8 December
Hilda came back today. She has had 3 weeks off. What with her husband home for a fortnight and also 'a week's gastric'. This seems to be a useful and catching complaint to enable the sufferer to have time off whenever she feels a strong distaste for work. We have a suspicion that Hilda has packed Rapley up. Fred, so far this week has continued to be astonishingly amiable, though we think it is mainly because we haven't needed his help much.

Wednesday 9 December
The morning passed quietly enough, until K discovered, quite by chance, that Jim the Pierrot has given her the wrong gauge for her spool job. This meant that the whole of 2 days work was incorrect and would have to be rectified. She was in a blazing rage over it and threatened to go home. Hilda got the horrible tapered socket to do and cattishly, we were delighted to see that for once she has not had a nice job picked out for her. She made a fearful fuss about it & did nothing but moan. We learn that Pussy's wife is expecting her first baby and she has gone into the nursing home today. Pussy in a great flap and went off at lunchtime.

Thursday 10 December
Pussy back again today, looking frightfully worried as the baby has not yet arrived. After lunch he departed again and later on, rather touchingly, sent a message to Laurie to say it was a boy. Hilda continued to moan and groan at her job, but nobody has much sympathy with her. Elsie has got an easy job at last and wears herself out by having a competition with herself to see how quick she can be. She felt exhausted at the end of the eleven-hour race.

Friday 11 December
Pussy arrived today looking as pleased as a cat with two tails, and beaming from ear to ear. Poor old Charlie, the foreman of the millwrights, looked worn out today as he had been on duty for 24 hours and had also to work all day today. The reason for this was because his opposite number on nights, Burgess, did not turn up, and is said to be ill. But rumour says he reports to Overton the slackness of the night men, and this has got round to them, and Burgess was afraid to come in last night for fear of what the men would do to him.

Hilda continued to moan over her job & Laurie continued to gloat over this – This job makes Hilda feel more gastric than before.

Els got a couple of unexpected bonuses. It is very queer because she had thought she was not going to get a bonus on either of these jobs. But the missing ones she queried have still not appeared. However, she will wait patiently for them till next week.

Saturday 12 December
Quiet day. We were the only women doing overtime on the lathes in the afternoon. The whole m/c shop looked very empty. Fred actually had the grace to say that he thought we could take more time off than we did, as we did overtime every night.

Monday 14 December
Dear Stan back with us once more. Els finished her job in less than the allotted time and started on a repeat. Hilda Carter returned on days. She is nearly demented as she hasn't heard from her husband in N. Ireland for 10 days and she usually has a letter every day. She really looks ill with worry. To our surprise Rachel Thurgood also appeared. Everyone gaped at her as they thought she wouldn't have the nerve to show her face with a lawsuit pending. However, on enquiry, we learn from her that there is to be no lawsuit. Her husband did consult a solicitor, but they came to the conclusion that she had a very doubtful case. As the lawsuit rumour has gone all round the m/c shop Rachel is being rather cold-shouldered in consequence. Hilda Greenwood continues to moan about her job and is doing her best to get out of it, but Stan says that if it is the last thing he does, he won't let her escape! Muriel very sulky today as she doesn't like the lathe or job she has been put on and doesn't mean to work hard on it.

Tuesday 15 December
Els, to her fury, has been told that her yesterday's work is incomplete as an extra recess should have been made in each bit. Els had pointed this out to Fred in the drawing and he had merely barked 'No recess'. However, Jim Pierrot now says they must all be rectified. This will take Els a long time to do, though if the recess had been made at the proper time it would have only taken a few seconds on each one. Els feels thoroughly disheartened and dispirited. Only 10 days to Christmas and we have not yet been told what holiday we are to have or when it is to start. Very inconsiderate. Hilda Carter arrived all smiles today as she had received 8 letters from her husband & also one from his Commanding Officer to say her husband was shortly getting leave.

Wednesday 16 December
Els had a better morning, but things went wrong again after lunch and she feels gloomier than gloomy. Laurie states that she has been told that Hilda Greenwood earns 1/3 an hour whereas the rest of us only get 1/1. Everyone very indignant about this and determined to find out if it is true. We forgot to mention that yesterday we had an interlude at 12.15 in the new factory. Sir Noel Curtis Bennett addressed the multitude through a microphone. In impassioned rolling phrases he told us, what we have so often heard before, of the horrors of Nazism. He tossed off many mixed sporting metaphors and even told us we might earn our colours for England in this greatest Test Match of all! Poor Els was very tired and could hardly bear it. If we had seen him on the stage we should have thought it a brilliant skit, though possibly a little overdone. Els scanned the faces around her and found them unmoved, but we think they probably all thought it very good. He finished his oratory with an appeal for the National Savings Movement, for which he tours up and down the country, voluntarily making speeches. Mr McGiveney then bounced up & said that he had persuaded the directors to open a Post Office Savings account for every employee and start each account off with an amount to be announced at Christmas. This seemed to us a practical stimulus to saving and one of the firm's

rare acts of generosity all of which seem to emanate from Mr McGiveney. This will cost the firm a good bit of money and we were surprised to see how apathetically the workers took the announcement. As usual nobody proposed any vote of thanks.

Thursday 17 December
A much better day today for poor Els. She got on much quicker with her 'bits' & felt more cheerful. K met Fred coming off nights and told him about Mr McGiveney's Christmas donation to the workers. Fred's only comment was 'Pshaw! That's only to avoid paying Excess Profits Tax'. Our view is that Mr McGiveney is all right as a boss and he certainly has a good face. But the firm has now grown too big for him and we doubt if he knows what his lieutenants perpetrate. We feel sure that he would give us stools and hot water, but there seems no means of getting at him, as all applications and complaints have to go via one's chargehand, shop foreman, works foreman, works manager to the directors, and everything possible gets sabotaged on the way. Ivy tells us that she asked Rapley if he and Hilda had quarelled. He said 'No' but that they had decided not to speak during working hours. However, he doesn't seem to have been able to keep up this good resolution as several times in the last 2 days he has stopped off at Hilda's lathe for a chat. Laurie Charman has also been doing a giggly sideline in Rapley and he hung over her lathe giving her help for quite a time.

Friday 18 December
First thing today Stan told Els that the omitted recess on E's previous job must be put in at once as 'Progress' was enquiring for the job. He thereupon set up her lathe and knocked off more than 50 for her in ¾ hour, utterly unmoved by all the other females who were awaiting his attention. Els kept the pile he was working on well replenished like the widow's cruse [*earthenware pot or jar*] and she afterwards was able to rattle along herself and get them done pretty quickly.

Apropos of a rumour that Hilda has had a rise (started by our arch-gossip Laurie) Stan told K that if true it was a great shame and he would enquire about it. He said the young ones were not consistent good workers and he wished everyone was like us four older ones (meaning Laurie, Mrs Hazelgrove, K and E). He told K also that he was having great trouble with Muriel whom he could not make do any work at the moment. She spends all her time ranging up and down the shop talking to everyone in turn, and even when she is at her machine she produces very little. This is really very awful because she can be both quick and good when she tries. Stan has threatened Muriel that he will go to Mr Hurst and suggest that she should be transferred to the Midlands if she doesn't pull her socks up. 'The Midlands' seems to be the bogey for recalcitrant industrial workers. Rapley being slightly off Hilda, we feel that now is the moment to catch him on the rebound if we want any little favours from him and K had a smack at him today. He came quite unasked to help her with her machine which needed adjusting while Stan was at tea. Laurie and Els exchanged amused glances while K and Rapley hung their heads together over the lathe. K made good going having made up her face for the purpose, and was making good use of her 'pools of loveliness'. She finally ended up by saying that when he (and Stan!) went back on nights, would he take Elsie and K with him. He agreed to this and we are now happy to think that we may be permanently free of Fred and with our dear Stan.

Saturday 19 December
Today they came round for a donation to a wedding present for little George Baker. These subscription lists come round fairly frequently either for leaving or wedding presents or for people who have been away ill for some time and need help. Recently we had one for a man who has been in a sanitorium for a year suffering from TB. Everyone was asked to give generously as the management had promised to double whatever was raised.

Monday 21 December
We hear that we can go on nights when they change over – as two new lathes have arrived. The only question is will the change be this Monday or in a fortnight's time. We understand we are to be put on the new lathes as Stan says the boys will ruin them. Old Mother Hazelgrove is now a grandma in earnest as her daughter gave birth to a son on Sunday. Laurie tell us that Stan has now been made a chargehand. We are surprised, as we always thought he was our chargehand, but apparently he has only been a 'setter' up till now.

Tuesday 22 December
It has been decided that the change from days to nights shall be next Monday, so we are specially delighted as we shall get an extra day's holiday, so we need not return to Croydon until Monday morning. A good many of the married women were given the afternoon off to do their household shopping for the weekend. Laurie's very indignant that we are leaving her next Monday to go on nights.

Wednesday 23 December
This week seems to be dragging dreadfully. Everyone is feeling it and we suppose it is because we are all looking forward to the Christmas break so much.

Thursday 24 December
Sad to learn on arrival that the day and night staff do not change over on Monday after all. This because the night shift men made a tremendous fuss as they didn't see why they should have their places altered 'just to suit Rapley', as they said. This means we shall have to come home on Sunday evening in order to start work at 7.45 a.m. on Monday. Everyone very gay and high-spirited today. About 10 a.m. we were invited by Lou to have a swig of cocktail out of a medicine bottle so we crept up behind her machine, which was mercifully in a corner, and had our secret drink feeling very guilty. However, she assured us that the odour of sanctity had been put on it, as the chargehand, George Baker, had had the first drink. There were several quiet little bottle parties going on and the atmosphere got gayer and gayer. We were due to finish at 4 p.m. and after lunch K and E set to work once more like smug girls. But some of them seemed settled

down and Muriel got hold of a piece of mistletoe and started kissing the
bridegroom-to-be George Baker, then Bob Slade (who was not amused) and
finally Stan and then Peters. This kissing has become pretty general throughout
the factory and there were clinging matches going on all over the place in a most
haphazard way. The Peccadillo was visited by about 8 different men who clasped
her in a long embrace, which she seemed to submit to like a dummy. Beyond
tidying her hair between each onslaught [she] appeared quite unmoved. Laurie
got furious with all this passion and finally pulled one man off the Peccadillo
muttering 'Disgusting! Disgusting!!' Muriel, being rather above herself after all
her kissing pecks, was suddenly set on by Reg Green and kissed in good earnest,
which left her flushed and panting. In the other factory we heard that an
impromptu band and dance was held and when Mr Overton (who is much feared
normally) arrived to protest, he was told to go to hell! Altogether everyone was
out of hand and not a scrap of work was being done. Finally, at about 3 p.m.
Captain Lines arrived looking very angry, and said everyone was to be out of the
building in five minutes. So off we went & felt very glad to get a little more time
to pack and tidy up. All the workers had been annoyed that the factory hadn't
closed at lunch time as nearly all the other Croydon factories had done so. [Xmas
break follows.]

Sunday 27 December
We both arrived back having had a pleasant 3 days, and the thought of no more
holidays for we don't know how long cast rather a gloom upon us.

Monday 28 December
Nobody would have known to look at the concentrating workers, quiet and
rather tired, that they were the same people who created the orgy on Christmas
Eve. The kissers and huggers seemed quite oblivious of one another and no one
has referred to it. In common with everyone else, we were inexpressibly tired and
were thankful to hear that we were closing at 5.15, though we shan't relish having
to make it up tomorrow.

Wednesday 30 December
Another interminable day with nothing but sighing and moaning on all sides. We
got quite a lot of work done nevertheless. No one left in the m/c shop for
overtime except the five centre lathe girls.

Thursday 31 December
Lou arrived all swathed up in bandages over one eye as she had got a piece of
metal in it and had to go to hospital. She sat looking very rorty [unwell] at her
machine all day with her bandage slightly askew, and her spectacles perched over
it. K had a job which she could sit at today. She was able to purloin a stool and sat
there all day working away. She felt as if she was driving a tractor. Stan and
Rapley eyed her but nothing was said – so K thought her reputation for hard
work has stood her in good stead. The worst of the week now over. Three days
running of eleven hours is a bit much we find.

Elsie Whiteman (left), Kathleen Church-Bliss and A.H. Fox-Strangeways, c. 1930. (*English Folk Dance and Song Society*)

Benacre, Milford, Surrey, 1935, taken when Kathleen and Elsie ran the tea shop/restaurant. (*Alison Speirs*)

Duppas Hill Road, Croydon. No. 25 is the first house from the right with a balcony. (*Stephen Bruley*)

Morrisons' No. 1 Factory, 1938, taken soon after the factory was opened. (*Audrey Clark*)

A group photograph taken outside the No. 1 Factory. Judging by the small number of women workers, this is likely to have been taken before the outbreak of war. The men seated above the women are managers and directors. Eighth from the left is Mr Young, ninth is Captain Lines, tenth is Mr McGiveney. Bottom row: extreme left (seated) is Eddie Cook. Top row, second from the right is Harry Mayhead. (*G. Lines*)

The Home Guard at Morrisons. Back row (left to right): Ken Cox, -?-, Geoff Collins, Ken Peters, -?-, -?-, George Ross, -?-. Middle row (extreme left): Eddie Cook. Front row: -?-, -?-, Ron Allen, -?-, Mr Proctor (Captain), -?-, Jim Sawyer, -?-, -?-. (*Ken Peters*)

An advertisement for Morrisons in *All The World's Aircraft, 1945–6.* (*Janes' Publications*)

An office staff outing, 1944. (*Audrey Clark*)

A Morrisons' identity badge. These badges were compulsory in wartime.
(*Audrey Clark, photographed by Stephen Bruley*)

PROGRAMME ══════ OCTOBER 26

PROGRAMME

S O U V E N I R

VICTORY

D A N C E

OCT. 26TH 1945

DANCING   SPOT PRIZES

Artists

DAPHNE KELF

of B.B.C. Broadcasting Fame

presents extracts from

"THE MUSICAL ECHOES"

featuring

CINTO and his Harp

PAT DUFFY

The Boy Soprano

SANDY SANDFORD

Radio's Comedy Query

From Variety Band Box—Stage Door Canteen, etc.

Music by

LYN CHARLES

and his

ORCHESTRA

COMPERE & M.C.   -   -   -   SANDY SANDFORD

Refreshments

MORRISONS ENGINEERING LIMITED

CROYDON, ETC.

A few Messages from well-wishers of Morrisons.

From SIR STAFFORD CRIPPS, President of the Board of Trade :

I send my best wishes to Morrisons Engineering Ltd. on the occasion of their Victory Ball.

While I was Minister of Aircraft Production I greatly appreciated the help and support I received from the Management and Workers at Morrisons. I am confident that they will bring the same industry and skill to bear on the tasks which lie before us now that peace is here.

R. Stafford Cripps.

From Lieut.-Col. D. R. REES-WILLIAMS, M.P.

It gives me very great pleasure to add just a word of appreciation about Morrisons of Croydon. During the War they rendered yeoman service to the country by working night and day, and by so doing earned the gratitude of the nation. In peace time it is my sincere wish that they reap the harvest they so richly deserve, and that we look to them, as we did in War, to help pull the country through.

D. R. Rees-Williams.

From G. R. STRAUSS, Esq., M.P.

As one who knows from personal experience the great contribution which Morrisons Engineering Ltd. made towards our victory, I confidently express the hope that this organisation will make an equally valuable contribution towards the reconstruction of our country.

I still remember vividly the day that I visited your works and gave you a message of congratulation on your achievements from Sir Stafford Cripps, the then Minister of Aircraft Production. I was deeply impressed by the efficiency of all I saw and the spirit prevailing in the workshops. May this spirit continue.

I send you my cordial greetings and good wishes.

G. R. Strauss, M.P.

From SIR HERBERT G. WILLIAMS :

During the War Morrisons Engineering Ltd. rendered a very notable service to the State by the efficiency with which they carried out all their contracts for the various Supply Departments.

Naturally, I do not know all the things that were done, because much of the information was confidential, but I am certain the Management and the work-people are entitled to the gratitude of the nation for the service that was rendered.

Herbert G. Williams.

From SIR NOEL CURTIS BENNETT, K.C.V.O. :

Its good indeed to know that Morrisons are holding a Victory Ball. May all those present enjoy the happy evening they richly deserve and by their continued loyalty and hard work uphold that wonderful spirit which made Morrisons such a shining example to all during the grim years of War.

Noel Curtis Bennett.

The programme for the Victory Dance, 1945. (*Audrey Clark*)

Stan Wallace, Elsie and Kathleen's
'setter' on the centre lathes, c. 1955.
(*Alison Speirs*)

Elsie Whiteman (left) and Kathleen
Church-Bliss (right) with 'Auntie',
taken some time after the war.
(*English Folk Dance and Song Society*)

1943

Monday 4 January

K had an awful day with her lathe going wrong. E also had a bad day with a new job which she was very slow over. Both worn out when we got home. Mrs Bellwood informed us tonight that we couldn't have the daily woman anymore as she was too busy. A gloomy thought.

Tuesday 5 January

Lou almost in tears, as her chargehand had asked her to go and work on the capstans for a while, as so many of the capstan girls are away. This would mean all standing & working a heavy machine, much too hard a job for a woman of her age. She refused to do it and George Baker was most insulting to her, she said. She was obviously most frightfully upset about the whole thing. Today we received our Trades Union cards at long last from the shop steward of the General & Municipal Workers' Union. As we have been members since 7 November this seems a little dilatory. As luck would have it we were also informed today by Jimmy Dale, the shop steward of the Amalgamated Engineering Union, that women were now eligible to join that union. So we are anxious to get transferred if possible.

Wednesday 6 January

Every few minutes, today, a job-chaser came up to K to see if she had finished her job, which was very irritating for her as she was getting along as fast as could be. Very bad management for them to be hung up for this job as they could easily have given it out before.

We have decided that we should like to change our rooms as it is now extremely uncomfortable with no one to do any cleaning for us. We are going to put an advertisement in the local paper.

Thursday 7 January

Els rather jealous as K was put on E's favourite job. However, E has got a very nice job of her own, so forebore to complain too much. Hilda and Rapley seem to be all 'on' again and they were seen on Saturday having a clinging embrace at a bus-stop.

Friday 8 January

Frightful fury all day. First of all, the new efficiency expert (whoever he may be) has reorganised the table accommodation in the canteen, with the result that everyone is packed tightly together with no easy access to the chairs. Also everyone's 'special place' is now altered, and teatime passed in an atmosphere because the m/c shop women had occupied their own particular table even though it now was placed in a new position. To add to this it was seen that a corner of the canteen is being partitioned off and when we enquired why, we learned that it was to form a nice little cosy tearoom for the office staff! This caused rage to everyone and complaints have gone in to Rapley and others. Personally, we are quite indifferent as to where the office staff eat their meals, but we think it is a pity to have labour and materials used in erecting a barrier between the classes. We feel annoyed too that a large amount of wood is being used for this partition yet we are told that we can't have any stools because of the difficulty in obtaining wood to make them!

The afternoon was passed in ructions in the m/c shop because Laurie discovered beyond all question of doubt that Hilda and Muriel were now earning 1/3 an hour even though they had flatly denied it when asked before. Stan was very upset about this when he heard it as he says Muriel doesn't deserve it and Hilda only gets it because of Rapley's favouritism. We think it is reasonable that they have a rise as they have been there 3½ months longer than we have, but we don't like the hole-and-corner way in which it has been done, Rapley having told them to 'keep quiet about it'. Laurie was absolutely enraged about the whole affair and was purple in the face with fury all the afternoon. She and Hilda and Muriel had a fish-fag row in front of poor Stan – Hilda accusing Laurie of getting all the 'good bonus jobs' while she, moreover, had a husband in the Forces! Laurie just managed to prevent herself adding 'And a sweetheart in the factory!' We said goodbye to Laurie and Lou today as we shan't see them for months as we go on nights on Monday and they don't come in on Saturdays.

Saturday 9 January
It seems such a long time since Christmas, and it is really a fortnight. K realised that unless she saw Mr Payne about the stools today she wouldn't see him for a month so she asked for an interview and later one of the awful little girls from the time office came up to her and said very rudely 'Are you Bliss? Mr Payne wants you'. K departed to see him. Mr Payne said that nothing at all had been done about the stools as far as he could make out, though it was true that there was a difficulty about the materials. He had delivered an ultimatum to the management that if the stools didn't arrive in a fortnight he would have to see what the factory inspectors had to say about it. As she was leaving K thought she would ask him about the usual procedure to get a rise in pay. He seemed surprised that we hadn't all got a rise in the machine shop and said that he was going to look into it.

We shall be sorry not to see Lou and Laurie for a month, and Laurie feels quite dejected at the thought as she says she has no friends now that she has had such a frightful row with Hilda and Muriel, and she is very depressed at the prospect of another batch of her interminable rods which she has already spent months doing.

Received 4 answers to our advertisement for rooms [*for various reasons none were suitable*].

Tuesday 12 January
Our first experience of nights at Morrisons was not nearly so bad as we had expected. The first quarter-hour break at 10.30 p.m. came as a surprise, especially as the girls are allowed to go 5 minutes early to get washed. The half-hour break at 1 a.m. is marred by the perfectly disgusting dinner served by the canteen. Badly cooked meat & veg swimming in a bath of greasy gravy. Really very unappetising.

Two very rough women do the canteen and Rapley and 2 other men help behind the counter and take the money. The atmosphere on nights is more free and easy than on days . . . but a good bit of work seems to get done in spite of the long conversations the millers seem to hold. But this possibly means that their machines are working with only occasional attention required. Some of them read while at their work which would never be allowed in the ridiculous red-tape of days. Rapley was very friendly and everyone else was nice to us. We had felt quite like new girls going into the 'closed order' of night shift. However, we found Marley and Mrs Margetson were also trying the experiment of nights so we had friends. We also met Ruth Treagus for the first time. She has been on permanent nights for some months. We had heard so much about her from Freda, as being the queerest little oddity & great fun & keeping them all in fits. She does not tally with the description at all. She is small and neat and very sophisticated – eyebrows plucked completely away and a thin pencil line put in, marvellously waved short hair, plum coloured slacks and a fur coat. There was no evidence of her 'keeping anyone in fits' though she talks for hours to Ken Cox on the mills. Reg came down to visit Els twice for a crack and the night passed surprisingly quickly. The second ¼ hr break at 4.30 a.m., we ate cheese sandwiches which fortified us until 6.30 a.m. when the women leave. The poor men remain till 7.30 a.m. We get 5 minutes grace after every break and no one takes any notice of the bell. But when Rapley blows his whistle everyone rises at once & goes back to their work immediately. During the breaks little card-playing groups start up all over the canteen, and cards are dealt and tricks taken between mouthfuls.

Wednesday 13 January
Tonight passed more slowly than the previous night, and K found herself looking at her watch a good deal, and Els found the night dragged more than before. Harry (our old acquaintance Godfrey Tearle) is our night inspector and seems quite amiable in spite of being a woman hater. He is overcome with sleep at about 4 a.m., puts his head on his arms and dozes off for a bit.

Thursday 14 January
Three nights this week our director, the Well-Scrubbed Pig (Captain Proctor of the Home Guard), has made a tour of the factory. Marley pounced on him during the first break and complained bitterly about the food & lack of fresh vegetables. He did not look at all pleased and we doubt if he will take any action. Marley wants to organise a round-robin to demand better food. However, we are not keen to ally ourselves to this complaint, as we don't want to start moaning the moment we get onto night shift. The hours drag slowly on till 6.30 a.m., and as Els wearied of her job and thought the night would never end and with still 5 more hours to go, she found herself saying at intervals through the night 'Heroines all'.

Friday 15 January
K had a long talk with Stan tonight and he told her the sad story of Harry May (Godfrey Tearle). Harry used to be the m/c shop foreman and was in charge of

all the machines and was the setter for the millers. During this time Jim Sawyer came new to the factory, having been a car salesman before the war. Harry gave him his first job on the centre lathes and Stan helped him, ground up his tools for him etc. and later on there was one of the inevitable rows which happen periodically in Morrisons – and cause[d] a reshuffle of positions. Harry ceased to be foreman and was relegated to the inspection bench, and Rapley became m/c shop foreman. Soon after this Sawyer wormed his way out of the m/c shop (we presume by his gentlemanly manner & his maroon shirts and his deferential air to the bosses) and is now head of the inspection bench over poor Harry May who gave him his first job. Stan thinks this is the cruellest thing the firm has ever done.

Sunday 17 January
We much appreciate our first long weekend and with the prospect of Monday free till the evening. We were not overcome with the usual gloom which descends on us about 7 p.m. on Sunday nights! About 8.30 p.m. we had an alert, which didn't surprise us very much, as Berlin was bombed heavily last night. We heard heavy firing and lots of planes and so trooped down to the cellar. The raid lasted about 1½ hours, but so far as we know no bombs dropped near.

Monday 18 January
The alert went again at 4.30 a.m. and very heavy gunfire and planes were heard. Fires were seen over S. Croydon and Purley Way but we heard no bombs. At 5.30, when there appeared to be a lull when we were standing in the porch, we saw a plane catch fire, heard machine gunning and then saw it come down in flames to the south of us. Later we heard that it fell in Caterham recreation ground. Three others were said to have come down in this area too.

We hadn't been in the factory more than a few minutes before the blue alert went up and everyone was rather grumpy expecting another noisy night. However, nothing came of it.

Wednesday 20 January
About noon we were awakened by the sirens. We heard gunfire so dressed & came downstairs, but it didn't last long. Later we learnt that about 30 fighter bombers had crossed the coast. Eleven were brought down. A girls' school, said to be Penge, was wrecked and many casualties. We went off to work feeling very tired and were infuriated to get 5 blue alerts before 1 a.m. The blue light seemed to be going on and off the whole time. However, no guns or planes were heard and we didn't have to go to the shelters.

Friday 22 January
May Nolan back today, slightly recovered from her gastric attack. She is never tired of saying how much she dislikes Marley and today told us that although Marley is always complaining how exhausted she is by her heavy work, Mrs Margetson says it is entirely her own fault, as she will force the pace of her jobs,

regardless of the machine and tools, in her effort to make 'double time' on all her jobs. Mrs Margetson also says that Marley is desperately jealous when she, Mrs Margetson, occasionally earns more bonus than she does.

Monday 25 January
The night passed fairly quickly. Elsie felt very vigorous as the result of a tonic which has restored her appetite. May Nolan has gone on days and Blondie Avery (Peccadillo) has come in her place. This makes it much more amusing for the men, as she holds court at her machine and they pay her frequent visits. She really is rather a sweet little thing though probably both fast and loose.

Tuesday 26 January
Blondie had great fun tonight with the men who had come on from Home Guard parade. She was being taught about the intricacies of the rifle and was squinting down it and cocking it in every direction – until Rapley suddenly appeared and she scuttled back to her machine, squeaking all the way.

Wednesday 27 January
The nights drag interminably this week – and our only entertainment is Blondie and her boys. Tonight Steve Everitt and Collins, two of the permanent night men, took it in turns to spend the greater part of the night chatting to her. About 3 a.m. Everitt and Blondie were nowhere to be seen and E wondered if they had gone for a little love in the air-raid shelter. However, they were discovered sitting on the floor together near Blondie's machine, screened by two tables; we couldn't see what was going on, but Rapley suddenly appeared and whistled them out of it. We have been rather appalled all this week, to see that few of the men seemed to be doing any work just now. They spend the greater part of the time talking to each other and lolling up against their machines. We can only suppose they have already done double time on their jobs and now have to kill time. Stan had a busy night making '6 'andles' for the new lathes – and was sweating with exertion.

Friday 29 January
Blondie away ill. K got a good bonus on her nice socket job – the original bonus of 10*d* being increased to 30/-! Els also got a bonus, but it was for 4/9 on a job she has never done so she queried this.

Tuesday 2 February
Blondie still away, but her place as chief entertainer has been taken by Helen, a new little thing on the capstans who came one night last week. She tells us she was three years in another factory and was sacked for saucing the foreman. She is definitely one for the boys and roams out of the section to our centre lathe men, whom she entertains each in turn, with her most peculiar allure. She is like nothing we have ever seen before and reminds us of a spaniel bitch puppy, flopping at every joint, her head rolling about as she talks and every part of her animated.

Wednesday 3 February
Helen again well to the fore. She does very little work and spends all her time in our section ranging from man to man. There seems to be nobody in authority to send her back to her machine as Rapley is out of the shop for long stretches. Reg does occasionally let out the sort of roar that one would use to scare cows and this sends her galloping back to her machine. She is a tiny rounded little thing with very pretty orange hair and snubby features.

Thursday 4 February
The week, thank goodness, is more than half over. In the brief intervals we bury ourselves in our two absorbing books, and for the rest are entertained by the antics of Helen. Blondie is away still and we wonder what she will make of her usurped kingdom, captured by onslaught and by such a different method of attack from her own, where the eyes are merely fluttered and the beaux approach.

Saturday 6 February
This was the last time of nights for a month and we think we have survived it rather well. We like Rapley better than we did, and he has been very amiable, though he spends a lot of his time out of the shop and rumour has it that he has a little lay down in the FAP.

We are rather shocked at the time spent in chattering by various couples. Stan said to Els tonight that looking down the shop at all these couples he thought it looked very bad and of Helen he said he wondered sometimes whether she was quite all there.

Sunday 7 February
Slept late and went in the afternoon to *In which we Serve* [*film*] which we thought was extremely good.

Monday 8 February
Back on days again today. The machine shop seemed to be filled with a seething mass of women and we didn't think there were any lathes for us to go on. However, K's job, requiring a revolving tool post, she was told to go on Laurie's lathe and this caused a most awful *crise*. Laurie was furious. At the elevenses she continued the 'straf' and replied in monosyllables to our bright but laboured chatter. We felt rather infuriated by her childishness, especially as we had no say about what machine we were to work on. Laurie continued white faced and silent all day, but we broke down her resistance at the tea interval and by the end of the day she was fairly amiable.

Tuesday 9 February
We are now involved in one of those absolutely infuriating women's squabbles. We often see them going on in the shop, but never before have we been caught up in one. We thought the *affaire* Laurie had died down and that we were all friends again, and so it appeared until at afternoon teatime she suddenly started

off again about how unfair it was that she had been taken off her lathe. Els tried to pacify her by pointing out that the nature of the job decided which lathe had to be used, but she wouldn't listen to argument and went on grumbling while the rest of the table goggled at her in silence.

Wednesday 10 February
The *affaire* Laurie has come to a happy conclusion. Having gone this morning in fear and trepidation, wondering what sort of reception awaited us, we found that Laurie was quite her normal smiling self and greeted us just as usual. So we responded, and all is now happiness and peace. We think her nice husband must have smoothed her down and told her not to be such an ass. Today was a day of wild rumour and surmise. Hilda Greenwood having been absent for 2 days, people began to ask why she was away and Rapley revealed to Hilda Carter that Hilda G. had got her release, and when Hilda C. said that she would be the next to leave, Rapley said 'Not for the same reason I hope!' So tongues are wagging and minds are exercised as to on what grounds she can have possibly obtained her release. Rumour varies between a baby or ill-health, or on account of her illicit attachment to Rapley. Anyhow, as everyone says 'It looks very fishy to me' and it's certainly very peculiar that she has been so secretive to everyone about it and went away without saying goodbye to anyone or collecting her tools & equipment.

Thursday 11 February
It is now stated, via Fred, that Hilda is going to have a baby, hence her release. This explanation seems to have stopped the gossiping tongues, but we shall believe in a baby when we see one. A middle-aged woman, Mrs Mason, has been transferred to the lathes from the 'drill' department. Poor Stan had a frightful day, nearly all his girls were in trouble with their work and wanted his help. He hurried from lathe to lathe all day and looked quite worn out by the end.

Friday 12 February
Els had the worst day she has had for many months. She has been engaged for weeks on a fiddling little spigot which, however, has gone swimmingly. Today, for some unknown reason, the whole thing went wrong. Stan had to alter the *modus operandi* and E accomplished practically nothing all day. Hilda Carter and Muriel are now thick as thieves. Hilda now uses a rather impertinent manner to Stan who obviously doesn't like it, but she gets no change out of him.

Saturday 13 February
Els' job went better today. Poor K sent in several bonus queries today. She was paid the miserable sums of about 3/- each for jobs she did at lightning speed and expected about £1 each on.

Stan arrived today and said 'No more nights for women' as the management have suddenly realised that the lathes are not full on the day shift, so they naturally see no reason to pay workers 'Time & a third' for nights when lathes arc idle in the day time. This means that Fred and Stan will both be on during the day shift and we have put in a plea to Stan to keep us as his charges as we cannot bear the thought of Fred again. Laurie tells us that Fred heard tell that we transferred to nights in order to avoid him! K really prefers days as she likes the 'life' that goes on round her, but as Els never takes any part in the life going on and keeps her eyes glued on her work, she really rather likes nights as she gets more done in the long unbroken hours. Stan told K that Hilda Carter is very saucy, and as far as he was concerned Fred could have her in future. He prefers the older ones.

CHAPTER THREE

Works Council

1943

Sunday 14 February

A quiet day mainly reading AND writing. By some queer chance all our literature has been connected with the Fall of France. We can now hardly separate one book from another and are filled with gloom at the picture one gets of the confusion and treachery amongst the politicians & even the army. We have been in Duppas Hill Rd a year today and can vividly remember the awful, dark, foggy day on which we arrived and the depression of hearing about the fall of Singapore on the 9 o'clock news. It seems hard to believe we have been industrial workers for a year. We have been in Morrisons 8 months and there is a rumour of a rise in pay shortly. This last week a Sick Benefit Fund has been formed amongst the employees. Everyone is asked to pay 6*d* a week, and if ill will receive £1 a week for 3 weeks & 10/- a week for a further 3 weeks. We think this seems a very good idea & we shall certainly support it. The scheme seems to have been worked out by a committee, whose origin is wrapped in mystery and is mainly composed of chargehands and office staff. We think this is a little irregular, as surely the workers should nominate their own committees.

Monday 15 February

Today we had both Stan and Fred to help us, and as luck would have it, none of the women were engaged on new jobs so they had practically nothing to do all day and lounged about looking bored. Fred went home early as he was so fed up. This morning we received a surprise visit from Frank Beecher, one of the Sick Benefit Fund Committee, telling us that a workers' representative was to be elected onto the committee, and would we please vote for somebody now! We were rather taken aback, as our minds were on our work and miles away from committees. We couldn't think of anyone off-hand, and then thought Jimmy Dale, the shop steward, was the obvious person. Later K learnt that Elsie had been nominated by Nancy and Lou who said that several of them, including little George Baker, had voted for her too. The result of the ballot was that Jimmy Dale, one called Bourne, and Els were elected and, as Frank Beecher so graciously said when informing her, she seemed to be quite popular. Els is amazed that she was elected, and feels very touched at being chosen, as she seldom speaks to anyone and keeps her old back bent over the lathe all day. Lou and Nancy obviously thought that someone who knew how to express themselves was the best choice. We fear that Laurie will be very jealous, but we can't bother about that. Tonight, Hilda Carter surpassed herself. Stan was tidying up his tool box and smoking a pipe. Hilda came up to speak to him and he replied to her without removing his pipe. Hilda seized hold of the pipe and snatched it out of his mouth. Hilda really is unspeakably rude. She little knows what she is letting herself in for, as Stan is adept at quietly paying out the insubordinate. Hilda will probably find herself being kept waiting on all occasions, and having all the most hateful jobs to do for some time to come!

Tuesday 16 February
K asked Stan what he had said to Hilda. He said he didn't say anything as he would only have got more sauce if he had. He said he had no time for Hilda – and puts her bad manners down to 'ignorance'. Anyhow we notice he doesn't do anything for her now and hands her over to Fred.

Wednesday 17 February
Stan and Fred have put Hilda Carter on to a rather more difficult job, doubtless to 'larn' her, and it is causing her some trouble.

We were delighted to find that the canteen managers have changed their bakers and we now have glorious fresh buns and cakes. We have estimated that they make £34 at least a week for cups of tea alone at 1½d each.

Thursday 18 February
The day passed quietly and at 5 p.m. Els went off to the Sick Benefit Committee meeting, looking so clean and sweet that she felt quite self-conscious. K, having told her that even if she was a 'Workers' Rep' there was no need for her to be a 'Workers' Disrep', which her appearance usually suggested.

Mr Payne was in the chair and explained the scheme again for the benefit of the 5 new members elected by the workers. As far as they could judge about 90 per cent of the workers want to join, but everyone has not yet been canvassed. During the meeting George Ross, hitherto unknown to us, but evidently a man of advanced left views, brought up the subject of the canteen, and asked whether this committee couldn't take it over, to run on a non-profit making basis, as is usual in industrial canteens. This was hardly the time or the place to discuss it, tho' everyone seemed to agree that the canteen over-charged. Mr Payne said that we must first deal with Sick Benefit, but that he visualised this committee growing into a Workers' Welfare Committee.

All the committee, except Els, Jock Ure and Miss Corney, wanted the firm to be dunned for an initial lump sum to start the fund off well. Els felt that the firm could give a donation if they felt inclined, but that it shouldn't be asked for. However, nearly all the others thought that they should try and get what they could out of the firm so that was that.

We met Ron, Laurie's nice husband, who is going to acquire a parcel carrier for E's bike. He has already overhauled E's disgracefully neglected bicycle, and he really is a peach. We reward him occasionally with a week's meat ration when we don't want it. We think Ron is a king among husbands.

Monday 22 February
Els did no work all the afternoon because her machine had gone wrong. At 7.30 p.m. Laurie and K and E went off to a meeting of the Local Branch of the AEU to be proposed as members. We made our way to an upper room of a fubsy pub having to march through the saloon, and then K marched back again to meet Mrs 'Islegrove' who arrived in a marvellous miowsquash cape over trousers and a long winter coat.

The meeting must have already begun, which we didn't at first realise, because we had been told the wrong time, but K barged up to the chairman and handed in our letter of introduction, which caused rather a hiatus. The meeting consisted of about a dozen chairs and 4 men and two others sitting at a chairman's table. The whole of the back of the room was filled with a *mêlée* of about twenty people transacting business and finances. These seemed to take no part in the meeting, but merely created a diversion of rustling paper and chinking change. The AEU motto is 'All men are brethren' and everybody is referred to as 'Brother So & So' which sounded to us rather self-conscious, but perhaps we shall get used to being Sister Bliss and Sister Whiteman, though we think we are just as likely to be styled 'Comrade'.

The meeting touched on a wide range of subjects, and feeling and argument ran high. Quite obviously the politics of the AEU are advanced left. The chairman was extraordinarily good and very much on the spot, and in spite of being starving we kept our interest to the end. The meeting touched on supporting the Labour Party in their action to uphold the Beveridge Report in its original form, a Production Drive meeting for the Croydon area, the inimical activities of the local Fascists, and many other things, but it was finished at 8.30. We found the most belligerent member comes from Morrisons, and he had a word with us afterwards. The enormous activity of the union and its huge membership scare us a little. Its potentialities are so great, and its danger, if swayed by hot heads, might lead to revolution.

Tuesday 23 February
Today during the tea break the conversation turned on dances and Muriel, aged 23, announced that she didn't dance. Her boy Reg was not fond of it, and both of them have agreed that it is not decent for other men to put their arms round Muriel, as she belongs to Reg. Hilda Carter, aged 19, also said she had given up dancing since she married. Her comment was 'Taking your boy to a dance is a sure way to lose him.' Rapley, who has been looking frightfully ill for weeks, went to the hospital today for an overhaul. He has had styes in both eyes and spots all over his face.

Wednesday 24 February
Lou's 7th daughter has left the factory and is joining the Land Army. We have been very much exercised in our minds about the iniquities of the system which allows skilled men to hang about in order not to earn more than 'double time' and today we posted (via Millie) the following letter to Sir Stafford Cripps, Minister of Aircraft Production. As Millie knows one of Sir S. C.'s personal

secretaries, she is going to warn him to be on the look-out for our letter. So we hope some action may be taken.

Dear Sir – We are centre lathe operators in an Aircraft factory and we wonder if you are aware of an industrial abuse which slows up production. We think it must be pretty general in factories which pay a low basic wage and individual piece-work bonus. Each job is given a time allowance (based on an average worker's speed) and if a worker completes the job in less than the allotted hours, he is paid a bonus of one hour's basic wage for every hour that he saves. In theory he can be as quick as he can, but amongst the workers it is the accepted practice that no one shall finish his job in less than half the allotted time. The reason for this is that if they do so, the management will cut the time allowance which will then operate very hardy on the average or slow worker.

We have often seen men standing about for hours on end because they have finished their job in less than ½ the allotted hours and they must therefore kill time before starting another job. This does not often happen with the women as they have not the skill and experience necessary for a great speed, but as every day the proportion of women to men increases (with consequent slowing up of production) it seems very wrong that the men who are still available should not be encouraged to turn out all they can.

If the quick workers were allowed to earn as much bonus as they could and the management restricted from altering the time allowances on jobs, the increase in production would be considerable.

Yours truly, E.W.W. & K.C.B.

Thursday 25 February
We had a postcard from Ronald [*Millie's husband*] today, which must have crossed with our letter to Sir Stafford Cripps, which we sent to Millie to address. Ronald says – 'Go easy about the bonus scheme – as it is a tangle of 40 years standing'. However, our letter has gone now.

K had a frightful day with tools that broke, but it made the day pass quicker. We have a new man turner in the shop this week and to our surprise we recognised 'Bill' of the Waddon Centre, the man who had such a frightful row with Powney and was suspended for three weeks. He has been back at his peace-time job, among the bacon and lard ever since, but was called up again last Saturday. He says he has forgotten everything he learned at the centre, but likes Stan very much so perhaps he will be all right.

Friday 26 February
Another letter from Millie today saying that Ronald seems rather upset about our writing a letter to Sir S. Cripps. He says again that the disadvantages of the bonus system are well known and that unless we quote a specific case with full details the letter will do no good. And that if the MAP gave orders for every man to be allowed to earn full bonus by working at maximum speed, there would be

dissatisfaction and even strikes amongst the workers. Millie says she has held up our letter until we write to her again.

K broke another tool today and can't imagine how she did it. She has been on the job for weeks and never broken anything and has now broken 2 in two days! Having got a new tool out of the store, she was almost too nervous to use it. Hilda Carter was in a rage with Stan this afternoon. Tears of passion gushed from her and she was purple in the face. The trouble was that she had been told to saw off her aluminium pieces instead of cutting them off with a tool. She doesn't like sawing and got sulkier and sulkier about it and finally refused to do any more work until she got a tool made. She stormed at Stan who took no notice of her temper & tears. He tried to explain that a tool couldn't be used on the job and that sawing was quicker. However, in the end he made her a tool and showed her what a paraphernalia it was to set it up for each operation. After that it was time to go home – so she will have to face her Waterloo tomorrow. Stan told K that he simply doesn't know what to do with Mrs Carter. He again said she was 'ignorant' and 'won't pay attention to what he says'. He has never had to deal with anyone like her and said he will have to speak to Rapley about her when he gets back. But anyhow she is just as rude to Rapley.

Sunday 28 February
We had a very good domestic day. We wrote to Millie and told her she could destroy our letter to Sir S. C. and we would do no more about it till we had time to consider it further.

Monday 1 March
K finished her job and had been looking forward all day to having something new to do, as Stan had promised this should be the last of her batch. But when the time came she was bitterly disappointed to be given another 450 of the little bits, so she expects to be on the same job for another 2 months. This is a bitter blow. Today, someone came round to make a collection for a nice woman who has been away having a baby. We were told that she was desperately hard up and that she was going to return to work almost immediately as she was in such straits for money. We hope they got a good sum for her.

Tuesday 2 March
A long boring day for K. She saw the factory life stretching ahead of her into infinity and felt she could hardly bear it. Els got on quite happily all day. In the middle of the afternoon Mrs Marley, who has been away for a month with a sprained wrist, appeared looking quite pretty and well-dressed. She came to say goodbye to us. She has obtained her release, and is going as lady supervisor to the Waddon Centre. We don't think she will be any more popular at Waddon than she has been here, where everyone cordially dislikes her. She is the only really educated person we have met in Morrisons, but we haven't wanted to cultivate her at all. We think it very feeble of her to give up. We are rapidly becoming the most senior in the m/c shop. Mrs Hazelgrove and Muriel are the

only ones on the centre lathes who have been there longer than we have. We've reckoned up that no less than 8 girls have come & gone since we arrived. They had swollen legs and pains in the head, nervous prostration, babies and/or a general disinclination for work. But the Old War Horses, Kat and Els and Laurie seem to go on while the younger ones fall away.

Wednesday 3 March
Nothing much happened today, but at night, just after dark, we had an alert, and gunfire and German planes, and went down to the basement for an hour and a half. Then at 4.30 a.m. another alert, and more gunfire and planes, but nothing in this neighbourhood. We had been expecting this as a reprisal for the heavy Berlin Raid on Monday.

Thursday 4 March
K's cold much worse as a result of being somewhat cold in the basement. Poor Stan had a frightful day with Fred away ill and Mrs 'Islegrove' rampant because her job was keeping her waiting. Laurie in her usual state of everything 'Not being good enough', as she always is when she tackles a new job and is nervous. At the end of the shift it was discovered that practically a whole day's work of Hilda Carter's was scrapped and she was almost in tears of rage and chagrin and helplessness.

Friday 5 March
K's cold still bad and she went to bed the moment she came in. We have got into conversation with a man at our dinnertime table. He has been very much interested in K's book *People in Production* by Mass Observation, which he has been trying to read upside down across the table. He is in assembly and hates it there. By his standards the work is a bodge, and during the 8 weeks since he came to the firm nothing has gone without 'a concession' – i.e. not perfect. This depresses him so much that he is trying to get a transfer into one part of the factory where by making the parts himself he would know they were all right. Our other companions at this table include Dennis who never utters, a nice, delicate-looking man, Joe who is evidently a student of nature, Old Jock the Sweeper and Ivy Barney and the man she is going to marry *en seconde noces*, Eddie Wratten. He is the complete antithesis of her first husband, as he is quiet and shy and reserved, but as she said 'He thinks a lot of me, and will be good to me'.

Saturday 6 March
No Laurie on Saturdays, so we were spared the slightly embarrassing situation which now arises at our morning break table where we used to enjoy Lou's high spirits and outspokenness, but since Ivy joined us at the table she and Laurie, who evidently consider themselves a cut above Lou, form a clique & murmur ill-natured comments on Lou out of the corners of their mouths. We are hideously embarrassed by this as we are so fond of Lou and feel sure she must notice their rude behaviour.

Monday 8 March

K and E were on fire watch duty last night, the first time E had officiated in Croydon. We slept fully dressed and were woken by the alert at 12.30 a.m. and hastened downstairs in our tin hats, and stood in the porch till the all clear went at 1.45 a.m. We heard and saw a good deal of distant firing, and on one occasion searchlights focused on the path of a plane right overhead, and the nearby guns opened up with the most continuous firing we have heard. White light lit up the whole road and we crouched in the porch till we reckoned the shrapnel would have finished falling. The plane was evidently hit as after it had passed us it veered again towards the coast with the shell fire following it. A very exciting night.

Laurie away with a cold and K asked for an interview with Mr Hurst for us both as we have decided to ask for a rise. This application should really go through Rapley, but he is still away with his malady. However, we were both summoned to the interview. E spent some time this morning collecting subs for the Sick Club.

Immediately after work we bicycled off to the meeting of the AEU held now at Ruskin House, Croydon. We met 'Mrs Islegrove' outside. The 'Three Sisters' entered among hordes of very rough-looking men. Our upper room was packed with these men. It transpired that they were there to be elected members of the AEU. Their proposer told a most interesting and appalling story of their firm who are sabotaging production by cutting the working hours down to 48 a week in order to evade the Essential Works Order. Their leader, who spoke very quietly and well, said it was a scandal, as there was masses of work to be done. The men are joining the union to strengthen their position.

There then followed an initiation ceremony, for which we were all asked to stand. Bro. Howard read us a little exhortation and statement of ideals to which even the most dyed-in-the-wool conservative could take no exception. We pledged ourselves to remove social injustice and to labour that there should not be want in the midst of plenty. Bro. Howard, our chairman, who read this, read it very well and we have taken a great fancy to him. He is an excellent chairman.

Our hearts turned over at the beginning of the meeting, because the question of a Newcastle strike committee was brought up asking for support in their action. We feared that everyone would vote to back them in the strike, but to our surprise and relief we found that they voted almost unanimously, condemning the action of the committee in calling a strike at the present time. There was also on sale *The New Propellor* the organ of the Shop Stewards' Organisation. We feel less like the Klu Klux Klan this week, and found 'Brother This' and 'That' coming quite naturally to the tongue. There seems to be a lot of very able men in the AEU.

Tuesday 9 March

A short alert during the afternoon – no incident near – and no going to the shelters. We again sent in our application to see Mr Hurst, and were summoned to the Presence, when we made our statement, & he agreed that we should have a rise. It now remains to be seen whether we get it or not on Friday week!

Wednesday 10 March
Laurie still away and Hilda and Lou both have dreadful colds. Almost everyone in the factory has had these – but ours are luckily better now.

Thursday 11 March
Poor Mrs Margetson heard last night that her boy in Bomber Command is missing from the raid over Munich. This is a real tragedy as he is such a lovely looking boy and she is devoted to him. Her daughter works in the factory and is the most appalling-looking girl. Only 17, but frightfully made-up, horrible dyed yellow hair and the most discontented sulky expression.

Friday 12 March
After lunch there was the usual Friday Bonus row. Mrs Hazelgrove threatened to get her release as she couldn't get her proper money in spite of many 'queries'. K also in a rage as she had been paid 3/5 for a job on which she was entitled to about 25/-. A notice has gone up to say a 'works council' is to be formed & details of the election will be announced later.

Saturday 13 March
After work at 4 p.m. we rushed home and changed and set off for London where K went to meet her Ma at the Royal Court Hotel and Els went to Madge. K having had an hour to spare, took a bus ride to see the Trafalgar Square 'Wings for Victory' bomber and also the one at St Paul's. Great crowd everywhere.

Monday 15 March
Els finished her job and was preparing to do a repeat of it, but there was no metal. She then clocked onto another job, but for this there was no tool, so she clocked onto yet another, and for this the card was mislaid for the next part of an hour. This was partly due to the new organisation (Mr Overton's latest pigeon) which involves fetching one's new job from the hatch labelled 'Movement Control'. This Ivy insists on calling the 'Birth Control Clinic'! However, Elsie occupied her idle time by collecting the Sick Club money.

Rumour has it that Stan has done something about K's missing bonuses, so we shall see on Friday if they are to be paid. At lunchtime today we had a talk with Joe Phillips, a nice delicate looking man who sits at our table. He divulged that he had been connected with the stage for 14 years and only left it when the blitz finished all theatrical engagements. Hilda Carter was in tears of frustration again today as her job was going wrong. She says she feels 'all anyhow' and is going to ask for her release on account of 'the nerves'. In the afternoon poor K got a blow in the eye from a large chip of metal. After two visits to the FAP she was told she had better go [to] hospital as it was her good eye. Luckily when she got there the doctor diagnosed no serious injury just pain from the blow. However, K had had to wait 3 hours, so as it was well after 6 p.m. she went home and got supper ready for E's return. E suddenly found herself summoned to a Sick Club Committee at which it was decided to hold 2 dances in aid of funds. A nice informal meeting. K asked Mr Payne about the stools again today and was told they were truly coming but the Lord knew when.

Tuesday 16 March
Lou in bed with flu and bronchitis. Ivy has a rumour that the works council is going to be a farce. She says that the management are going to nominate the Workers' Representatives. We feel raging about this and shall eagerly support any protest which is made. However, we will wait and see what the management actually do, before getting too much worked up.

Bob Slade, the 'ginger fellow' in the Home Guard, left today to join the RAF. A tremendous lot of the young men are now being de-reserved and we lose some from the factory every week.

Wednesday 17 March
A notice from the management announced that the works council would consist of 3 representatives from the management and 5 from the workers (3 men and 2 women). The men to vote for a man and the women for a woman, every worker to have one vote. We think this a very unsatisfactory method and that there should be nominations put forward and then an election to follow (votes not according to sex). So Ivy's rumour that we were to have no option as to who represented us has come to nothing. We thought of getting hold of Bro. Joe Moroney to see if he could do something about a more satisfactory method of election, but during the morning Mr Payne came by, and K pounced on him and 'told him what'. He was most sympathetic and said he would put it before the director at once but didn't hold out much hope of anything being done about it. He spilled a bitsful to K about the difficulties of his position and the management's complete lack of any idea of cooperation with the workers. Soon after this Nancy Deacon came along to Els & asked her if she thought K would allow herself to be put forward for the works council, so Nancy went off and asked K, and then busied herself up and down the shop, canvassing all the girls for her candidate. We think she also carried her propaganda torch over to Lou's daughter in the drills; we suspect that Nancy and Lou hatched out this plot over Lou's sick bed when Nancy went to visit her yesterday. She really is a very public-spirited little thing. We are both very much thrilled with this development and very much hope that K will get on the council.

Thursday 18 March
Laurie back again after two weeks away with flu & bronchitis. She doesn't look at all well even now and her husband would really like her to get her release, as he thinks the factory life is too much for her.

The new paraphernalia in getting out new jobs in the machine shop, seems at present to cause nothing but delay and muddle. Els was held up for hours a few days ago and yesterday Hilda was on an idle time card all the afternoon. This was the first time any woman centre-lathe operator has had to go on idle time and it seems a perfect scandal as there are piles of work to be done, and the m/c shop is always working all out. Today Hilda was given a job (but one which is usually done on the capstans) and spent most of the morning in tears of rage, because she didn't like it. If looks could have killed, Stan would have been dead more than once!

Nancy went on with her canvassing for the works council. During the afternoon one of the men in the tool room brought round a petition asking the management to permit only men of not less than 3 years engineering experience (and women of 2 years) to represent the workers. Further, that no chargehands should be eligible at all. This petition met with short shrift in the m/c shop and never got further than Bros and Jock the Sweeper. The petitioner turned tail, with Laurie screaming after him that the women had already made up their minds whom they wished to vote for and she knew he couldn't produce anyone better from his side of the factory! It was really rather like an 'Eatanswill' election. Anyhow all these alarms and excursions have stirred up the apathetic. Nancy has got the promise of a good many votes, but the details department have also put up a good candidate, Mrs Grace Dobson, so K's prospects don't look so rosy. But Nancy has been assured that there is no cooperation amongst the girls in the No. 2 Factory, as they all vote for their best friends on the same bench!

Gossips Laurie and Ivy have both parted with scandalous stories about Hilda Greenwood. Apparently, she and Mrs Barbara Lloyd have both found themselves in the same hospital, as sequel to illegal operations [*almost certainly abortions*]. Barbara Lloyd was very ill and nearly died. Hilda is reputed to have denied taking any improper actions, but the doctor said 'Don't tell me, my girl!' The authorities are trying to find out where they got it done.

Friday 19 March
Today the 'Eatanswill' Election waxed fast and furious. Men chalked up on their tool boxes 'Vote for Dale' and the women not to be outdone used every available space with, 'Vote for Bliss' – 'Vote for Bliss and prevent Blitz' – 'Bliss the Workers' Woman'. Everybody was going round and getting very excited over all this and canvassing went on, and more chalked up notices with 'Vote for Bogie Allen, the Working Man's friend', 'You'll get no baloney from Dale or Moroney' (our Bro. Joe Moroney).

It appears that Grace Dobson agreed to stand in order to split the vote in the No. 2 Factory as so many workers don't wish to vote for Anne Smith, the shop-stewardess, whom they consider slack and unenterprising. They would prefer to vote for Grace Dobson whom they know and like.

Elsie had a very dull day as far as work was concerned, as she finished at 11 a.m. and got nothing to do for the rest of the day because of delays for various reasons. While she was standing idle the Hippo came up to her, and said 'Your friend didn't know she was so popular, did she? Anyway, she's got a bit of "class" on her side, even if she has got a dirty job'.

Nancy Deacon has worked like a black for her candidate. Even writing a note for the girls on nights, and arranging for Lou, who is away with bronchitis, to record her vote through her daughter. Laurie, whom we always consider rather jealous, showed up to great advantage over it. She was very nice about it, and supported K's candidature with enthusiasm, saying very charmingly that we had got Els on the Sick Club, and now we would get K on the works council. We were delighted to find tonight that we got our promised rise this week, so that our princely pay is now 1/3 per hour.

Saturday 20 March

We arrived this morning and found the following notice chalked up on a large piece of board on a lathe:

> Production Bonus – Workers' Welfare and a SQUARE DEAL.
> Vote for Bliss
> She's all for this.

So K now knows the feelings of the parliamentary candidates when they drive round their constituencies and see what their agents have perpetuated. Nancy had a nice note left her by May Nolan saying she had canvassed the night girls and she was herself 'only too pleased' to vote for K.

Els had another dire morning getting colder and colder while a bolt was made for her lathe, and she did no work at all.

Towards the end of the morning a notice appeared on the board to say that the elected members were:

> J. Dale
> Mrs Dobson
> J. Moroney
> Miss Bliss
> Lancashire

So our Kat is now a Works Cow to the great delight of all, and not least ourselves as we didn't like to contemplate how disappointed we should have been if she hadn't got on to the council. Nancy was almost tearful with delight. She certainly is a most public spirited little thing. It is all due to her canvassing that E is a Workers' Rep' on the Sick Club and K a Works Cow.

During her idle morning Els had a talk with Bros (the Boy With the Shirts) about the elections. He told her that he, Jimmy Dale and George Ross were all members of the Communist Party, but that it was uphill work in the firm – and Jimmy Dale was losing heart, and would really like to hand on his trade union work to somebody else if he could. He said the men were either afraid of supporting the union or else satisfied with their own conditions & apathetic to other reforms. He said that the boys of his own age whom he tried to interest in politics were only keen on their own amusements. He said that women trade unionists could do a great deal as they were less afraid than the men as they had less to lose.

We are both amazed (and very proud) that we find ourselves representing the workers on their committees. We always thought that we cut absolutely no ice whatsoever and see ourselves as a couple of old 'Squeaks Aunts' in our dirty old caps and overalls, our drab clothes that we go to work in, trundling slowly along on our upright bicycles with the huge wicker baskets. We can only suppose that as we neither swank nor grumble and always work hard we have earned respect.

Sunday 21 March
We were invited to hear Churchill's 'fireside talk' in the Bellwood sitting-room as our wireless is still away. Extremely good. Churchill says after the war there must be no more 'drones'. We have been saying just this for months so have a friendly feeling.

Monday 22 March
Elsie's new job is a brute: the tools won't cut properly, and the whole thing (as set up by Fred) seems incredibly difficult. She feels as bad as she did when she first came. K had a talk with her fellow committee member, Mrs Dobson, and they both agreed that they may need to smooth down the violent Communist 'demands'. In the evening we dragged ourselves to the AEU meeting which was not quite as absorbing as usual, as there was a lot of formal enrolment of new members. But there was an interesting discussion on 'absenteeism and persistent lateness' which is rife in a neighbouring factory and the union's advice and methods of dealing with it. The question of supporting a Communist candidate for the AEU General Secretaryship also came up and we and Bro. Moroney were the only dissentients!

Tuesday 23 March
Another awful day for Els, and she and Laurie almost think they will ask for their release, as they can neither of them manage their new jobs. K and the rest of the works council were summoned to meet Mr Young, one of the directors who is to be the chairman. The meetings are fixed fortnightly for Thursdays. The workers' reps will have a preliminary meeting on their own to discuss points and general procedure.

Wednesday 24 March
Els had a bad morning, but all went well in the afternoon, so she felt more cheerful. After dinner K and her co-reps met just outside the factory and considered their plan of campaign. George Ross, a Communist who did not get on to the works council, (he also serves on E's Sick Benefit) added himself to the meeting. Ross has a lean and hungry look and the air of the firm working-class agitator. When we came back we found a letter from Ronald congratulating Kat on being a Work Cow.

Thursday 25 March
Els had another awful morning as her job is the devil, and Fred sets it up for her each morning with great rapidity and inaccuracy, so that this morning he made her one object which was quite incorrect and would be scrapped, and then left the machine for her wrongly so that the first one Els took off will probably also be scrapped. E was particularly upset over this as she had had her doubts, and so asked Fred if all was quite OK before she began, and he assured her it was. Later in the day, however, all went well, and she made up for lost time.

At 12 noon Els was summoned to a Sick Benefit Committee – where poor old Payne grumbled that he got no support from the management and was properly browned off. At 5.30 K packed up and went off to the first of the works council meetings. The management's reps were Mr Young, Capt Lines, Mr Hurst. Mr McGiveney, the managing director, welcomed the delegates and proceeded to give the council his blessing. Mr Young then took the Chair and the meeting then formed its rules. Meetings to take place fortnightly on Thursdays at 5.30. Everything passed off very amicably and we think the council should do good. K feels rather like a babe in the wood as she is prepared to think that the management means as well as they sound, whereas the other workers' delegates are deeply suspicious.

Friday 26 March
Work during the day was better for Els as she got on all right with her job. K had a great day, a rosy flush mantling her neck and face while she rushed round the shop telling them about the meeting yesterday, and explaining about a delegate from the machine shop for a sub-committee to serve under the workers' representatives at the works council. It seemed quite like the dear old days to see K with a note book and that questing look, and when she gathered the girls all round at the tea table and 'told them wot' all the girls of the machine shop agreed that they had got a winner in K. Laurie very angry because she expected her rise this week, and it didn't come – once more nothing is 'good enough'.

Saturday 27 March
Life in Industry looks like being much more interesting for K in future – for the tedium of the job she has been on for months is now broken by visits from boyfriends who serve on the committee with her and come to discuss their procedure.

Today, Ivy Barney and Eddie Wratten got married and the firm collected £7.0.0. for a wedding present. They went off today to stay at The Huts, Hindhead, for their honeymoon, at our recommendation.

Sunday 28 March
Letters and domesticity all day. Our line of drying handkerchiefs had to be removed from the window as Mrs Bellwood said it lowers the tone.

Monday 29 March
K handed in yet another 100 of her bits and was preparing drearily to start on a repeat when she discovered to her joy that there was no more metal available. So another job had to be found for her. Laurie came in a great state today as her husband had been in great pain all the weekend. He insisted on going off to his work, but at lunchtime Laurie departed to go and see how he was. At 5.15 the first of the works council sub-committees was held. This consisted of a workers' representative from each department of the factory. Ken Peters represented the m/c shop. And we were very pleased to find that nearly all the girls voted for him. This we think a great compliment to him as he takes very little notice of any of them, but works quietly on by himself all day. He is said to

be a good supervisor and those who know him, think he will speak his mind on the committee. Els was almost the only one working overtime on the lathes today as K had to go to the meeting and both Stan and Fred packed up and off. The meeting took place in the canteen in a hideous din of metal bashing rising up from the factory below, but it was very interesting because everyone was full of talk. Our much discussed 'double time' problem that we wanted to write to Stafford Cripps about, was also considered and it was decided to make a test case. The welding department agreed to clock off, however little time they took, and then see whether the management cut the time on the job. In any case we hear that it is not allowed by the gov't to cut job times without the operators' agreement.

Tuesday 30 March
Els had an awful afternoon with her lathe gone wrong, and stood and watched the millwrights dismantle it for 4 hours. K spent all day chasing about after a job. The new 'Birth Control Clinic,' or 'job card routing system', seems to be causing chaos. Laurie very delighted because she is going on part-time until her husband has recovered.

Wednesday 31 March
Laurie presented each of us this morning with a natty little navy blue peaked munition cap which caused quite a stir in the shop. The men all chy-iked [*made fun*] when they came in and either galloped down the shop because we looked like riding ladies, or called 'Tickets, please' because we had an air of the Southern Railway. We look much more spruce and smart, and many have congratulated us on our improved appearance.

The Sick Benefit Fund dance last night was a great success and made £9.7.6 clear profit. Mr Proctor attended and made a speech we hear, and Mr Carlton is revealed by Nancy Deacon to be an excellent dancer.

Thursday 1 April
April Fools Day, which was driven home to us because we found on arrival that the night shift had coated all the handles of the machines with grease! A simple-minded not very funny joke. After this Nancy roamed round the shop, her eyes sparkling and sending about a dozen people, one after the other, on a fool's errand to the time office. She told each one so gravely that they were wanted in the time office, that everyone was taken in and there was quite a procession and the clerks in the time office got quite hysterical. K was 'had' amongst others, but Nancy's plum was Stan, who set off almost at a run looking fearfully purposeful.

These committees are getting almost more than a joke, Els had to go to a Sick Club meeting at 5 and K shortly afterwards went to the works council, where a certain amount of business was done, but K thinks that the management are really rather afraid of the workers' reps – and the chairman takes the business through too fast. Their whole attitude is 'telling the workers what' and not really seeming to want to know the workers' ideas and suggestions. However, Jimmy

Dale held his ground on one point and insisted on the management examining a technical improvement which would save 3,000 man-hours. This suggestion had been sent in months ago, but no notice had been taken of it. The management announced that they hoped to install a wireless in the factory shortly. They stated it was to be played for ½ hour in the morning and ½ hour in the afternoon. No exchange of ideas was encouraged. K came away feeling rather annoyed as when anyone 'tells her what' her immediate reaction is to take the opposite view! The other representatives don't seem to mind this so much – perhaps they are more used to being brow-beaten. After the meeting Moroney asked K if she had noticed that Mr Lines always signalled to the chairman, by scratching the tip of his nose, whenever the discussion became awkward. Els thinks the workers should have an elbow-rubbing signal, which may mean nothing, but should be quite obvious that two sides can play at this silly, ill-mannered game.

Friday 2 April
K was put on one of the new electric lathes today which was quite an adventure for her. However, she soon got into the way of it and now prefers her Rolls-Royce to her Austin 10. Fred is really now remarkably amiable, now that all the responsibility of the section is taken by Stan. He laughs and jokes and doesn't mind how much he helps you. At the moment he is in a slight flutter as his wife in imminently expecting her first baby.

Tuesday 6 April
A dire day for us both as neither of our jobs would go right. Poor Laurie returned looking very worn. Her husband has been desperately ill with shingles affecting his eyesight, and he is now in hospital and only just off the danger list.

Wednesday 7 April
We were much touched to be invited to a select wedding drinking party at the Hare & Hounds, given by Ivy and Eddie Wratten during the dinner hour. We and Nancy were the only women and the rest of the party consisted of Ivy's boyfriends from the m/c shop. K had one glass of port and waxed boisterous on this. K's port resulted in a phenomenal increase in her production during the afternoon. Stan says he is going to keep a bottle for her in his cupboard to ginger her up.

Thursday 8 April
Hilda Carter still continues to be very intractable and rude. There was a blaze yesterday about the opening and shutting of windows and today she was very turbulent and making derisive 'moues' at Stan's back whenever she had truck with him.

Friday 9 April
K worked very fast against time all day and finished her job. Fred is now remarkably amiable and he is very much interested in K's works council so comes round for a crack at all odd moments.

Saturday 10 April
K very sick to find she is back on the first job she ever did when she came into Morrisons, but her sulks turned to smiles when she found she now considers it quite potty and even pleasant on the new electric lathe.

Monday 12 April
[*K and E ask for Wednesday off to go to Milford to sort out urgent business regarding the change over of the Benacre tenancy.*] We consider that since we do all the overtime there is to do, and much more than most of the women in Morrisons, Mr Hurst's grudging consent came very ill. First he stipulated that only one should go, and when we explained that being a joint concern we must take action together on anything that might arise. Then he said we must make up the day we should miss on the following Sunday, until he realised that Morrisons is to be closed on Sunday, and finally he said we could go. All our friends consider that in view of our unimpeachable record for attendance and overtime Mr Hurst's attitude was infuriating. Many people simply take a day off when they don't feel workish – and nothing is said. Our friends urge us not to ask permission another time.

[*It now transpires that their day off on Wednesday is not necessary.*] Tomorrow we shall have much pleasure in returning Mr Hurst's grudgingly-given day-off back to him.

Wednesday 14 April
[*Problems continue with the tenancy of Benacre.*] With all these alarms and excursions we find it very difficult to keep our minds on our work. To add to this K's job has been frightful with an essential tool not in stock, and unsatisfactory 'bodging' only results in scrap. The only comfort is that Stan and Fred are neither of them any more successful. Finally the job broke down altogether and the whole of the ailerons will be held up until the proper tool is forthcoming.

Thursday 15 April
Grilling hot weather these last few days – and we feel like wilting tomatoes in a greenhouse, with the blazing sun beating through the frosted glass onto us all day. Rumour has it that Mr Proctor has ordered a sun blind for his office window which is immediately above us so we are going to cash-in on the idea and shall demand a sympathetic response.

Another council meeting for K. Rather heated on several points and K, stated that we had now waited 31 weeks for our stools. Mr Young agreed that this was a 'hell of a time' and said he would look into it. But we don't feel very hopeful all the same.

Saturday 17 April
Delighted to find that we were to stop at 12.15 today, so had plenty of time to wash and clean ourselves up before starting off to London to spend the night with Susan Greenall at the Savoy Court Hotel. London had the air of a continental city with its crowds of lightly-clad people drifting about and sitting under the trees and the many foreign voices & uniforms everywhere.

Monday 19 April

E, K and Muriel all on idle time for hours today as no jobs could be found for them. This we think is due to the inefficiencies of the new efficiency experts. Finally, we were both given tool room jobs to do and fussed about as nervously as we used to do at the centre and felt quite unable to take the first cut! In the evening a sub-council meeting was held and K brought up the subject of the terrific heat and bad ventilation. This was a fearful day of meetings, and after the Sub-Council, K went with the works council to attend a meeting of chargehands with the efficiency experts. Very interesting meeting as the EE.'s were bombarded with questions. After this we went on to the AEU meeting.

Tuesday 20 April

After more idle time today K and E both were doled out with entirely new jobs, never before done in the factory – part of the new contract which Morrisons have just received. E's job looks rather fascinating as it is brass, but has only a ¼ thou. limit. The first operation, however, is quite easy so Els got on all right with it, but for the fact that her machine is always going wrong and she has to stop while the millwrights are fetched and dicker about with it. Morrisons, since they have received all this important new work, are a secret factory and any careless talk may land the talker in gaol without the option of a fine.

Thursday 22 April

K's job, which went rather badly yesterday so that she felt she couldn't do anything at all and must ask for her release, is now going swimmingly and she is thoroughly enjoying it. Another really journalistic article, designed for Morrisons' bulletin, was brought round to K by Moroney. K went over it, correcting grammatical mistakes and gathering up the stray ends of sentences which had gone adrift. But perhaps, like Lancashire, Moroney will take no notice at all and the article will appear in its original form.

Two or three days ago, Stan, wearied of Hilda Carter's rudeness and general unmanageableness, reported her to Mr Hurst, a thing he has never done before in his engineering career. It seems to have had a most salutary effect on Hilda who is now quite polite and smiling & pleasant.

Saturday 24 April

[*K to Hindhead for the Easter weekend and E to Benacre where Millie and Ronald are staying.*] The gloom which always descends on us on Sunday nights at the prospect of work next day reached almost the density of fog at the end of this Easter holiday and we could not bear the thought of work at the factory at all.

Tuesday 27 April

Laurie arrived in an awful state again. Her husband's neck is now all swollen with glands and the eye specialist fears he may lose his whole eye. She is a most unstable person and only her very nice husband keeps her level-headed and sane. Everyone seemed very tired after the holiday and we were thankful to come home at 5.30.

Fred all smiles today as his baby – Averil – pronounced with a long A as in April – was born during the weekend. Fred looks as pleased as punch.

Wednesday 28 April
To our great surprise Mr Rapley returned today having been away ill for 2 months. He looks quite well and fat in the face. It was nice to see him again, as he is always nice and amiable in spite of his unfortunate weakness for the young ladies. Since we now have no affection for George Bradford we are glad to welcome Rapley back again.

Thursday 29 April
Once more a day of committees. E's Sick Club seems to be paying out each week almost as much as it receives, and some of the men have resigned because they complain that it is too much of a women's benevolent fund. This comment received no sympathy from the committee. K went off to the works council minus Moroney who was absent. This meant that everyone else took a share of the talking – because generally Moroney is the council's mouthpiece. There was a frightful row between Lancashire and the management because Lancashire had made a rather damaging and not well-substantiated statement at the Sick Club Dance to Mr Proctor. He was thoroughly on the carpet and they went at it hammer and tongs. Grace Dobson revealed afterwards that her heart was thumping in her chest with the upset and K thinks it was one of the worst rows she has ever been present at. After this the meeting settled down again fairly amicably – though K had a passage of arms with Mr Lines on the question of sun-blinds for the m/c shop windows. Mr Lines was very snubbing and said the sun only came in about 3 p.m. and it wasn't worth considering. K flew at him and said 'Excuse me – the sun is on those windows from early morning till late evening – and it's like working in a greenhouse'. Mr Young came to her assistance and said he completely sympathised with her, and he would see that something was done. At this Mr Lines subsided looking most inimical. K hates Mr Lines as he is always very rude to everyone at the meeting and cuts everyone dead when he meets them in the factory. He has never been known to utter a pleasant word or 'good morning' to anyone.

Friday 30 April
K back on her old lathe again today and not particularly liking it. It felt very small and shaky after the big electric lathe. There was a scene today because Lancashire put up a notice on the board purporting to come from the works council, but which in fact had never received their sanction. This was particularly unfortunate as the actual information on the notice was incorrect and Lancashire finally landed in Mr Hurst's office on the carpet once more. We all feel annoyed, as this young man is being so precipitate, that he will get the works council into serious trouble if he doesn't look out. Horrified today to see that Mr Rapley's eyes are already getting inflamed again. Laurie right up in the bows again today as Ron is getting on nicely and they hope to let him out of hospital

in a week or two. K furious because she has now waited 8 weeks for one particular bonus and didn't get it paid today.

Saturday 1 May
In the afternoon the machine shop was almost empty, excepting for the two old War Horses and little Lily Sturgeon, as [*many of*] the men had . . . gone off to a ceremonial Home Guard parade for Wings for Victory Week. [*Mrs Bellwood is putting up the rent by 5s a week so K and E make another attempt to find alternative rooms and also hope to find something more comfortable.*]

Monday 3 May
Els won a grapefruit in a 3*d* raffle and gave it to Jimmy Dale for his wife who has been ill for some weeks. She was apparently delighted with it. He said she had never eaten one before. Laurie arrived today in an awful state again as Ron seems to have had a relapse and his glands are all swollen up again. In the evening K went to a sub-council meeting which was quite interesting. This was followed by the usual chargehands meeting to which the members of the works council had been invited. K was rather embarrassed to find herself the only woman amongst about 25 men, Grace Dobson having gone home with a headache. Her position was driven home to her by the efficiency expert who at the end of a long speech said 'Oh, Bugger it!' and then turning to K with 'Oh! I beg your pardon!' There was a general laugh and everyone looked at K, who was covered with confusion at being made so conspicuous. This is almost the first time she had heard 'language' at Morrisons. We ought to have gone to the union meeting tonight but were too tired.

Wednesday 5 May
On leaving for work this morning K appalled to find that she had lost her cheque-book wallet which also contained £5 in notes, a cheque from Ronald, all her clothing coupons, both her & E's sweet coupons, besides innumerable letters and papers of importance. . . . K spent a wretched day worrying about it – only slightly alleviated by Mr Rapley's consideration in providing her with many pennies for the telephone calls and by a personal visit from Mr Young in the afternoon to tell her that he had 'looked into' her missing bonus and would see it was paid on Friday. No Laurie again today and in the afternoon we learnt that she had telephoned to say that they feared Ron had scarlet fever. Poor man, this seems really too much on top of all his other troubles. We wonder if he will have sufficient strength left to get over it. In the evening we were thrilled and delighted to have a visit from a charming young woman bearing with her K's missing cheque book wallet with all its contents intact. K felt like kissing the young woman, whom she ultimately persuaded to accept £1 as a reward.

Thursday 6 May
Laurie came in and said that Ron had not got scarlet fever – though his temperature had been up to 105. In some miraculous way this fever has had a

good effect on his injured eyes and he is now really on the mend and Laurie hopes to have him home at the end of the week.

Friday 7 May
We said goodbye to Laurie today for 3 or 4 weeks as her husband is coming home from hospital and she has been given indefinite leave to look after him. We lent her £5 to help her cosset up her invalid.

Saturday 8 May
An alert at 7 a.m. coincided with the wireless news that both Tunis and Bizerta had fallen, which came as a great surprise as we hadn't dared to hope for this news so soon. The alert lasted about an hour, but we heard nothing and set off to work as usual. The afternoon dragged . . . we rushed off to clean up and get ready to catch the 5.05 to Balcombe. [*Met friends.*]

Monday 10 May
K arrived to find her machine had been dismantled so she had to start a new job on one of the electric lathes. Elsie completed 240 'Bits o' Brass' and was pleased to find they were all passed by inspector even though they had only a ¼ thou limit on the diameter. Els spent the rest of the day with the usual infuriating wait, getting all the tools out for one job and then discovering there was no material available. Finally, she got started on a horrible steel job, which is going to take for ever.

Tuesday 11 May
Elsie had a dreadful day on her new job and feels as tired & depressed as she did when she first went to Morrisons. We are interested to see that in the Royal Academy one of the 'pictures of the year' is Dame Laura Knight's 'Miss Ruby Loftus screwing a Breech-Ring' [*see cover*]. She is working a centre lathe so we have a fellow-feeling for her. We think the tense attitude is typical of women centre lathe operators, a contrast to detachment and sober confidence of the skilled men.

We are so fed up with our parsimonious landlady.

Wednesday 12 May
Another awful day for Els and she was in black despair all the time and finally came home shaking with exhaustion and frustration. The minutes of the works council were sent down from the office at teatime, though they ought to have arrived yesterday. K much annoyed to see that the minutes this time were even more biased than usual. Any accusation against the management is slurred over or omitted altogether, and any snub administered to the workers is heavily emphasised.

Thursday 13 May
All this week the news from N. Africa has been wonderful and today all German resistance seems to be finished. K came back from the works council sick as mud, having fought a battle over the inaccurate minutes and only being snubbed for her pains. Altogether a very unfortunate meeting, a lot of time wasted in argument, neither side being willing to give way. Lancashire lost his temper and

K was in suppressed fury and a lot of subjects which should have been raised were forgotten. K feels very depressed about the whole council and thinks nothing good will come of the meetings. She doesn't think she can endure Morrisons till the end of the war.

Friday 14 May
An alert in the early hours and as we were on fire watch we stood in the porch till the all clear went an hour later.

There were various repercussions over the works council meeting. Moroney obviously thought it was all a storm in a teacup, but as he wasn't at the previous meeting he was hardly in a position to judge. However, K has decided that she is not going to break her heart over the works council. Unlike the majority of the works people, she began with the idea that the works council held the promise of increasing production and improving the workers' conditions. She has now come round to the view of the majority that the management do not really wish to cooperate with the workers at all, so in future she will not expect anything and won't lay herself open to disappointment.

Saturday 15 May
After work we went off to London and had a pleasant evening at the Phyl's. And so on to Madge. Ronald came up to lecture K on her cynical attitude towards the management and the works council.

Monday 17 May
Three alerts last night, plenty of noise but no bombs.
Committee meetings galore today – Sick Club, sub-council and the Union where we were nearly dropping off to sleep with fatigue all the time.

Tuesday 18 May
Alert again last night. K was discussing with Stan today the relative abilities and speed of the women centre lathe operators and K said that though Els took a tremendous interest in her work, no one could say she was quick. Stan cut in quickly with 'Ah! but Elsie's really good.' K had to come off post haste to tell Els this, as Els has been so depressed this last week and has been considering transferring to the canteen to peel potatoes. It's been so hot for the past week that we've hardly been able to bear life in the factory. The sun glares through the permanently closed windows and bakes us. Mr Proctor of course has a nice sunblind over his window just above us! At 7 p.m. we trailed off to a fire-guards lecture (compulsory) where a nice middle-aged man reeled off masses of information about incendiary bombs which we were too tired to take in. We cannot attend the compulsory fire-guard practice on Sunday so we are kindly allowed to go on Saturday afternoon instead.

Wednesday 19 May
Several alerts again last night which is very fatiguing. We don't take any notice of the gunfire until the Duppas Hill gun goes off and then we snatch up our

coats and hasten off the top floor. These broken nights make us very disinclined for work next day, but we don't take a day off as Muriel does after she has had a night's fire-watching! Els started a new job, an easy one which she has done before & she got on like a house afire. K also had an attractive new job and everything went well. We took sandwiches today as K had an informal meeting of the workers reps to discuss their agenda for the next council. Moroney, with true Irish volubility, gossiped at great length about Morrisons, until K decided she must be most unwomanly and take the lead or she felt nothing would be decided for the agenda. Keeping them firmly to the business in hand, she succeeded in getting quite a lot done. Moroney looked slyly amused when K said firmly 'now what do you want me to write down?' every time they strayed into discursive chat.

Thursday 20 May
Two alerts last night & heavy gunfire. We were up and down several times. Dreadfully hot again and the m/c shop is sweltering. Everyone weary with insufficient sleep and the heavy, thundery weather. Lou very upset today as she has been wigged by the moth-eaten little personnel manager, Mr Davies, as she stopped out on Monday afternoon. They were slack in her section and as she had no job to do she stayed at home to get upsides with the housework. Considering what a splendid worker she is and how public spirited, we think she is justified in taking a half-day when work is slack. She feels very aggrieved and it is just another example of the firm's lack of any imagination & their inhumanity.

Friday 21 May
We were on fire watching last night and prepared for a wakeful night. The alert went at twelve and we went downstairs and sat on a rug on the doorstep for our fire watching duty. We were joined soon after by Mr Bellwood and the all clear went at 12.15 and there was no other disturbance during the night.

   After work we went to tea with Laurie Charman to see Ron, who was very nice and looked better than we expected, though he looks terribly thin and frail.

Saturday 22 May
An alert last night & terrific barrage. Bombs were dropped in Mitcham. A day of rush. Work stopped at 12.15 and we rushed off to a horrid lunch at the Civic and then to do some quick shopping, which was very successful, and then on to a hair wash, and finally to a practical exercise of fire fighting specially arranged for our benefit. We threw ourselves into it with great zeal and after 1½ hours came away quite exhausted with torn stockings and grazed hands and chipped shoes from crawling about to put out incendiary bombs on the gravel. [*Away for the rest of the weekend.*]

Tuesday 25 May
We look forward with sober confidence to the end of the Battle of the Stools. We are told that 12 metal chairs were seen being delivered today. However, a horrid

fear assails us that perhaps they are destined for the firm's new orchestra about which rumour is rife.

Els was getting on very nicely with her present job and thought she would make a good bonus when Stan came along to say she had to break down on it and do another which Mrs Hazelgrove regards as her own special property. The rest of the day was spent setting it up and E only had time to get one off.

Wednesday 26 May

Els arrived to find that the future for her job had been upset by the night-worker and Stan and Fred spent the whole day failing to get it right while Els sat about miserably. At 5.15 she decided to go home as there was nothing for her to do. This is the first time she has missed overtime since she has been at Morrisons, but she made good use of the time and had a nice supper ready for K's return.

Today is a red letter day – THE STOOLS HAVE ARRIVED – there is one for each woman in the m/c shop and everyone is delighted. We have waited nine months for them! Els and K really feel they have done something to relieve the lot of the workers – but what a struggle it has been.

Thursday 27 May

Today Elsie's job was finally set up correctly and she got to work on it. Stan told her that Mr Rapley had promised it should be completed today. This did not take into account the entire waste of yesterday, so Els was in a fever trying to get done with absolutely no hope of succeeding. However, Stan came to the rescue and rattled off a good many for her while she chatted to him of this and that and the job was finally handed in just before closing time.

K went to another works council meeting in the evening. Rumour had gone round that there was a terrific row pending as some of the chargehands had sent in a round-robin complaining that their authority was being usurped by the works council. So K went off in fear and trembling as she hates unpleasant interviews. However, everything passed off most amicably – a great deal of work was done and we consider it's the best meeting we've had so far. K created quite a stir with a polite speech as a message of thanks for their stools from the women of the machine shop. The management preened themselves and looked tremendously pleased with this. Mr Young commented 'It's not often we get thanked for anything. I am glad somebody's pleased.'

Friday 28 May

Went to tea with Laurie and were delighted to find Ron looking very much better.

Saturday 29 May

After work this afternoon we rushed off for a quick clean-up at Duppas Hill and then off to London [*for a dinner party*]. Back to sleep at Madge's. An alert, but we heard nothing and it only lasted ½ hour.

Monday 31 May
When K's machine went wrong . . . she went off to fetch old Charlie Sawyer the millwright. He flung his arms round her and gave her a smacking kiss on the cheek. They then linked arms and marched off mateyly to the m/c shop amidst jeers and cat-calls. Another sub-council meeting in the evening and the health of the worker was discussed. It was suggested that a periodic medical examination ought to take place to prevent the spread of TB and a 'Certain Disease' which was delicately alluded to.

Tuesday 1 June
We were woken by the alert at about 2 a.m. and two planes, flying very low, whizzed over the house. Terrific gunfire was let loose and we bounded downstairs in record time. However, no more was heard and the all clear went in 20 minutes. We heard later that bombs had been dropped at Thornton Heath.

Elsie is engaged on a most loathsome little job. It is boring, fiddling, stinks of paraffin oil.

Wednesday 2 June
A notice went up on the board inviting the workers to the formal opening of the canteen on Friday. It was worded in the peculiar way Morrisons have by which they manage to convey a back-handed jab even in an invitation to a party. 'Morrisons' Aircraft Symphonic Orchestra' is to play to us so we shall see this much talked-of band in the flesh at last. Rumour has it that there are 15 players whose minimum wage is £5 pw and it is therefore asking between £4,000 and £5,000 per annum. Who is paying for this and why? Is it a means of avoiding Excess Profits Tax or is it Postwar Planning? We hear they are to play to us at all the breaks, but what is the BBC for, if not to broadcast music to factories? Perhaps the orchestra will go on the air and be used as an advertisement for Morrisons' Aircraft. Personally we would prefer to see some of the money spent in improving the cloakrooms which are completely inadequate and where there is seldom any hot water.

Thursday 3 June
The electricians are as busy as inkle-weavers fixing up cables and wires to receive the loud-speakers as *Music While You Work* is to be a feature of Morrisons in future.

Friday 4 June
This was the day of the opening party for the new canteen built for Morrisons by the Ministry of Aircraft Production. K was rather much exercised in her mind because while others sometimes look quite well dressed in their outdoor clothes we invariably are the shabbiest people in the place and she thought it behoved us to look more presentable at the party. Consequently she took her 15 guinea coat and skirt wrapped up in a piece of newspaper to change into before the party. Els also took a respectable skirt and her magenta coat.

The new canteen is built across a wide road from our factory and . . . we all trailed over according to instructions. A narrow gate in the barbed wire fence admits us, another avoidable industrial bottle neck. It is a large, square airy building, with kitchens and serving counter recessed at one side. It is supposed to seat 450. When we got in Morrisons' Aircraft Symphonic Orchestra was playing a selection of light music, and they were first class, conducted by Mr Payne. We had no idea we had a really professional conductor in the firm. And he has got together, from his musical past, a band of professionals whom it must be a joy to play with. We recognised two men who used to work in the factory, but we hear that they entered Morrisons with the understanding that they were to join the orchestra as soon as it was formed.

We made our way through the scrimmage to a couple of chairs where we could watch the proceedings in comfort. After the orchestra had played for a bit Mr McGiveney spoke. He said that this great expensive building had been put up by the MAP for the benefit of Morrisons' workers and that this was an indication of their satisfaction with the output of the firm. He then told us several stories of his own industrial youth, implying that we all had cushy jobs nowadays and said that we mustn't allow ourselves to be softened by this comfort now provided!! After this we surged up to the barriers for refreshments and nearly died of the scrimmage.

[*Entertainment followed and then dancing.*]

Mr McGiveney and Mr Young took the floor also and finally the band struck up the Lambeth Walk . . . and thus finished the party which we had very much enjoyed. We were amazed to find just what a large proportion of the employees are under 18.

Saturday 5 June
An alert last night – but only one German plane raced overhead. A lot of the girls were 'out' this morning after yesterday's dissipation. We chatted to Stan about the party and he tells me that Mr Payne is very much in with the musichall world. Costello told K today, apropos of the new chief inspector, Mr Willis Hole, that he distrusted anyone with a double-barrelled name! He thinks it is always a sign of swank and snobbery. He little knows that Kathleen Bliss is really Miss Church-Bliss or he probably would not have chosen her to confide in.

Monday 7 June
The new canteen was in use for the first time and is certainly very nice. But the organisation of the breaks is not good yet and there is terrific congestion. A queue from the counter stretches and holds up all the others in a hurly burly outside. There are only two breaks instead of 4 so double the number of people have to be served in the time. No. 1 Factory has a long walk round the outside, as it is forbidden to use the direct route through No. 2 Factory. This will be jolly in the rain.

In the middle of the morning Els, who is a canteen steward, was summoned to Mr Peckham's room and asked if she would take duty on the canteen door for half the dinner interval. This meant she lost half her precious rest time and hopes it will not occur again. The orchestra played throughout lunch and was much appreciated. It certainly is excellent, though we can't see the justification of spending all that money. Els finished her 250 little horrors and found to her dismay that she has to do another 400, as Stan says they are 'wanted urgent'.

Tuesday 8 June
Mrs Hazelgrove had a fierce row with Jim-the-Pierrot who told her off for her abrupt manner and said he didn't allow 'his staff' to speak to him like that, and wouldn't allow her – he wondered her chargehand allowed it. Mrs H. snapped back that her chargehand never gave her cause. She knew the sort of man Jim was, liked everyone to beg and pay to him, but she was North Country and he'd have to get used to her sharp ways. It was just how she'd spoken to Mr Hurst last week. With that she 'swep' off – triumphant as always and unpopular as always.

Els again found that she had to steward at the door for dinner again. Apparently, Mr Peckham had gone off for the day without making any arrangements, so the same poor devils had to forgo their hard earned rest. The orchestra seemed better than ever today and after food was finished most people sat about in silence listening to it. After work we paid our promised visit to Mrs Parachute Marley at the Training Centre. She was very amiable and looked in much better health than when she worked at Morrisons – as well she might with her easy hours. But we found we liked her no better than before. In fact almost everything she said annoyed us. We went into the workshops to visit our teachers and saw Old Powney and Mr Evans and Chris Crow. They, one and all, told us that Gawge had left six months ago and now had a job as works foreman in the London Passenger Transport Board at Chiswick. To which K quickly, but quite untruthfully, interposed to say that we had come to see Mrs Marley! The staff at the centre is tremendously reduced and we were struck with the lack of trainees. The place seemed practically empty and what trainees there were were women.

Wednesday 9 June
The management has still done nothing about arranging for stewards for the canteen doors at dinner and so Els again had to do it, but this time Mr Proctor said that the stewards could take half an hour before the dinner for their own meal, so this was quite pleasant, though doesn't help production or Els' bonus. Rather hard on those who work on piece-work rates.

With the early tea break at 3 p.m. the day now seems interminable, and though K and E took sandwiches and had a snack at the lathe at 5.30 we felt faint and exhausted by 6.45 p.m. K is going to bring this early tea menace up at the works council, as it is particularly trying for people who do overtime.

Thursday 10 June
Very hot today, but K has got a nice boy working near her who is gradually breaking a window for her to let in some air. Today he gave it a good biff, inadvertent like, and a star-shape crack appeared.

Works council for K tonight. She created quite a diversion by saying that though barbed wire rose higher every day round the factory, the slender could still slither under the gates on to the premises. This was hardly believed by the management, but K told them she had seen with her own eyes some of the juvenile workers using this method of entry.

All the workers' representatives complained about the tea break being three o'clock, but got no sympathy at all from the management. Mr Lines quoted grim stories of his own tealess industrial youth and Mr Young said 'think of the Merchant Navy – they don't get tea every three hours.' This, even if true, seemed no good reason why we shouldn't be fortified with tea if possible.

Friday 11 June

Poor Ivy, who has been away for weeks, today went into hospital for a serious operation. It seems terribly sad so soon after her marriage to Eddie.

Els clocked on to rods to her chagrin, cooperating with Hilda Carter who has gone off for yet another week with her husband on leave. Els and her five mates still continue to steward at the dinner break, and as no other arrangement has been made yet we suppose that we shall continue until further orders. However, they are making an adjustment of Els' time so that this half hour shall not count against her bonus. Glorious Whitsun weekend began today. [*K and E away for weekend.*]

Tuesday 15 June

Ivy's operation was performed yesterday and it proved to be a very grave one, though no details are yet known. Poor Eddie looks wretched.

Stan told Els today that he had followed her instructions on tomato-growing from seed in the sitting-room and had had a great success. Mrs Hazelgrove arrived in rumbustious spirits this morning, full of tales of her orgy of drink at her 'Hubby's-mother's' Whitsun party. The whole thing is an eye-opener to us as she always seems so prim and righteous. We should have expected her to think the whole affair 'simply disgusting'.

We had an alert last night and the searchlight beams were straight up over the house. A minute later we heard a peculiar noise like a plane diving. We also dived off the top floor as we thought something would be coming down shortly, but nothing more happened. The all clear went soon after, though the guns were still banging away in the distance.

Wednesday 16 June

A very long day and all was vanity and vexation of spirit. We have had a naughty idea that we might wangle an extra week's holiday, pleading our unimpeachable attendance and overtime record, our poor, tired, pale faces, and our lack of husbands in the Forces to give us a week's leave every 3 months.

Thursday 17 June

K began the day by trying to enlist Stan's sympathy for our extra holiday idea. He thought we richly deserved it and thought the long hours were getting us down.

We have worked out that we who do the full overtime, do an extra week's work in every two months. After this K had a little chat with Rapley on the subject and he says he will put it to the 'Old Man' (Hurst) but he doesn't think anything will come of it, tho' he is most sympathetic.

Friday 18 June
An alert last night and we sat on the doorstep, being on fire watch, till the all clear.
  Mr Rapley came to K today and said that he had caught the 'Old Man' in a good mood and he thought we were going to get our extra week's holiday. We can hardly believe this grand news. Rapley says we must write in formally for the extra week's leave. We visited Laurie and Ron and were pleased to see him looking much better.

Saturday 19 June
We handed in our formal application for extra holiday today, skilfully worded. It was in fact veiled blackmail as we hinted that we should not be able to continue our long overtime hours without a longer holiday.

Monday 21 June
To our astonishment we heard today that Mr Overton, the production manager, has said farewell to his office staff and has left the firm. Mystery surrounds his departure & he is believed to have quarrelled with the efficiency experts.

Tuesday 22 June
Els' job is going very badly and she is depressed and low. Rapley said he thought we could fix up rooms for our holiday, though the official notice has not come yet. [*K and E start to make plans for a week at a guest house in Kingswood.*]

Thursday 24 June
We can hardly keep our faces straight at the prospect of our holiday which we have not mentioned yet to our fellow workers, lest it should unsettle them and put ideas into their heads.

Friday 25 June
Our offical notification of holiday came today and we also heard that there is no afternoon work on Saturday, so we shall be able to get off without any rush and also do some shopping before we go. We forgot to mention that recently Elsie has been in most dreadful woe, as she has lost all her clothing coupons – 30! – in the post. Many letters to and fro have produced an application form which has to be signed by a JP. So K got on to Dame Beatrice Lyall, to get her to sign it. In the course of conversation Dame Beatrice let out that Ma had written to her, asking her to use her influence to get conditions in Morrisons improved. And Dame Beatrice got extra inspectors put on in the area to tighten things up. K was simply apoplectic with rage, as she considered she was quite capable of writing herself to Dame Beatrice if she wanted her to

intervene and that it was a gross breach of confidence on Mum's part to act without our knowledge on information obtained from the diary. We presume that Morrisons do not know that the extra inspection was an inspired one or else they wouldn't have much difficulty in tracing the complaint to us, as we are always agitating to get things better and are the only people in the factory likely to have outside influence.

Saturday 26 June – Saturday 3 July
We had quite a send-off for our holiday and everyone was very nice about it and didn't seem to grudge us the extra week. By the end of the week we felt unbelievably recovered and on Saturday returned to Croydon to repack for our official holiday.

Saturday 3 July – Sunday 11 July
[*K spent the week with her mother. E visited family and friends.*]
On Sunday evening K and E met again at Duppas Hill and strangely enough felt quite ready for work. This may partly have been because of the wonderful news of the invasion of Sicily. We hear that Croydon had quite a sharp daylight raid on Friday afternoon.

Monday 12 July
We went off to work quite cheerfully, but this soon evaporated as we found that there were no jobs for us nor suitable machines vacant. We spent a long time moving about on idle time and then Els was issued with a batch of rods, which though uninteresting may bring in a bonus. K was awfully cross as Hilda had got her electric lathe, but that is what comes of going away. Of course Peggy Hazelgrove, who had also been away, managed by threats and complaints and by being generally very selfish and disagreeable to get put back on her own electric lathe.

The day was intolerably boring. We disliked everyone, excepting Lou and Nancy, and even Stan failed to charm us. The main excitement of the week seems to have been the raid on Friday afternoon. At about 5.10 p.m. the planes swept in and machine-gunned the Croydon streets. May Nolan had a piece of shrapnel ricochetting through her window and Ivy and Eddie had a bomb in their road. Several people seem to have had quite narrow escapes and an aircraft factory was hit and 6 people killed. If it had happened a few minutes earlier the streams of people coming out of the factories would have been an easy target.

Wednesday 14 July
A terrific horde of fortresses were making white streaks in the sky as we went to work. The whole air was humming with them.

A charmingly worded letter of thanks from Laurie to her fellow workers appeared on the notice board today. They had made a collection for her and her husband to help in his illness. Later on another notice appeared advertising an 'Outing' for Morrisons on 4 September. Up the river in steamers starting at

Hampton Court at 9.30 a.m. and returning to Hampton Court about 9 p.m. We have enrolled for this beano, with sinking hearts. Costello has not yet returned to the factory after the holiday. We do hope that this does not mean that he has got a transfer, as we both like him so very much and should miss his quietly humorous presence if he disappeared from our daily round. Another inspector, transferred to Morrisons from a neighbouring factory by the National Services Officer, came today and we don't take to him at all, a bumptious little creature called Peter Joseph.

Thursday 15 July

Many derogatory comments have been made today about the new little inspector who struts about in an uppish manner. Elsie was purple in the face today, tearing along on a job and doing double time. She hopes that the bonus on this job may recoup her for some of the lean weeks she has had in the past. K also racing along neck and neck with Mrs Hazelgrove, with whom she was sharing a job.

Friday 16 July

An alert last night, and we were on fire watch duty so went down to the porch, but no gunfire and the alert ended in 20 minutes.

K finished her new job and was given a horrible one in hard steel, but just as she was about to begin Stan came along and told her she could return to her old electric lathe on which Hilda Carter had been working since our holiday. Stan has been determined to get Hilda off this lathe as she is so saucy he can't do anything with her. Hilda was in a rage about all this and cast evil looks at K and Stan.

Saturday 17 July

We found to our surprise that there was no afternoon work, so went off early shopping and E bought a nice pair of shoes. In the evening we sat at our open window watching the fair which is encamped on Duppas Hill for 10 days.

Tuesday 20 July

Today Jock returned *The Song of Bernadette* which K had lent him. He enjoyed it very much and wants to borrow some more books to read. An awful afternoon for Kathleen. Her job would not go right and she could not get any help out of Stan. In the end she sat by her lathe and sulked.

Wednesday 21 July

Elsie is feeling rather cheered, as although she has a most uninteresting job, she is getting terrifically quick and is rattling along in double time. This will help up the old bonus in due course. K arrived this morning determined to 'coué' her job into going better and better, but by 9.30 a.m. she was in despair again as nothing would go right. However, later on she tried a little experiment in the setting of the machine, although she had been told by Stan that it couldn't make any difference. But to her delight she found 'the finish' improved immediately. So then she had to use guile and tact to get Stan's approval of this change. And mercifully he was rather amused at her insubordination and allowed her to continue. Once more K is having a passage of arms with Hilda, as for some reason best known to himself, Fred set Hilda up on K's electric lathe (which was unoccupied for a short time as K was on another job). However, when Stan saw what was toward he said 'Oh well – she won't be there for long!' and as soon as Hilda cleared up before overtime he pounced on the electric lathe and proceeded to set K's job up on it. Hilda was in a rage and went round muttering imprecations. We wonder what is going to happen tomorrow when K and Hilda both arrive early ready to start work on the electric machine!

Thursday 22 July
This morning Mrs Hazelgrove arrived to say that 'her Joan' was ill and that therefore she was going straight home again. This left another electric lathe vacant and K fondly imagined that her quarrel with Hilda would smooth itself out and that they could both have an electric lathe. But no! K was put on Mrs Hazelgrove's and Fred took over the one there had been the argument about yesterday. This left Hilda in more of a rage than ever and she rushed round blaspheming at 'Mr Wallace' and threatening to complain to Hurst. K felt rather sorry for Hilda and thought she was being treated unfairly. It certainly doesn't pay to get on the wrong side of Stan. He always gets even with the recalcitrant. These new electric lathes are much in demand as they are much more accurate and nearly all jobs can be done more quickly on them. By ill luck Els is the only woman who has never been on one and Stan cheered her last week by saying that he was planning to put her on one this week when one of the men went on nights. But alas, when the day came, another man got the lathe, as his old machine is going out of commission. So poor Els is now stuck on her old original lathe and sees herself there for ever more. Added to this only a few jobs are suitable for this particular machine and all of them horrible ones. So Els is cast into gloom. After tea K went to a council meeting and came out as depressed as usual. She is sick of the management's snubbing manner to the workers' representatives and feels the whole atmosphere is very unpleasant. The management seem to delight in 'scoring off' the poor representatives and always try to make them look fools. They obviously don't like it when too many questions of welfare are brought up and when awkward questions are asked about production they hedge and seldom give a straight forward answer.

Saturday 24 July
A kind present of lettuces from Stan this morning. We raced off from work. [*Another round of social engagements.*]

Monday 26 July
We started the day with the news of Mussolini's resignation. Terribly hot at work and we nearly died of the 11-hour day, especially as we both have horrible jobs

which go wrong all the time and tax the patience of a saint. Added to this Stan hates the heat as much as we do and it has the effect of making him very reluctant to give anyone any help.

Tuesday 27 July

Hotter than ever. We soaked right through our clothes and are getting sunburnt through the glass. K spent the day raging inwardly against the directors for making us work in these frightful conditions and doing nothing to improve them. She also has a private strafe against Stan who was continuing his tiresome policy of non-intervention.

Wednesday 28 July

Another baking day. We went with practically no clothes on but still dripped. K kept her roller towel near at hand and kept wiping her face on it like a tennis champion. The heat makes her very bad tempered. Neither of our jobs are going well and Stan still seems very unwilling to help. K felt so wretched, she contemplated 'getting her release'.

Thursday 29 July

Another sweltering day. K and E had decided to do no overtime, but by the time the evening came we both felt we could manage to stick it out with the long August weekend drawing near. K finished her loathsome job, thankfully, and was hoping for something better, but to her horror was given 300 more of the little brutes to do. This will take her the best part of 3 weeks and she can hardly face it.

Friday 30 July

Another baking hot day, only made bearable by the knowledge that it would finish at 4.45. K wears nothing but slacks and a blouse and overall, and E has got out her cotton bib and brace overalls. So we can't possibly wear less, though we are still extremely hot. Rapley asked K to approach Mr Hurst for permission for the girls to leave off their caps during the heatwave. So she wrote in a polite note, but received no reply. Today E received 18 clothing coupons to replace her lost 30. She feels rather sad about this. [*K to Hindhead with Ma and E to Milford with Auntie for the bank holiday weekend.*]

Tuesday 3 August

A new girl has come to the machine shop. So, with the new boy who came last week, the lathes are now all occupied and Lord knows what will happen when Peggy Hazelgrove and Laurie return. The new girl is called Eileen Savage and is a fine, strapping young woman. She has come from Harper's Automatics where she has been doing 'roughing down' work and is rather appalled at the fine limits which our work entails, especially as she has never used a micrometer before.

The new inspector, Peter Joseph, has not reappeared and rumour has it that he is trying to get his release. However, his place has been taken by a very nice young man, Graham Welby. He is very lame and is an ex-RAF air-gunner. He has an artificial leg.

Wednesday 4 August

Els finished her loathsome job, but found to her dismay that she has to do another 50. Her lathe has been behaving most peculiarly for some days past and today she at last persuaded Stan to give the order to get it repaired. So E went on idle time for an hour and after that the machine went much better. Why this couldn't have been done days ago no one knows! K hates her job which is hard work and not always satisfactory even when done (caused by an error on the part of the previous operator). She watched the clock miserably all day and felt life really wasn't worth living. Lou's daughter, Betty, who has recently joined the ATS, returned today to visit her old factory friends. She looked radiant and loves the life.

Thursday 5 August

Alarms and excursions for Elsie today. She had barely got started on her horrible job when Stan asked if she would like to change to her old 'spigot' job which she had done once before. She agreed and only realised that it meant transferring to an electric lathe when Hilda marched up to her white with rage. She had been ordered to take over Elsie's job and was supposed to watch E [*to*] learn how. But all she did was to lean against E's machine and read a novel until Bradford came up and jumped on her. Els had great difficulty in teaching her the job as she kept on tossing her head in temper and looking everywhere but at the machine. However, E won her by gentleness at last. Stan certainly is very unfair to Hilda and won't lend her any of his tools, as he does to the rest of us. But of course her manner to him is simply preposterous and we are not surprised he bears malice. Els had a great day on the electric lathe and was as nervous as a kitten of all its strange handles and gadgets. However, the day passed in a flash for her with all this fierce concentration. K had a good day and her job went better. As it was cooler she didn't hate the factory quite so much.

Friday 6 August

On Sunday the firm is to play Fields Consolidated at cricket, and this evening teams captained by 'old Hursty' and Mr Young are to have a trial to select the team. Both the captains are very keen on cricket and when a possible match was mentioned at the works council both their faces lit up with a wholly unusual vivacity.

Monday 9 August

We heard this morning that Morrisons won their cricket match yesterday afternoon against Fields Consolidated 120–60. The machine shop was well represented – Ron Allen, Ken Peters, Les Harris and our darling Stan all being in the team. The new inspector with the artificial leg also played and kept wicket and made a sensational catch. They all seem to have enjoyed it very much and hope for some more matches before the end of the season.

K had a meeting of her sub-council, the last before the new election for the works council. Bro. Moroney read a report on the council's work and the results of their labours. The data for this was supplied by K from her little note book. She doesn't think anything would have been done about a report to the sub-council unless she has set it out for Moroney.

Tuesday 10 August
Hilda Carter is going off for 10 days as her husband will be home on leave again. K has been having a terrific race to get started off on a new job before Hilda goes as she was terrified that she would be saddled with Hilda's utterly beastly job on that utterly beastly machine on which poor Els has already spent so many long days. To K's delight she finished her job and and got well started on another. However, it was rather a disastrous day for K as during the morning she got the hem of her overall caught up in the revolving lead-screw of the machine and before she knew where she was she was dragged down by it and her arm scraping against the whirling chuck. She couldn't turn off the machine as she couldn't reach the lever from her entangled position so she uttered a yelp and Fred, who was luckily standing near, came rushing to switch off the machine. She was at length disentangled and found to have lost the sleeve of her blouse and overall and had a wide graze on the upper arm. So off she went to the First Aid, accompanied by Els, where it was dressed and *sal volatile* administered. Luckily it didn't seem very bad and after dinner she returned to work feeling she had had a very lucky escape from a serious accident. After work we went, by previous arrangement, to see Ivy and were pleased to find she looked much better than we expected.

Wednesday 11 August
K has a most colossal bruise on her upper arm. She went off to FAP three times to have it dressed and found the bruise measured 4" x 7". By the evening she was feeling rather wan and headachy so Els tried to persuade her to cut overtime which she was reluctant to do. However, Stan urged Els also to go home as he said we do more than our share, so Els concurred and off we went feeling most delighted to have an early evening.

Thursday 12 August
We were greeted this morning with the news that Mr Hurst had come round the machine shop on the ramp during overtime last night and was horrified to find that there were only seven people working in the whole machine-shop. He demanded that the names of all those who had cut overtime should be sent to him. This would happen on the only night in our sixteen months at Morrisons that we have defaulted.

Later in the day Bradford came round telling everyone that in future they must do 3 nights overtime a week or else produce a very good excuse. He had the grace to tell us that he knew it wasn't necessary to tell us we must do the overtime as we never miss.

This evening almost every machine had an operator and the whole place looked busy. We feel that we have really done the country a service by going early yesterday and so drawing attention to the slackers about overtime – May Nolan,

Audrey Avery and Hilda Carter never do it and many of the others only once or twice a week if they feel like it.

A notice appeared on the dining tables today advertising a 'talent spotting' programme to be held on Friday when the orchestra normally plays 'Request items' for the workers.

Friday 13 August

The canteen at dinner time was packed today. All those who normally bring sandwiches and sit outside came indoors to listen to the local talent. However, only two items were produced at such short notice, neither of them very good. Graham Welby, our nice ex-air-gunner, with the artificial leg, sang us 'You are my heart's delight' and he was followed by the much-disliked chargehand, Lavender. He is a dago-type little twerp, and loathed as being both inefficient and an arch-crawler. He played the accompaniment to a song which he had composed and the chorus was sung by one of the girls. Mr Biffo, who conducts the orchestra when Mr Payne is away, acted as compère.

Great excitement is raging in the factory. Peter Joseph, the new little Jew inspector, has demanded a meeting of the Canteen Committee which exists but never meets. He considers the canteen is a scandal and outrageously dear. He has asked everyone to write down their complaints and he will see that they are brought up at the committee. He has demanded to attend the committee himself and also that the canteen manageress shall be present. Our own view is that the canteen cooking isn't really so bad, but that everything is too expensive for working-class pockets.

Sunday 15 August

A domestic morning and then by bus to Cheam to visit Bert and his family whom we have not seen for about nine months. They were as charming as ever, and the conversation turned to what we are all going to do after the war. Bert is . . . drawn to the idea of a road-house. He made broad hints to be taken into partnership at Benacre, but we explained it was too small for a third partner and anyhow his taste for a swimming pool, cocktail-bar & a 'nice tune-up' for a bit of dancing in the garden, would not be ours.

Monday 16 August

The heat wave seems to have returned. We sweltered all day and could hardly endure it. K had a works council agenda meeting during the dinner hour and the day dragged on to 6.45. It is most amusing to see the machine shop full of all the girls who used to cut off home at 5. o'c. However, we expect they will get even by staying out a day to make up.

Tuesday 17 August

An alert last night, but the all clear followed soon after. Hotter than ever today. K took her thermometer and had it sitting under her table in the shade and in the afternoon it went up to 82°F. Every one finds this sudden burst of hot weather very trying and it must affect production very adversely. If we had electric fans to make a breeze it might not be so bad. K's bruised arm is on the mend, but the bruise now extends from shoulder to elbow though paler in colour. Darling Stan has given K a nice new job. We think largely because she jokingly said she would get a transfer to No. 2 Factory where it is always fairly cool.

Wednesday 18 August
The thermometer registered 76°F when we arrived this morning and was soon up to 84 where it remained. K keeps it in the shade under her table. Everyone is most intrigued with it and frequent visitors come to view it. Today was the day of the canteen committee. Six representatives from the workers were invited to attend and everyone showed a great deal of interest. The heat in the m/c shop was terrible. Els is getting sunburnt through the glass.

Thursday 19 August
Everyone agog this morning to hear news of the canteen committee. The meeting lasted 3 hours and was extremely stormy. Mr Proctor started off with a gubation [*speech/oration*] on the terrible food he had had to put up with in the army in the last war. This seems to be the management's only reaction to any criticism. Peter Joseph listened for a while and then interrupted to say that the workers didn't want to hear all that, but they wanted to state their own complaints. Mr Proctor then said 'Well – you are going to listen to me whether you like it or not'. After this Peter Joseph said 'Well – unless you want to have a Government Enquiry, you'd better let us talk,' on which Mr Proctor sat down and the meeting then proceeded. Complaints ranged from cracked cups, what happens to our butter ration and inefficient committees, to uninteresting menus, and high prices. One of the representatives described the meeting as a 'major victory'. It now remains to be seen what improvements are actually made. Knowing Morrisons we don't feel too sanguine. However, the old committee is to be removed and a new one elected by the workers so that is all to the good.

   At 10 o'clock K went off to a works council meeting, the last of the 6 month's session. It was very amicable for once and ended with felicitations on both sides, and Mr Young said he hoped the same five would be re-elected to serve for the next period. K made an impassioned speech about the heat in the m/c shop and after the meeting Mr Young came down to see for himself. The sun was blazing onto us and he agreed that conditions were very bad. K batted her eyes at him and made him come up and have a word with her. But they didn't arrive at any satisfactory conclusion and we expect to swelter for the rest of time.

Friday 20 August
Another amateur concert during dinner hour today. The place was packed and Mr McGiveney, Lines and Proctor came and leant against the wall to listen. One

man played the *Warsaw Concerto*, but it was largely drowned in the clatter of crockery. Then a wild girl played the mandolin, but she looked very anxious and was still in the counting stage. Then Mr Biffo announced that Mr Lavender would play another of his song compositions and that this time the chorus would be sung by Sally Fillingham. Sally is the true factory type, bursting with high spirits, completely unselfconscious, and with the wild, free gestures of the very rough. Most of the girls are at great pains to doll themselves up for their public appearance, but Sally rose from her seat in her filthy white overall, with the usual grease marks all over the backside and walked onto the platform giving the double-handed boxer's salute. She is a tall, fair girl, with thin, stringy, loose limbs and a long, thin face which lights up. We have always been interested in her since we heard her singing like a lark in the shelter one day during an alert. She has the roughest gin-and-fog voice and was one of the firm's first girl employees. When she began her song there was an almost immediate breakdown, as Lavender's songs seem utterly tuneless and quite unsingable. Everyone roared with laughter as this had happened last week with the other chorus singer. Sally had an altercation with Lavender, accompanied by much arm slinging while the audience shrieked. She started off again and there was another breakdown. Finally Mr Biffo said 'Never mind – sing something next week instead', but Sally said 'Oh! no I don't. I came up here to sing and sing I'm going to' and she broke into a modern dance hit and the orchestra joined in. She sang awfully well and was received with thunderous applause. The double bass and the pianist had tears streaming down their faces at Sally's altercation and the directors were also howling with laughter. Even the grim Capt Lines, who has never before been seen to smile, was purple in the face and mopping his eyes. Sally really is a find and has all the makings of Gracie Fields.

The concert then ended with some dire crooning and a very young girl, Pansy Williams, playing the piano with wonderful rhythm. She played popular dance music and quite spontaneously the workers gradually joined in, until the whole room was singing with her. It is quite evident from the packed room and the vociferous applause, that the workers much prefer to come and see what talent there is amongst themselves than to listen to the grand professional orchestra provided by the firm.

Saturday 21 August
[*A nest of baby rats was found in some rubbish under the inspection table.*]

The other excitement during the day was that Peter Joseph had an almighty row with the chief inspector, Mr Willis Hole, and walked out without permission as he was refused a Pass Out. We are told he is a bookmaker and goes to the greyhound races on Saturday afternoons to make his little pile. He has always had permission to go early on other Saturdays (much to some people's annoyance) and today when he was refused he completely lost his temper and walked out. This constitutes a 'refusal to return to work' and he will be reported to the National Service Officer. We wonder what will happen on Monday. Work till 4 p.m. & then we rushed off to London [*for a weekend with Madge*].

Monday 23 August
Everyone came in agog to hear the latest about Peter Joseph, but he did not appear. About 10 o'clock he arrived looking very natty in a gent's navy striped suit, but he refused to 'clock on' until he had seen one of the directors. After this interview he went off to report to the National Service Officer to try and get his release. Peter Joseph's comings and goings rather complicate the arrangements about the new Canteen Committee. He is the obvious candidate to be nominated from No. 1 Factory as he had demanded the original complaints meeting, but no one knows now whether he will remain in the firm. One woman also has to be nominated and poor Els has got stuck with this. She doesn't altogether relish being on the same committee as Firebrand Joseph, but feels she must accept as a reluctant duty. There seems to be a great dearth of women willing to take an active part in factory affairs. They all plead husbands and homes and their only idea when asked for nominations is 'Oh! Elsie or Kath will do it.' After work we dragged ourselves off to a Summons meeting of the AEU. This was a complete failure. Moroney, the chairman did not turn up, and the Minute Book arrived 40 minutes late. It was extremely dull and we much miss Brother Howard who has now joined the RAF. He always made the meetings interesting and was a most excellent chairman.

Tuesday 24 August
After various interviews today Peter Joseph obtained his release and departed during the afternoon with hardly a backward glance. He didn't even say goodbye to Costello who has been a true friend to him through all his adventures. For one who has been in the factory such a short time he has certainly caused a stir. Though we think he has an unpleasant personality, we admire him for having the courage of his opinions.

Hilda has come back from her 9 days leave and has demoralised Muriel already. They vamoose to wash and tidy up half an hour before dinner and come back looking radiant, but afterwards it seems a pity to get dirty again so they hang about idly for the remainder of the time. We also have a new addition to the m/c shop, a pretty little fairy called Rosie who has transferred from the welding suffering from eyestrain. She seems very quick and intelligent. She has been a wedding cake icer in civil life.

Wednesday 25 August
The result of the Canteen Committee nominations went up on the board today and we are appalled and disgusted to see that Elsie is the only nominee from the whole factory! Peter Joseph had been nominated, but as he has now left, this falls through. No. 2 Factory hadn't taken the trouble to nominate anyone! However, this is to be rectified. Poor Els goes into the whole affair without relish. It is not very stimulating to try and improve conditions for people who grumble freely but are not prepared to take any trouble for themselves.

One the way home we saw a flat to let at no. 25 at the bottom of Duppas Hill Rd. [*K and E subsequently arranged to leave the Bellwood's and rent two large, unfurnished rooms and a scullery.*]

Friday 27 August

An emergency meeting of the works council was called by the management today to discuss the question of the outing on 4 September. Apparently the Ministry of Aircraft Production forbade another local factory to have their outing and Morrisons fear that they may also be forbidden. The management aver that their permission had never been specifically asked although they had agreed in principle to the idea of an outing. They said they had no idea it would involve a whole day's holiday and couldn't countenance the plan. So it is all cancelled and Morrisons have generously promised to pay all expenses incurred. Actually, we had thought it was a rather queer idea for wartime so are not surprised it is cancelled.

Tuesday 31 August

[*Mrs Bellwood is not pleased to receive notice from K and E and tells them that no. 25 has bugs. This does not deter them from moving.*]

Wednesday 1 September

A notice went up today to say that there would be a tea dance on Saturday in lieu of the outing and that if successful they would be held once a month on Saturdays.

Thursday 2 September

The new loud speakers have been tried out and *Music While You Work* blared out for half an hour this morning. It may be all right for those who are near a loud speaker, but Els is not one of these, so to her it is Bedlam. She thinks she may have to ask for her release on account of the £600 wireless!

Friday 3 September

News on the wireless this morning that the 8th Army have invaded Italy. Today was the National Day of Prayer, and just before 11 all the machines were turned off in readiness for the broadcast service. However, nothing happened and we stood about waiting, and quarter of an hour later the machines went on again, so we all went back to work having had no service at all. Typically Morrisons, we thought, not to try out the apparatus hours beforehand to see that all was satisfactory.

Another amateur concert at dinner time, at which the performers were mostly the same as before. Pansy Williams played and sang and is really extraordinarily good, wonderful rhythm. Jock Ure recited a long poem. We had been granted the afternoon off to prepare for the move tomorrow.

Saturday 4 September

[*The move went relatively smoothly and by the evening K and E were settled in no. 25 together with furniture borrowed from Millie and Madge.*]

Monday 6 September

So easy are our new arrangements here that we found that we had time to wash up and make our beds before leaving for work at 7.15 a.m. Even though it was

Monday morning we went off quite cheerfully with the thought of a pleasant little home behind us. Unfortunately, when K asked for a new job the only one available was the ghastly tapered socket job which E has done so many of. Stan said it was a rotten job, but anyhow he set K up and helped her whenever she got in a mess with it so she hopes she will successfully complete her 50 in due course. Stan says that in future we shall all take turns in doing this hateful job – so that no one person will get stuck with it for weeks.

The works council has asked for nominations for the new committee, Lancashire and Mrs Dobson are not standing again so there will be two vacancies anyhow. K has been proposed by Nancy Deacon and Peggy Hazelgrove.

Tuesday 7 September

Els asked Costello if he would stand for the council and he agreed, so now we have five men to vote for: Dale, Moroney, Costello, a man on the night shift called Higginson and our darling Stan. There is only one other woman nominated besides K – a Miss Rhodes from No. 2 Factory – so they will automatically be elected to the two women's places on the council so all the workers' votes can be used for the men. K had a dreadful day on her job and feels very gloomy. Els went to a Sick Club meeting. One of the men members of the club has sued the club for non-payment of benefit. He was not entitled to any benefit as he has not complied with the regulations and there has been a considerable row going on on this subject for some time past. At first he sued the firm, who denied responsibility as it is an employees' Sick Club. It was thought that the matter would end there. But today the case came on at the County Court and the man withdrew his case at the eleventh hour. So costs were given against him and the Sick Club came out triumphant. Everyone agrees that the man is a twister and are thankful that he is getting his release shortly.

Wednesday 8 September

We discovered that another woman, named Nellie Barford, has been nominated for the works council, so the women will have to have an election after all. Mr Hurst strongly advised that there should be two votes given to each employee to vote for one man and one woman and this obviously better scheme was adopted and necessitated much adjusting of plans. K was busy here and there all the afternoon.

Thursday 9 September

The wireless has been toned down now and is quite pleasant, and Els no longer thinks she will require her release on account of it. The only stupid snag is that *Music While You Work* in the afternoon coincides with our tea break when we don't need music at all, so that the music certainly fails in its object of pepping up production.

In the evening we did a lot of cooking and were still sitting at the meal table, too tired to make a move for washing up, when the front door bell rang and in came Laurie Charman and Ron, to our great delight.

Friday 10 September
Up very early to clear up the litter of last night's party. The concert at dinner time today was a great success. A young lad sang two songs about the moon in a really lovely voice. Grace Dobson astonished us by singing beautifully with a voice which might well have made a fortune for her if she had had the opportunity. There was quite a good screeching soprano and a man with the manner of a professional entertainer also performed. The hall was packed, fuller than it has ever been before. There was quite a lot of activity during the day over the works council Election and May Nolan spent the greater part of her time canvassing most threateningly, for K and Costello. But there were no funny posters or slogans up this year. During the tea interval various collectors went round with boxes for the ballot papers and Nancy Deacon did some more canvassing, while so engaged telling anyone who didn't seem to have made up their mind that they had better vote for Costello and K. May Nolan visited her metal bashers, and old Grandpa Fraser said 'I'll vote for Kathleen Bliss – that's the woman we want – she does her duty'.

Saturday 11 September
Els had an awful morning as her machine went wrong continually and Stan, beyond saying he didn't know how to repair it, did nothing at all to help! Finally, she transferred to another machine while her own was mended but had a rotten day all the same and didn't get much done. The result of the works council election was announced today and K came top of the poll with 164 votes, next came Jimmy Dale with 94, then Moroney 72, Costello 57, Mrs Barford 51, Higginson 41, Stan 30 and Miss Rhodes 20. This is very gratifying, though of course there were only 3 women to vote for, as against 5 men candidates. K can't imagine where all these 164 supporters came from as she only seems to know about 70 or 80 people. However, she is quite pleased with the result and thinks Mr Hurst will be slightly astonished as he had advised that everyone should have two votes, one for a man and one for a woman candidate, as he had feared that if everyone only had one vote no women candidates would receive any votes at all!

Monday 13 September
We both had a bad day as it was terribly hot and exhausting. We hardly knew how to endure it till 6.45. We do feel that if only we could leave every day at 5.15 we shouldn't loathe the factory life so much. It's these exhausting late nights that finish us off. K had several congratulations on being top of the poll. A notice has gone up to say we can buy industrial clogs – coupon free – price 9/3d. We all went up to the office this afternoon to try them on. They don't seem too bad and will certainly save our other shoes.

Tuesday 14 September
Els had an appalling day with her job. It took Fred all day to attempt to set it up, but most of the essential tools were lacking. By 5.15 p.m. he had still not got it done and Els had grown hourly more nervous in anticipation of 'screw cutting'.

The afternoon was enlivened by a fierce row with the Security Police. For some weeks past these men have been prowling round the factory peering at everything and everybody and generally creating an atmosphere of suspicion and discontent. Nobody seems to know what they are looking for. This afternoon they found a pram wheel set up in one of the vices and naturally knew that it was not part of an aeroplane. They pounced on Eddie Cook (the chargehand on the autos), a very nice man with a most alarming temper when roused, and asked him a lot of questions to which he replied with a furious face and fierce gesticulations. We don't know what transpired, but the question is being brought up by the works council. The sub-council for the new works council met today and K's new woman colleague, Mrs Nellie Barford, appeared for the first time. She seems pleasant, but says she has never done anything of the sort before and seems rather shy and retiring. K was made sec. of the council. As Moroney said, she has always done all the secretarial work, and now that Lancashire has retired from the council K may as well have the doubtful honour of the official position.

Wednesday 15 September
Another dreadful day for both. Fred experimenting all the morning unsuccessfully with E's job. Stan was very busy all day as most of his girls wanted help, so he has very little time to give to K, who spent most of her day messing about, drilling 24 lousy little holes (as Bert would say).

Thursday 16 September
An alert about 10 p.m. last night. Some gun-fire but not much. K started off almost in hysteria as Stan told her she had got to make 24 plug gauges without any help from him. He merely made her a drawing and left her to it. She felt perfectly frantic and hadn't the least idea how to begin. However, after fiddling about for some time, she managed to evolve a method and by the end of the day felt quite at ease in the job and rather enjoyed herself. Els had a lovely morning cutting screws and felt very pleased with herself when all went well. However, as there was no finishing tool she wasn't able to complete the job and had to interrupt on it and start another job. So she had not the satisfaction of seeing a finished batch. The rest of the day was spent fussing about setting up the new lot and she didn't get going properly until 6 p.m. The 'Gestapo' were on the prowl again today and every time they marched round the m/c shop all the metal workers 'downed tools' till they had gone.

Just as we were boiling up our hot water bottles preparatory to lying down fully dressed on our beds for fire watch duty the alert sounded. Luckily, the all clear went in about 10 minutes so back home again and no more disturbances during the night.

Friday 17 September
K continued with her gauges and quite enjoyed herself. Elsie's machine broke down again so she was out of a job for some time. We learn with delight that there is to be no work for the centre lathes on Saturday afternoon so we shall be free.

We can't quite understand it as the milling machines are all working. For some reason we seem to be short of work.

The lunchtime concert today was not so good as usual, though we had another wonderful young boy who sang *Darling* with a magnificent voice. We then had our dear little Nancy Deacon singing *Smiling Thru*. She has a sweet voice, but was very nervous and didn't do herself complete justice. However, she looked so charming perched up on the platform like a little robin and smiling up at Mr Biffo that E and K were moved to tears. [*The entertainment continued, including an attempt at a 'Morrisons song', which K and E thought dreadful.*]

Saturday 18 September
Elsie's machine was still out of action so she had no work to do until late in the morning. K got yet another tool room job to do today and finds these odd jobs rather interesting though nerve-racking. Anyhow, they make the time pass quicker. Stan teases K about these jobs and says she is a 'tool room turner' now! (Tool room work is the cream of the engineering trade, though actually what K is doing is not particularly difficult.)

Monday 20 September
Stan seems to be determined to make poor K an engineer. These tool room jobs are rather disconnected and involve lots of different operations. Stan insists on K struggling along by herself.

Tuesday 21 September
The day was enlivened by a fearful row between Mrs Hazelgrove and Stan. For once Stan kept her waiting while he attended to some of the other girls and she lost her temper and rushed off to Mr Rapley to complain. Stan was in a rage and threatened to 'pack up' being our chargehand. Mrs Hazelgrove said she wished to see Mr Hurst and ask for her release. However, the new little deputy works manager, Mr Heseltine, came to see her instead and pretty well snubbed her. We are delighted she came off second best as she is poisonously selfish and always wants all the attention. We used to think it was because she had got the war on her mind and couldn't bear to waste a moment. Now we realise it is simply greed and that she doesn't like to lose her bonus by hanging about. We have never seen Stan so fed up.

Wednesday 22 September
A long tiresome day for Els. She couldn't get any help from Stan and wasted a long time in consequence. K had a pretty good day on her gauges and quite enjoyed doing them. Very hard frost. Everyone perished with cold as so many of the windows are broken. K asked Mr Rapley if he could get them repaired and said it was as well to ask now before the weather got too bad, as last year it had taken 3 months before anything was done. To K's great surprise a labourer appeared in the evening to say he had come 'to repair the window by Miss Bliss' lathe.' This was done satisfactorily and he has promised to do the other ones tomorrow.

Thursday 23 September
K had a works council during overtime. She brought up the vexed question of whether workers may read a book while waiting for a job and though Lines and Young agreed they might, Hurst was quite determined that in no circumstances at all should reading during working hours be permitted, so there was a deadlock and Mr Hurst said he would look into the question and it should be brought up again at the next neeting.

Friday 24 September
Mr Biffo organised the workers' concert today as our nice Graham Welby, the lame ex-air-gunner, had taken umbrage because he was accused of wasting 4 hours collecting talent. Utterly untrue and merely Jim Sawyers' jealousy, but Graham said 'Never no more.' The concert was not remarkable.

Monday 27 September
K was disgusted to get a repeat of her wretched job. Today was a Canteen Committee meeting. Els's first appearance on this, and she sent in a number of small items which she had collected for the agenda. The chairman of the meeting was Mr Proctor, known to us as the Well Scrubbed Pig, and he, in the usual managerial manner, tried to rush through each item and make difficulties instead of meeting them. However, E held on politely but tenaciously until she had got him to agree to do something about all the points. Mr Proctor certainly did not succeed in riding roughshod over Els. We wonder whether the directors wish they had never admitted us to Morrisons Ltd. We certainly keep them on the hop. Els came out feeling rather triumphant.

Tuesday 28 September
K has a streaming cold and Els a sore throat, so we both feel very miserable. Luckily it was a short day so we went straight to bed by 7.30.

Wednesday 29 September
Our colds both slightly better today. Els was very pleased to note that 3 of her canteen proposals have already been put into effect.
   Poor K is on the Lateness & Absentee Committee to her sorrow. Now she will have to lecture the bad boys and be a proper schoolmarm.

Thursday 30 September
Everyone seems to have colds, but ours are now better. Lou and Costello will both be away tomorrow we imagine, as they looked wretched. The Lateness & Absentee Committee met today. The management's representatives are Mr Davies and Miss Barr. The former is the queerest little man, who looks like a little old wizened monkey and chatters away very much like one. We feel sure he is a very nice man, but utterly unsuitable for the job. Miss Barr is a modern miss, wearing rather mannish white satin shirts, but looking extremely feminine in them. She looks very young, but seems very capable and assured. We believe she

is the liaison officer between the NSO and the firm. K senses that the little old wizened monkey drives Miss Barr nearly dotty. Two delinquents were brought before the committee and their shocking record laid in front of them. K thought Moroney conducted the proceedings very well and lectured them forcibly and well. K chimed in and found she could wig with the best. One of the bad boys had been late 25 times in September alone. He is one of a family of 10 and Moroney is going to visit his mother if he doesn't improve. Both the culprits were put on probation for a month and if they do not mend their ways more drastic action will have to be taken. Mr Davies gave K a list of about 15 people who are persistently late and absent and they will all have to be dealt with in due course. Els thinks a tonic, provided by the management, might pep some of these people up.

Friday 1 October
Another concert today. During the week we had handed in a verse we had written for the Morrisons Song and Mr Biffo announced that the concert would start with this and that the verse he had been given was 'quite good'. Then Larry, the naughty boy who wrote the unrhyming chorus last week, leapt onto the platform and called on Mr McGiveney, Mr Lines and Mr Young to sing a line each of the original song. This they did with great aplomb and distinction to everyone's amazement. The insufferable Mr Lines revealed himself as quite a comedian. Larry then roared out our verse and everyone joined in. It runs as follows:

> How we work at Morrisons!
> Don't we earn our pay!
> Sweat & toil in grease & oil
> Roll on Saturday!
> Biffo's Band is simply grand
> Their work is all play.
> But I fear that I'm stuck here
> Till my hair turns grey!

[*Much of the rest of the concert was taken up with a visiting pianist from the BBC.*]

Monday 4 October
We learned today that Croydon had quite a raid on Saturday night. Fortunately, we were away so missed it. The aerodrome was deluged with anti-personnel delayed-action bombs and as there were air exercises on at the time our pilots had to be signalled to land elsewhere. The bombs were exploded next day.

Wednesday 6 October
K went on a new job, and was as cross-as-may-be about it, as she doesn't see where that munition maker's fur coat is coming from as the timing is poor. Alert at 8 p.m. lasted till 9.30 but we heard nothing.

Thursday 7 October
Els finished her job and started a repeat. At about 10.30 K's machine broke down utterly and she went on Idle Time for the rest of the morning. Then George Bradford said 'They are very short of operators on the capstans – would you mind going there?' So K, nothing loth, tripped off to the capstans and whirled away for the rest of the day, flushed and excited and piling up the production.

Friday 8 October
An alert last night at 8.30 p.m. and we were on fire watch so dashed out. Terrific barrage and waves of planes. It was a long alert, with quiet intervals, then more gunfire etc. just as we thought we should get the all clear. Our bombers were going out at the same time. We saw lots of flaming onions and our planes dropping red flares to light their own tracks. Rather cold sitting in the Bellwood porch [*Fire watch* rendez-vous *for Duppas Hill during alerts*], and the all clear did not go till 11. o'c.

K started work on the capstans but came back to the centre lathes when her machine was ready. Mrs Hazelgrove was at her most infuriating today. She has got a new job and is frightfully cock-a-hoop because it is rather tricky and she goes strutting about, quite convinced that there never was anybody so good as Mrs Hazelgrove at anything ever.

The dinner time concert today was enlivened by a verse to the Morrisons Chorus composed and sung by three girls from the canteen. It received a great ovation.

> Here we are the Canteen Soaks
> Waiting for the breaks
> Trying hard to give you Folks
> Food like Mother makes –
> Some like spam, and some like jam
> And some prefer a 'Grouse'
> But if we ever please you all
> We'll go out and get soused.

Patching, the man who is so keen on music, from the anodic section, sang to his own accompaniment very well. Jack Reeves, the man who appears like a broken-down music hall artist, entertained us with a flow of risky stories. The next entertainment was by the band itself who composed an extempore foxtrot on the theme of three disconnected notes called out to them from the body of the hall. This was really very clever indeed and brought down the house.

Sunday 10 October
Got up rather late and we were busy doing household chores. Ron Charman came round to see us, bringing Elsie's old shoes which he has patched up

marvellously. He says Laurie would really like her release from Morrisons as she isn't at all well and doesn't feel she could stand the factory life again.

Monday 11 October
We feel very much annoyed because our nice Joe Phillips, whom we sat with at dinner every day, has been dissuaded from serving on the sub-council. He alluded darkly to stories that Moroney is a 'Proper crawler' to the management, and we learnt from Grace Dobson that Joe's foreman, Bert Page, has been getting at him and saying derogatory things about the Works' council. Certainly, the chargehands and foremen are jealous of the council and one or two of them will do anything in their power to sabotage it. They don't like the workers having direct access to the management as it can undermine their authority.

Wednesday 13 October
The *affaire* Phillips continues and we spent the dinner hour trying to pump Joe as to why he won't serve on the council. K felt strongly that if 'remarks were being passed' about the council, it was her duty to go to the fountain head and find out what was the matter. So after a good deal of chin-wagging she got hold of the foreman of the Details Section, Bert Page, and asked him what was wrong. However, K didn't get much out of him, except that he isn't interested in works councils and didn't think Joe was a very strong-minded representative. So nothing much was gained tho' possibly the air was cleared a little.

Thursday 14 October
We learnt today that the 2nd XI Football match on Saturday is to be played on Duppas Hill. Stan is playing in the match so we have invited him and his wife to come back to tea with us afterwards. Sub-council meeting tonight, rather badly attended. Fire watch but no alert.

Friday 15 October
Not a very interesting concert at dinner time today. The only outstanding feature was our little new deputy works manager, Mr Heseltine, who told very good funny stories and finished up by reciting Stanley Holloway's *Albert & the Lion*.

There has been a lot of trouble lately as many of the girls lose a lot of production time idling in the cloakrooms. Today Mr Hurst swept down and ordered the cloakroom attendant to remove all the towels until just before clocking off time (This is always done in the men's cloakroom.) This caused fury as the girls say, very naturally, that it is most unhygienic for them not to be able to wash their hands after going to the WC. K went off to investigate and tried unsuccessfully to find Mr Hurst. She had a long talk with George Bradford touching on the iniquity of removing the towels, considering the anatomical differences between men and women. K will seek out Mr Hurst again tomorrow.

Saturday 16 October
K wasted a tremendous amount of time hunting for Mr Hurst, but couldn't find him, so the girls had no towels all the morning. Els heard on the wireless, to

her astonishment, that she had to register among the 1895s in the afternoon.
So she rushed off at dinner time and found, as she had always suspected, that
no women were born in the 'sparrow's year' as there were only 3 other people
registering with her. These she thought looked younger than she expected, but
they all admitted that they were not, 'at present' doing any work!

[*The tea party with Stan and family passed off well.*]

Sunday 17 October
An alert last night but nothing happened here. Our weekend of entertaining
culminated in a visit from Mum who came to lunch and tea.

Monday 18 October
An alert last night – and planes and gunfire. Poor Mum, spending the night in
London, had a noisy time. K spent nearly all the morning hunting for Mr Hurst,
and finally ran him to earth, and asked for the return of the towels. He said it was
all a mistake and they should never have been taken away at that time.

Tuesday 19 October
An alert last night. We got up and watched the gunfire and flares and
searchlights from the back and front of the house. We saw a plane caught in a
great cone of searchlights with smoke streaming from it. It began to lose height
and then disappeared from our line of vision. We hear that one plane was
brought down, so probably this was it.

Els had an awful day, fiddling about with her job for which the tools were not
cutting properly and Stan could not be persuaded to do anything about it 'just
now', so she spent the whole day messing about with it, and accomplishing
nothing, which was extraordinarily wearing.

Wednesday 20 October
An alert last night. Some gunfire, but the all clear went in three-quarters of an
hour.

K had a council meeting in the morning and thought it a very amicable
meeting. She brought up again the vexed question of whether workers may read
when their machines break down or when they are without work for some
reason. Mr Hurst has resolutely set his face against this in the past, and wretched
women have been known to sit all day doing nothing. However, today Mr Hurst
was over-ruled by Lines and Young and in future anyone may read if they are
without work.

Els' job continued to be infuriating and she hardly got anything done all day.
Finally, she got Fred to help her, and a new tool was found and she got on like a
house-afire tho' enraged that she had wasted so much time through no fault of
her own.

K was told in the council that Mr G.R. Strauss from the MAP is coming to
Morrisons on Friday to see the Works and is to meet the Works' council. K is
also on E's socket job, so we shall have to Box & Cox with the tools. Els spent a

couple of hours on Idle Time because of a machine breakdown and had a quiet read.

Friday 22 October
An alert last night at 3 a.m. and as we were on fire watch we rushed out onto Duppas Hill. A good many planes were about and we heard one heavy bomb in the Kenley direction. All the management in a fever today preparing for the visit of Mr G.R. Strauss from the MAP. He was scheduled to arrive at 12.45 to hear the workers' Friday Concert. He arrived pretty late for this, but as the concert wasn't up to standard it was perhaps just as well. We learnt afterwards that though Mr McGiveney had assured Mr Strauss that there was no 'window dressing' and that he saw us just as we are, he had, in fact, altered the programme and been round to each performer to ginger them up. This had a disastrous effect on most of them, especially on Sally Fillingham who seemed to be trying to force her rough factory-girl manner, and as it wasn't spontaneous it didn't ring true. During the afternoon the works council were summoned to meet Mr Strauss. So K and the others trouped up to Mr McGiveney's office. Mr Strauss seated himself at McGiveney's desk and announced that he had a message from Sir Stafford Cripps to thank Morrisons, both management and workers, for the excellent job of work they were doing. Not only were they producing a lot of stuff, but it was also of a high standard. He wished this message passed on to the workers. This sounded sincere and everyone felt rather pleased. He then went on to ask if Morrisons had any special problems which they would like thrashed out by Sir Stafford C. Moroney, mercifully, was ready with a good flow of words and finished up by saying that the relationship between the management and the workers was pretty amicable. Costello said that he thought the works' council had greatly helped this, as the workers now felt that they had a direct access to the management when they wished to air their views. Mr Strauss then said that he would tell Sir S. Cripps that there were no special problems from Morrisons. At this K bethought her of double time – which has hung like a black cloud over us ever since we came into industry. So she thought that she must speak now or for ever after hold her peace. So, purple in the face, she said 'W-e-ll!' and launched herself into the gist of the ill-fated letter which we had once written to Sir Stafford Cripps but never posted. This created a stir and all the management said that K was quite mistaken and that there was no limit to the amount of bonus which a worker could earn in Morrisons. Mr Hurst also said that no job timing had been cut for the past two years. K said that she wasn't specially indicting Morrisons but the whole practice in industry which causes limited output. A long discussion followed and Mr Strauss said that this question ought to be on the agenda for the next council. He also said that in future he would be very grateful if a copy of the minutes could be sent to him each month as Sir Stafford was very much interested in Works' councils and felt that the ideas of one factory could often be adapted to solve the problems of another.

This brought the meeting to an end and K fears she has disturbed a hornet's nest. However, Moroney seemed to think she had brought forward something which needed to be said even though storms will ensue.

We expected Laurie and Ron to coffee in the evening but the alert went at 7.15 and a good number of planes went over and there was a lot of gunfire. Also several distant bombs. Needless to say our visitors didn't arrive.

Today we learned the horrible news that we have to work tomorrow afternoon and also overtime to 7.30 p.m. (11¾ hour day!) all next week.

Monday 25 October

No alert last night – the first free night for over a week. Mercifully, we were told today that the new order about extra overtime could not apply to the women until the firm has obtained permission from the Labour Exchange. So we are to carry on as before for the time being.

Just as we were getting supper Ron Charman came in bringing Laurie's release application form and a screwdriver to do a few odd jobs, but he hadn't been with us many minutes before the alert went, so he went home again as Laurie is nervous.

Wednesday 27 October

Horrified this morning to hear that the Labour Exchange has given permission for the women to do extra overtime until 7.30 three evenings a week. This we feel is a bit much. We always understood that women were not supposed to work more than 52 hours per week. This new order will bring it up to 56½. Very shortsighted we think, as we are quite tired enough already.

K started her screw-cutting and was flushed with excitement all day. We got home just before 8 p.m. and by the time we had had supper and washed up it was bedtime.

Thursday 28 October

While working today one of E's steel sockets broke in half! This was caused by the previous operator drilling a hole ⅒th inch too long; . . . it only goes to show how frightfully important it is that every detail should be exact. After that every measurement should be examined by inspection. K had a frightful morning as her screws wouldn't go right. She was nearly in tears of mortification as Stan seemed to think she wasn't able to manage the job. However, in the end he discovered it was the tool which was at fault and when he had put this right everything went perfectly correctly. K and Moroney attended an Absentee Committee in the evening and two delinquents were brought up before them and lectured. Both rather unsatisfactory young people and there is not likely to be much improvement. It was reported that the two culprits who had been wigged a month ago are both much better timekeepers now.

Friday 29 October

At the concert today K and Moroney were expecting to sing the 'Absentee' verse which E and K have composed to the Morrisons' Song. However, the inspection dept. had decided to give a complete programme, so all the other efforts were crowded out. Mr Willis Hole, Head of inspection, a man without

charm, took the lead and announced all the items. It was an all-male programme consisting of solos and duets and quartets. On the whole the workers
were rather bored.

Monday 1 November
Another alert last night. Heavy gunfire and bombs near enough to shake the
windows. We learnt later that one of the German planes blew up and we think
perhaps we heard this as we heard a most peculiar noise which we couldn't
account for. A long day today, but luckily we are now to leave at 7.15 p.m. so as
not to clash with the incoming night shift. We had our tea-break late and Els
was requested to act as Gestapo and report on the behaviour of some rowdy
boys from the other factory who have been giving trouble in the canteen.
However, they were as good as gold, so there was nothing to report. We both
had a good day on our exacting job and are also pleased to learn that we have
been given a good time allowance on the job, so should get good bonuses in
time.

Tuesday 2 November
Another alert last night with heavy gunfire, while it lasted, but it was soon over.
We hear that the Sunday night plane which was destroyed blew up over Sutton
Green so that must have been the noise we heard. We are both rather happy in
our jobs. Though very tricky it is interesting and the day passes pretty quickly as
we have to concentrate so hard. At 7 p.m. the alert went, and we thanked our
stars that it wasn't a late night as the gunfire was terrific and the shrapnel
pattered down on the roof. We shouldn't have cared to have been cycling home
in it.

Wednesday 3 November
At dinner time we went off to visit Lou who lives close to the factory. She has
been away for a fortnight with ptomaine poisoning and still looks rather bad.

Thursday 4 November
K got a bit of metal in her good eye and so had to go off to hospital to get it out.
When she returned at lunch time she had to have a pass out and go home as her
eye was all bandaged, and of course she couldn't see properly out of her other
one. Els worked quietly on by herself, and as the time drew towards 5. o'c., she
decided that she had reached an age where she might be directed into 'part time
work near her home' and so decided not to stay to overtime and having made it
all right with Stan she departed. She found K fast asleep on her bed, where she
had been ever since she came in as she couldn't see to read. An alert at 9.25 p.m.
and as we were on fire watch we went round to the Bellwoods, but there was no
firing and no searchlights up, and the all clear went in ½ an hour.

Friday 5 November
K went to hospital this morning and was pronounced cured, so came back to
work for the rest of the morning.

The lunch time concert today was not very interesting, mainly women's solos singing the most deadly songs. K and Joe Moroney had come all ready to sing their duet on absentees, as Mr Biffo had said he would have it done today. However, nothing happened and the programme drew to a close without our song, so we are not going to trouble about it any more, and Joe Moroney says he is not coming again as he does not normally stay to dinner. As it is not now going to see the light of day it may as well be entered here:

> I won't be an Absentee,
> Better late than never.
> For there's no doubt if I stop out
> The War'll go on for ever.
> And if I lose time then its clear that I'm
> On the side of the blinking Hun.
> So I won't be late at a quarter to eight
> Nor yet at half-past one.

This afternoon Stan told us that he is to go on nights in a fortnight. Two new women are coming in on Monday and the lathes will be full by day. K & E will have to go on nights too probably which is a black outlook but preferable to days with only Fred.

Saturday 6 November
An alert last night with the heaviest gunfire we have had for a long time. Bombs near East Croydon station hit a nursing home. Flares were dropped over the aerodrome.

Monday 8 November
An alert last night. We heard gunfire and bombs, but it did not last long. We hear that Putney High Street got it badly.

K had a record day with her screws. Els is greatly cheered because she had a word of high praise today. During extra overtime 'Bill' the capstan floor-inspector came into our section, and coming up to Els he said that he had examined a batch of her screw sockets and he wanted to tell her that they really were 'remarkably good'. He was doing a batch of one of the men's work at the same time and the contrast in the quality of the work was astonishing. Els was overcome with pleasure at this and feels that perhaps she is not such an old hen after all.

Laurie came in this morning to collect her things, having got her release. She seemed sorry to leave now that the time had come but the doctor thinks a lighter job would be better for her.

Tuesday 9 November
An alert last night, but it didn't last long, heavy gunfire. Reg had to go out at 6. o'c. on Monday morning to help deal with the bombing tragedy at Putney

Dance Hall. He worked the grab which lifts masonry. He said it was a dreadful sight and 245 dead had been brought out by the evening.

Wednesday 10 November
No alert last night. The first free night for over a week. K started a new lot of the sockets. We don't mind how long we do this job as it is interesting and has a generous timing for the women. Els and K are the only two of the women who stay on for the extra half hour's overtime.

Thursday 11 November
Another night free of alert – tho' K heard distant gunfire. A record day for Els with her screws. At lunch time E realised that for the first time since 1918 the 11. o'c. Armistice time had passed by unnoticed.

K went off to a sub-council meeting in the evening, which had a record attendance as the subject was 'double time and over'. The general feeling was that if unlimited bonuses really were allowed production would benefit. Cases were quoted where times of jobs have been cut in the last two years, in spite of Mr Hurst denying this. The sub-council members authorised the council to bring up the whole matter at their next meeting with the management, and if unlimited bonus was agreed upon, they would like a signed statement by the management and works council posted on the board, as otherwise nobody would believe that it was really true.

Poor old Mrs Hazelgrove was talking to us this morning when she first arrived when she suddenly flung up her arms and fainted dead off on top of us! When she'd recovered she was sent home and we expect she'll be away some time.

Friday 12 November
Not much of a concert today. The only bright spot was the naughty little girl from the time office, who is about 16. She sang *Put Your Arms Around Me – Hold Me Tight* with great assurance and cheek and was tremendously popular. Today K had an Absentee Committee and had to interview a young woman who turned out to be an unmarried mother, persistently late due to getting her child off to school in the morning. She is going to be allowed to come at 8.30 in future as the excuse seemed reasonable and she is a very good worker. She burst into tears and hadn't got a handkerchief, so rushed out of the room. K had to pursue her to the ladies' lavatory and continue the interview there.

Monday 15 November
Els had a complaint from the men on Sunday work that the canteen service on Sundays is appalling. So she wrote a little note about it to Mr Proctor and will have to see what happens next Sunday.

Wednesday 17 November
Those dreadful long 11½ hour days are too much. We came back dead to the world & went to bed almost immediately.

Thursday 18 November
Poor Els broke a front tooth on a canteen roll and fears she has swallowed it. This will mean endless visits to her dentist and makes her very miserable. It is also very uncomfortable besides being unsightly. Having been in the wretched factory 11½ hours the alert went just as we were leaving. We went down to the shelter till the factory all clear went a few minutes later and then made our way home. There were several flares to be seen and planes heard, but no gunfire. E has done our socket job in under double time and Stan said the time allowance ought to be cut a bit. So this was done and Els fears she will never get 'double time' again. Anyway, it was nice while it lasted.

Friday 19 November
No more alerts last night for which we were thankful as we were on fire watch. The Absentee Committee met [*dealt with one case, another did not turn up*]. Mr Young sent for K and Moroney and told them they had carte-blanche to suspend delinquent absentees and in fact could deal with them how they liked.

Monday 22 November
Council meeting for K and a good bit of business done. The vexed question of unlimited bonus earnings and double time came up and the meeting got so heated that it was decided to call an emergency meeting in a week's time to discuss this subject only. K brought up a suggestion of a 'punctuality bonus' to encourage those who are only a little bit late to make them put a spurt on. This suggestion has always been frowned on by the rest of the Absentee Cte, and she was much surprised to find that Mr Hurst received the idea with warmth and Mr Young asked him and K to get together & produce a detailed scheme.

  In the middle of the afternoon K and Moroney were summoned to an Absentee Cte to see Miss Ray, who had failed to appear at the last meeting. She had had the unmitigated nerve to stay out for 5 days without any adequate excuse and then walked in during the afternoon to get her money. This girl has only been in the firm since September and has hardly done two consecutive days' work since she arrived. Her only excuse is that she can't get up in the mornings! The Absentee Cte decided to suspend her for two days and suggested she should apply for her release as she was really more trouble than she was worth. She filled in the form there and then, and we hope it will be the end of her.

Thursday 25 November
Els' tooth still bad and aches more or less all the time. Unfortunately, she can't get an appointment with Mr Power till next Wednesday. [*K embarrassed as she unintentionally snubs Mr Hurst.*] The alert went about 7 p.m. before we left the factory, but luckily the factory all clear went before the end of the shift, though the public all clear didn't go till nearly an hour later.

Friday 26 November
[*E had to travel into London to get her troublesome tooth removed by gas.*]

Saturday 27 November
The annual stock-taking today and we got off at 12.15. Today K was sent for by Mr Hurst to discuss the vexed question of the amount of time wasted by the girls in the cloakrooms. The main trouble is that the cloakroom attendant is a completely illiterate old woman and has no control over the girls at all. In fact Mr Hurst says she actually warns the girls when he is on the war path! K quite sympathised with Mr Hurst's difficulty, but could only suggest they got a new cloakroom attendant and found some method of putting the wash basins out of use for about 5 or 10 minutes before each tea-break. The girls know quite well they are not allowed to leave their machines or benches until the whistle blows, but some of them try to wangle a few extra minutes by every ruse.

Sunday 28 November
[*E became ill while at Madge's.*]

Monday 29 November
Els' temp up to 101 this morning so she stopped in bed and K went off to Morrisons by herself. In the morning the works council had a very important meeting when bonus earnings were discussed. They talked for hours and it seemed as if they would get nowhere. However, suddenly the management agreed that bonuses were to be unlimited and that no times should be cut, except when they were obviously absurdly overtimed, and then only by arbitration. The workers' reps could hardly believe their ears and went out feeling that something had really been accomplished and that production would go up by leaps and bounds. When K came back at dinner time she found E's temperature up a bit more, so arranged for Mrs Brooke's doctor to come and K didn't go back to work. The doctor pronounced it to be flu and Els is to stay in bed for a few days.

Tuesday 30 November
When K arrived at Morrisons this morning she was promptly informed that Mr Hurst had sent down for her on Monday afternoon, so now he knows K took the afternoon off to look after poor Els.

He sent for her again later (K really feels that Mr Hurst is incapable of making any decisions now without K's help!) to discuss some of the details of revised bonuses which had been brought up at the works council. K was rather horrified to find the rate-fixer up in Mr Hurst's office too, as she doesn't care for him. However, it was quite an amicable interview and K was delighted to get an increase of time for the centre lathe women on one particularly hateful job. This job has always caused dissatisfaction and the women have several times been refused extra time on it so K feels she has really accomplished something.

Wednesday 1 December
Flu is absolutely raging in the factory and on Monday there were 15 absentees from the m/c shop alone! Today Lou was the only woman on the mills and the whole place only looks about half full. A short alert during the evening and distant gunfire.

Thursday 2 December
Stan told K today that he believed there were 190 workers away with flu. However, it seems a short sharp variety and most people get back to work again pretty soon.

Friday 3 December
K had a dreadful day. To begin with her m/c broke down and the millwrights were all day repairing it. She had to transfer to E's machine, which is a beast. The question of unlimited bonus earnings is already beginning to cause a bit of trouble. This afternoon one of the capstan girls, Hilda Fisher, came to tell K that her chargehand, Len Quirk, had refused to allow her to send her job in when it was finished as it had been done in a few hours less than 'double time'. When she protested that this was not allowed, Len said that if she did send it in, he would take care that she never did 'double time' again as he would set her machine running slower. K was appalled at this story, especially as a somewhat similar story had been told her by Muriel yesterday when Fred rounded on her for sending her job in too quickly. After consultation with Stan K decided to explain the situation to Moroney and then go up to see Mr Hurst and tell him the trouble without giving any names. This she did and there ensued a most frightful half hour. Mr Hurst tried to bully K into giving the names of the chargehands involved. It felt just like the Gestapo, and K only stuck out by dint of making herself deaf to all his talk and then repeating again that she didn't intend to give any names as they were doubtless only two of many others doing the same thing. . . . He finally said 'Well I can't make you tell me if you won't. I'm very disappointed, but I must say I rather admire you for sticking to your point.' He said he was going to have a meeting of foremen and chargehands and tell them what was expected of them. K compromised by saying that if, after they had all been warned, she heard of more cases of jobs being held up, she would give him chapter and verse. K came out purple in the face and quite exhausted and later saw all the m/c shop chargehands trouping upstairs to Mr Hurst. She gathered from Hilda Fisher that Len Quirk pitched into her for spilling the beans to K. A hornet's nest has certainly been disturbed and Els thinks there may be 'Murder in Morrisons' yet!

Saturday 4 December
K went off in fear and trembling wondering what sort of reception she was going to get, but nothing happened and K learned from Stan that Mr Hurst lectured all the chargehands impartially, but said he didn't know who was the culprit. After work K and E met and went off to London to the EFDS Annual General meeting

and had a lovely time seeing old friends. [*Later went to the theatre and were joined by Tommy Adkins.*]

Sunday 5 December
A lovely weekend, and so nice to find that we can pick up our friendship with Tommy just where we left it and talk for hours in the old way.

Monday 6 December
E went back to work today, but didn't feel very grand and so went home before overtime.

Tuesday 7 December
Els's lathe going very badly, and as she still feels far from well, this was all the more annoying. We were both glad to come home early.

Wednesday 8 December
Els rushed off after dinner to visit the dentist again and had to have another tooth out. She felt very wretched when she got home and found her temperature was slightly up, so will not go to work tomorrow.

Thursday 9 December
Els spent the day in bed, and Bradford told K to tell E to stay out the rest of the week and not urge herself back too soon. This afternoon K heard that Welby, our one-legged ex-air-gunner, has gone for an audition for an ENSA tour.

Friday 10 December
K heard today that Welby did get taken on by ENSA and is to go out at a salary of £12 a week plus expenses. The tour starts quite soon. Later Stan came to K with an awful story that Welby owes a lot of money round the firm, and the workers don't think the debts shall be paid before he gets his release. Nancy lay in wait for him at the pay desk to secure 9/- off him owing to Meg Nolan.

Saturday 11 December
Everyone flabbergasted to learn that Welby was sacked yesterday. It is said that he owes £50 to various workers.

Monday 13 December
E back at work, still not feeling too grand.

Everyone still talking about Welby. Costello told K that the men in inspection have long known that Welby is not to be relied upon. They even wonder whether he really is ex-RAF at all, as he has made one or two unknowledgeable statements about RAF affairs – pensions etc. All this is rather a blow to us. He is such a friendly looking, personable young man, always in such good spirits in spite of his dreadful lameness.

Tuesday 14 December

K unutterably bored all day and hardly knew how to endure it. E's lathe went wrong and she had to move to another, but she is feeling much more recovered today so is greatly cheered.

Wednesday 15 December

K was indescribably bored today, and looked more than a little sulky. Mr Hurst sent for her to discuss the 'punctuality bonus' for which there was supposed to be a sub-committee. K was particularly incensed to find that while Mr Hurst sat at his desk, she had to stand throughout the 'committee meeting'. Anyway, he went back on the 'punctuality bonus' idea, so that is off. He talked on and on and scolded at K as though she were an absentee herself and K is sick to death of him.

Thursday 16 December

To our great surprise Welby appeared at work today. He looks rather pale and subdued and instead of being the centre of a chatty little group, he kept very much on his own. We feel rather sorry for him, though he is certainly a dirty dog to defraud his fellow workers.

Friday 17 December

Els and K are cast into gloom. They have screwed sockets for several months, quite successfully but today there was a complaint from the storekeeper that too many of the little 'chasers' have been broken in the process. These things break very easily, especially now that there is a shortage of good tool steel. We are always exceedingly careful, but somehow the teeth do seem to chip off. Stan is rather worried as he doesn't think we do anything wrong in the process, so doesn't know how to stop the breakages. As each set of chasers costs about 30/- and we have damaged half a dozen sets, the situation certainly is rather serious. Added to which K got two enormous bonuses on these jobs today so it makes her feel more self-conscious than ever. Altogether rather a bad day as K's work wouldn't go right and we both felt our *amour propre* has been wounded. We went about all day saying we wanted our release.

Saturday 18 December

Welby still seems to be with us so perhaps the story of his being sacked is one of our factory rumours. He says he is shortly getting his release to go on the ENSA tour as compère and singer. We felt very much aggrieved today as the machine shop had to work in the afternoon, although many of the other sections went home. Mr Hurst had arranged that each shop could decide for themselves by a majority vote whether they worked or not. But we didn't understand this in the machine shop, and thought we were being asked if we were willing to work, and reluctantly agreed. As it turned out the 500 hp engine was roaring away all the afternoon with only 3 centre lathes working and no one at all on the mills, capstans or automatics. A terrible waste of fuel we thought. We still feel rather gloomy and depressed. Don't quite know why, but think it is probably because of the broken 'chasers'. Stan also seems rather aloof and gloomy, so perhaps there is some connection between all these things. He went off to play centre forward for the 1st Eleven this afternoon looking radiant in his film-star's overcoat. Our foreman, George Bradford, has disgraced himself this week by being late two days running through over-sleeping. He says they have to put their alarm clock at the bottom of the stairs 'as it frightens Nipper'. We suggest that the baby should go at the bottom of the stairs and the alarm clock come into the bedroom.

Monday 20 December
An alert at 5.30 a.m. but all clear by 6.15. K went on to a new job today, the one Mrs Hazelgrove regards as her own personal property. E felt very peculiar and shivery all the morning. [*E's condition worsened and she had to go home.*]

Tuesday 21 December
K got a pass out in the middle of the morning in order to be on the spot when Dr Stewart should visit Elsie. K had some difficulty in getting out. Dr Stewart decided it was another go of flu. A short alert at 6.30 in the evening with gunfire.

Thursday 23 December
[*E remained ill and consequently had to cancel her trip to Phyl's for Christmas. K also stayed at Duppas Hill to care for her.*]

24 December
K went off to the factory alone leaving E still in bed. Our Xmas chicken was handed over and K was aghast to find it needed plucking and drawing. However, kind May as usual stepped into the breach and removed the chicken, promising to return it ready for the pot on Christmas morning. Her only stipulation was that she should have the feathers to make a pillow for her sister's forthcoming baby! There was the usual Xmas Eve hugging and kissing and no one did much work. There were no bottle parties this year, probably on account of the extreme difficulty in obtaining any drink. Hilda and Muriel paraded the place, decked out with mistletoe in the hair, and kissed all and sundry. Somehow none of this seemed very spontaneous this year. K found herself rather out of tune with the jollifications. She would much rather have gone on quietly working all the morning, but didn't like to be thought too smug so stopped about 10.30 and leaned idly against her machine like everyone else. As usual the firm gave everyone a Savings Certificate as a Christmas box.

Christmas Day
E felt better and was quite able to do full justice to the roast chicken and etceteras which K cooked. We had a lovely day listening to the wireless and quite enjoyed ourselves.

26 December
[*Mum made a surprise visit.*]

27 December
[*K now has a cough and a temperature.*]

[*The diary breaks for two months.*]

1944
27 February
We have been in no mood to write in the diary, so now enter a few notes. K went from bad to worse and Els got more and more worried about her and exhausted with running up and down to the telephone [*unlike 15 Duppas Hill Road, no. 25 had a phone*] and the front door. Kind Madge came to stay for ten days and was a ministering angel coping with all the cooking and housework whilst E nursed K. K finally got pneumonia and was rushed off to a nursing home in an ambulance at 9 p.m. New Year's Eve. [*On 8 January both K and E began an extended period of convalescence which they spent away from Duppas Hill, first in Kingswood, Surrey, then Cornwall and finally a few days at Madge's.*]

Monday 28 February
Returned to Morrisons today, feeling more than a little nervous after so long an absence and fearing that we should have forgotten how the lathe worked. We had to start extra early as E's bicycle tyre had perished, so had to walk. We have sent an SOS to Ron Charman to see if he can purchase a tyre for us. We had quite a welcome at the factory. All our friends seemed very pleased to see us and many others whom we hardly know came up and had a word. We started off with the usual standing about waiting for jobs and machines, but finally got started. We were both nervous and amateurish, but found that it all came back after a bit. A good many people seem to have left, including Old Mother Hazelgrove. May Nolan told us that when she came in to get her final release she was dressed up to the nines and was flaunting up and down the shop patronising everyone. May also told us that Lou was very miserable while we were away, as Hilda and Muriel were so offhand and rude to her at the tea table and she had no one friendly to talk to. Hilda, we found, was engaged on quite a difficult job. We suppose that with so few women available Stan has had to teach her some of the more difficult jobs and she seemed quite elated with her success and altogether in a better frame of mind. Old Joe Phillips was very pleased to see us again and kept places for us at his table at dinner. He thinks E looks 100 per cent better than she did before Christmas when he thought she had looked truly awful. He says we haven't missed much and the factory has gone plodding along in the same old way.

Tuesday 29 February
An alert last night about 10 p.m. Heavy gunfire, but it didn't last long. An uninteresting day. We heard that last week a rocket shell case, about 3 ft in

length, came through the roof of the factory. Luckily everyone was in the shelters.

Wednesday 1 March
Message from Ron to say that he had got a tyre for us and will come today and fit it. We invited him and Laurie to tea. We both feel fed up with factory work and almost wish we had got our release when the opportunity offered. We are both bored to tears, and nothing amusing seems to happen. To add to this Stan seems more than usually disinclined for work, and wastes a lot of one's time. A nice new man, middle-aged, has come to our dinner table. He is a police instructor of ju jitsu, and the conversation turned on this today and he promised to teach some of the boys. Ron Charman brought the bicycle tyre and fixed it on E's bicycle. He came up afterwards and had a meal with us. He said Laurie had unexpected visitors so couldn't come, but we suspect that being very neurotic she suddenly felt she couldn't face going out. Ron was obviously rather embarrassed about it as it is about the third time she has cried off at the last moment, although she always seems very eager to keep up with us.

Saturday 4 March
K's hand swollen and painful this morning and when she went to the FAP they told her to go off to hospital. She spent the whole morning there having it X-rayed etc. and a break at the base of 5th metacarpal bone was recorded. So it was put in plaster of Paris and she returned just before the end of the morning.

After dinner, cooked in our new hay box cooker, we went off shopping and got K's bicycle repaired.

We have got through our first week all right. The days pass much quicker not doing any overtime, but it has seemed a very long week nevertheless, and we are obviously rather tired as we slept for a couple of hours this afternoon.

Monday 6 March
K went off to hospital and saw the specialist at the fracture clinic. He said she must have much more plaster round her hand, so now it is all swathed up and huge and she can't get into any of her coat sleeves, but manages to work all right with the other hand.

Wednesday 8 March
We still don't seem to be able to settle down to work. Nothing amusing seems to happen and K spends all her time looking at the clock. E is having a race with herself so has no time to look up. An alert early in the evening, but no gunfire and the all clear went in half an hour.

Thursday 9 March
Another dreary day, enlivened for K by Fred having set her work up wrong, so that it was very peculiar. Stan came to the rescue and was astonished that Fred had been so careless. After this she progressed quite fast.

Came back this evening to a delicious stew cooked in the beautiful hay box cooker made by Pagie [*friend?*]. This is the minimum of trouble, and will give us plenty of nourishing meals.

Friday 10 March

The Bulletin (Morrisons' news rag) was issued today. An article by Mr Young on the vexed question of double time, and explaining about the sub-committee of two workers and two management which has been set up to arbitrate in questions of re-timing of jobs. A very good article, and if the management perform what they promise it should be very fair. It amuses us to think of a director writing an article in the magazine all as a result of K's 'double time' outburst to Mr Strauss in the works council.

Monday 13 March

K went off to hospital in the afternoon and disgusted to learn that she had to keep on the plaster for another fortnight. She had a sub-council in the evening and had to conduct it herself as Moroney didn't turn up and Costello is still away.

Tuesday 14 March

K seemed to spend the day fussing round after works council business, but as she is well ahead with her job this didn't matter.

Wednesday 15 March

An alert last night and heavy gunfire – all clear went in 1½ hours. When Els got to work, Stan warned her to hide her bits at night as the man on her lathe is on the same job and has been seen to exchange his dud work for someone else's. What a dirty trick.

Thursday 16 March

An alert last night early at 8.50. Distant gunfire, the aerodrome landing lights were on, and we counted four of our own trainer planes coming in to land before they were able to switch the lights out.

Els is in involved in a row over the Canteen Committee. It is now nearly five months since it met. The Works sub-council had asked K to bring up the question of the Canteen Committee meeting regularly and also to ask about providing National Milk Cocoa for the under 18s. Els contacted Miss Corney who was quite disinclined to have a meeting. However, Els held on till Miss Corney agreed that if E would produce some items she would ask Mr Proctor to call a meeting. Els then contacted Mr Lancashire, her co-committee representative, but he is Proctor's yes-man, and saw no reason at all to have meetings. In fact he was simply poisonous, and said that any complaints about the canteen were all engineered by the works council who were jealous that it wasn't their pigeon. Els blazed back at him, and told him he was completely mistaken and couldn't imagine what his justification was for saying so. She arrived back all hot and bothered, and dished up a number of items to warrant a meeting.

An alert in the early evening, but the all clear went in 30 minutes.

Friday 17 March
On fire watch last night but luckily no alert.

St. Patrick's Day today, and a great many Irish Melodies in *Music While You Work*. All the Irish workers were wearing the green. Poor Moroney says that since the banning of travel to Ireland the people in the factory who don't like him make his life a burden to him by jibing at Ireland and the Irish.

Monday 20 March
Els had her canteen meeting after work, and found, to her delight, that Mr Proctor was quite willing to have meetings every two months. In fact, he was altogether more amenable than at the previous meeting and was quite ready to listen to the various suggestions E brought up. An AEU meeting and most interesting talk by Miss Heinemann [*Margot Heinemann, left-wing intellectual*] of the Labour Research Department. The talk was on post-war planning as it affects the unions, and was followed by a discussion. She seems a most able young woman.

Tuesday 21 March
A short alert last night. We hear that Morrisons' Orchestra is going on an ENSA tour for a few days next week, and are to give a command performance before the King and Queen. The Queen slightly altered the programme Payne had sent her for her approval. After work we went off to have tea with Ivy and Eddie Wratten.

Wednesday 22 March
A noisy raid last night. Terrific firing almost continually for quite a long time. We heard that bombs were dropped in Jim Moore's road, and he was fetched away from night shift to help the rescue parties.

Els very pleased to hear that they now have soup on nights, and as Harry Mayhead said, the men were agreeably surprised to have something done for them on nights.

K had a council meeting and held forth uninterrupted nearly all the time.

Friday 24 March
On fire watch last night and the alert went at 12 midnight. Our new *rendezvous* is the steps of the shelter on Duppas Hill. We don't much care for this as it is quite 200 yards from home, and we have to go stumbling across the bumpy mile, falling into pits on the way and it seems a very exposed and unpleasant position when you get there. There was not much firing locally, and the raid only lasted ¾ hour. Els has had a frightful time with her job the last two days. Nothing went right with it yesterday. The lathe kept going wrong. Stan wouldn't bother to help and she got practically nothing done all day and finally the lathe conked out altogether and she went on idle time. Today also she started off on idle time, but by 10.30 she was put on another machine and all went well and she raced along.

Saturday 25 March

An alert last night. Nothing happened for about ¾ hour, but after that the barrage was the most terrific thing we have ever heard. There was an incessant thunder of all manner of guns for about ½ an hour on end with blinding flashes lighting up the whole sky, masses of flares and incendiaries. Nothing fell nearer than S. Croydon but we heard the bells of the ambulance and fire service cars going past the house and saw fires in the distance. We stood at the door and watched and then when the noise was too deafening we huddled on the hall floor and watched. The noise of shrapnel falling on the road was like a cascade of tin cans. Altogether a wearing night and the usually intrepid little lodger from the flat below was in a great state. We think she has perhaps not looked out before and anyway the noise was pretty alarming. At the factory this morning everyone was comparing experiences. They all agreed that they had never heard or seen anything like it before.

Sunday 26 March

E's birthday. We went off to London to the St. Matthew Passion at the Albert Hall and met Kate and Joan [*friends*] for a picnic lunch in the Park. Afterwards back to listen to Churchill. Kathleen's Aunt Ida rang up to hear how we were after Friday night's raid. She said Haw-Haw [*British peer broadcasting for Hitler from Berlin*] had announced that Croydon had been the target that night and a lot of damage had been done. So no wonder we thought it rather a night.

Monday 27 March

Our dear Bernard Costello back once more after an absence of five weeks. Els had another frightful day with her lathe going wrong. There is great rage in the machine shop today because Helen Tucker, of the capstans, has been revealed as an unutterable little liar and fraud. [*A collection had been held for her after her brother 'died of TB', it now transpires he is alive and well.*]

Bernard told us some interesting facts about Friday's heavy raid. He has a friend who is in the Home Guard unit who were manning the rocket guns in one of the south London suburbs. It was the first night he had been on duty when the guns had gone into action. He said he was simply terrified as they had incendiary bombs all around them (which were dealt with by the ATS), the grass around the predictor was all alight and the noise of the guns themselves was like dozens of express trains tearing through a station all at once. After the incendiaries a packet of HEs [*high explosives*] came down but didn't touch them.

Tuesday 28 March

An alert last night about 12 a.m., but we only heard very distant gunfire. Helen Tucker did not come in today, evidently unable to face her angry fellow workers after they had told her off so roundly yesterday.

At lunch time today Mr McGiveney announced that the orchestra would now play part of the programme which they were going to perform at the Command

Concert on Friday. It is to Queen Mary, in her country home, that the orchestra is to play, and not to the King and Queen.

Wednesday 29 March
Helen Tucker arrived this morning and was immediately sacked by Mr Payne.

Thursday 30 March
Els spent the greater part of the morning watching Stan do a tool room job on her lathe. But as she has now got back on to an electric lathe she was quite pleased to watch, especially as she feared that if she started agitating she might be sent back on to one of the old lathes again. Stan's job was very fiddling but interesting. We have felt so much annoyed that we have not been on the electric lathes since our absence. It doesn't matter for K as her job cannot be done on an electric lathe but is a plum job on any machine. E on the other hand has only once had an electric lathe for one batch of jobs and she thinks it is because some of the other girls 'create' so much when they are put on the old lathes, and are so unmanageable and mess up their jobs, so it is less trouble for Stan to put them on the best lathes for peace and quietness. It comes very hard on poor Els, for though, of course, she does the work accurately on the old lathes, it is more difficult and takes longer, and bang goes her bonus through no fault of her own. K has been so annoyed about the injustice of this for E that she has been thinking that the time has come for us to get our release.

Friday 31 March
An alert at 3.30 this morning, and as we were on fire watch . . . we went up to the air raid shelter on Duppas Hill and stood on the steps with Pa Bellwood. A few flares were dropped and there was distant firing. It was icy cold out there. The all clear went at 4.30 and we boiled up our bottles and went to bed again for an hour but then we had to get up to go to work.

There are frightful ructions going on in the firm over the management's job timing adjustment scheme. (This arose out of K's question to Mr Strauss MP on double time.) Two men had had a big time cut on a job, and as they are earning 'quadrupal' time it was felt that they were earning a disproportionate bonus and often took home £15–£20 a week. In certain other cases time has been increased on jobs and in fact the management has added very much more than they have taken away. But there is great trouble over this particular time cut, and Joe Moroney, who is the inspector on this job, has come in for a lot of criticism. Joe Moroney tells K that he knows that No. 2 Factory are getting up a vote of no confidence in the works council and the union, and Joe certainly seems to have lost his hold on the workers in No. 2 Factory. He is said to be a crawler to Mr Hurst. We don't know enough to have an opinion, but anyway his blarneying Irish manner would lay him open to this criticism, although this manner probably means nothing. A propos of all this Bernard Costello gossiped to

K today and told her that some union people have a poor opinion of Joe and consider that he is a 'guvnor's man'.

Saturday 1 April
Today, after waiting more than 18 months, K received permission to change her air-raid shelter check, so she is now legitimately entitled to go to E's shelter. K went to hospital and had the plaster off her hand. She seems to have lost her fifth finger knuckle as a result of the injury.

Monday 3 April
Els got onto an electric lathe today, at last, and got on like a house afire with her job. Lou came in looking very gloomy. During the afternoon Costello came round and asked K if she could make an effort to attend the union meeting in the evening as Bro. Marley, the AEU District Secretary, was coming to give advice on the time cutting row. So after a hurried supper K went off to the union where she had a most exciting evening. She was only sorry that E wasn't there too to watch all the fur flying. The meeting was largely composed of Morrisons' workers, and the two men involved in the big time cut were both present, as they were putting up for union membership. In informal chat before the meeting began they both averred that though they were quick workers they were not 'tear-arses'! (As K was the only woman present she was thankful to have heard this word before from a friend factory reminiscences – or she might have found herself asking innocently, what it meant.) The fun began when Moroney rose to his feet and indicted one of the tear-arses as a saboteur of production, as now that the job time is cut they are 'going slow' as a protest. Moroney was white with rage and voluble. He opposed the election of these men to the union on account of their action. Then another member bounced up and asked 'on a point of order' (a thing they dearly love in the union) why these two men were present at the meeting before they had been elected. After high words for and against, the men were asked to leave and they departed slamming the door. Later Bro. Marley the 'District Sekiterry' arrived and made a statement on the bonus earnings at Morrisons. He was amazed that double, triple and even 'fourple' time. (as Mr Hurst calls it) can sometimes be earned and said that other factories in Croydon seldom earned more than 42 per cent. He thought the rate-fixer must be out of his mind. He spoke quite nicely about Moroney (who had now gone home), and said that he considered Moroney stuck up for the workers, and K explained how the works council was elected and it was agreed that if the Morrisons' workers didn't like Moroney being on the works council they had only themselves to blame as they had elected him themselves. K was amazed at the way the men vilified each other. Anyhow, it was a most interesting evening and the workers from the other factories were sitting goggling.

Tuesday 4 April
Els had a frightful day. Her electric lathe was not available, and she went on one of the old ones and everything went wrong all day. Finally, an hour before the

end, Fred did something which made it all right, and she raced away having wasted pretty well all day. K went to an Absentee Committee and it was decided to suspend three people who have been late every day for a month. They are quite hopeless and moral pi-jaws [*persuasion*] have had no effect, so everyone is fed up with them. K wishes they could be given the sack, but this is not so easy under the Essential Works Order.

Wednesday 5 April

Today began in an 'atmosphere' as Muriel, for some unknown reason, refused to lend E her drill chuck, even though she was not using it herself. We were furious about this, as Muriel continually borrows our spanners and tools, and we thought it ill behoved her to be such a dog-in-the-manger. K swore she would never lend her anything again. Stan tried to persuade E to complain to the foreman but E thought this was rather petty, so decided to do nothing. Later in the morning E found she couldn't do her work at all without a drill chuck, so she bearded Muriel again and said she must have it. So M gave it up meekly and the crisis passed.

Looking round our dinner table today we suddenly realised we had an amazing collection of companions. We are all very friendly and it is a permanent party which sits together every day. First there is our voluble old Joe Phillips, with his stage past, who is a fund of unreliable information on every subject connected with the war and industry. Then there is a nice little ex-milk roundsman. Next to him is a newcomer and a burly ex-Police ju-jitsu instructor called N. Graham, an awfully nice man, with a good steady face. Next to him is our ex-burglar Peter Catford, famous for robbery with violence. Our good looking Dennis Ellis completes the table, not remarkable for anything much except his pleasant manners, but he is a very nice boy and a good engineer. Today, when only Joe and the policeman and K were left at the table Joe asked the policeman whether he knew that he sat next to an ex-burglar every day. (Catford's past is well known in the factory, but he seems to be a reformed character now.) The policeman said he had recognised Catford immediately, but of course he never said anything to him. He said that one of the police sergeants had been awarded the King's Medal (comparable to the VC) for arresting Catford and his brother when they had loaded revolvers in their possession.

Thursday 6 April

Mr Proctor interviewed the works council today and explained to them the very serious coal situation. All factories have been told that they must reduce electricity by 10 per cent and gas by 25 per cent. This is a tall order and drastic economies will have to be made. Today all heating was off: in future there will be no more hot water in the cloakrooms. This is a bitter blow, and K pointed out to Mr Proctor that 500 people boiling kettles at home to get clean wouldn't save much fuel. He hadn't thought of this, but promised to restore the hot water if he could get the 25 per cent cut in any other way.

Friday 7 April
Easter Weekend We went off to work this morning in our best clothes, with an old skirt to change into for work. Just before dinner Mr Young addressed us over the radio on 'Pay-as-you-Earn' and spoke very well and clearly. During the last ten minutes of the afternoon we took it in turns to change our skirts in a corner of the m/c shop, pulling the inspection door to make a screen. [*K went to Hindhead and E to Auntie in Milford.*]

Tuesday 11 April
Everyone incredibly tired after their holiday and the whole shop seemed to be yawning its head off. The double time hornets' nest seems to be getting worse and worse, and today Jimmy Dale spent an hour and a half arguing with Mr Hurst over the tear-arses [*and*] their iniquities. They now say that when they were apparently earning 'fourple' time they were [*doing*] what is known as 'fiddling the cards' i.e. cheating over clocking on and clocking off the job. Anyhow, the result was that Jimmy finally got fed up and said he wished to resign from the works council at once and also from the Rate-Fixing Sub-Cte. He came rushing down to tell K this and she spent some time trying to pacify him. In the end Mr Young sent for him and told him that he wouldn't accept his resignation until the sub-council had had a chance to discuss it. Today Mr Hurst sent for the works council to inform them that he intended to suspend two people who had taken French leave and clocked out at 1.30 instead of returning to work. Unfortunately for the young people, they ran into Mr Hurst in Waddon Road and he recognised them. When they come in tomorrow Mr Hurst will send them home for a day as a punishment. He also told us that two girls have been cheating over clocking on in the morning. One always arrives late and her friend clocks on for her so that she apparently loses no time. Mr Hurst caught them at it last week and they are now awaiting sentence.

Wednesday 12 April
A dull day and an alert in the evening just as we'd got settled for the night. Lasted about ¾ hr and flares were seen in the distance. We heard at least one bomb which shook the house a bit.

Thursday 13 April
Everyone electrified this morning to find Mr Hurst and Mr Young on the gates at 7.45. As they seldom appear until after 9 a.m. everyone realised that something was up. And sure enough at 9.30 the works council was sent for and Mr Young reported that 171 people had been late this morning and 17 of them over ¼ hr late! This represented 30 hours production time and Mr Young said that if the MAP got to hear of it they would raise Cain. At the end of the morning he addressed the workers through the loud-speakers on the sins of bad time-keeping. He then read the names of 6 persistent late-comers who had come in over ¼ hr late this morning. He also said that if things didn't improve the firm would have to prosecute. Everyone was appalled at the number of hours lost and

the talk created a great stir. All those with guilty consciences are in a flap and May Nolan is in a perfect fever so we hope she'll come in early in future. Sub-council this evening quite a good meeting.

Friday 14 April
An alert early this morning and as we were on fire watch we rushed out onto Duppas Hill. Not a very noisy raid but masses of searchlights making a huge cone in the distance. Back to bed again in ¾ hour. Both very tired and yawny today and Els very bored as she was on idle time during the afternoon when her machine broke down. Mr Hurst and Mr Young were again watching the clocking on in the morning and later in the day a notice went up to say that there had been a great improvement in time-keeping only 37 people being late. Every Friday the names of all persistent late-comers will be read over the microphone; this was done today. The near-misses for the list like May Nolan were in a state of nervous apprehension.

Monday 17 April
Terrific works council meeting. The tear-arses, having been proved to be 'going slow', the management wished to send them before the Nat. Service Officer with a view to prosecution. They wanted the works council to back them in this action and asked the council each in turn what was their view. Moroney was for indicting them forthwith – Mrs Barford also. But Costello was in favour of their being given a week's warning to return to normal speed, and Jimmy and K backed him up. Mr Young then said that he would like the men summoned to the meeting at once, to state their case and if the workers' reps were not satisfied with their explanation, he wished them to be warned then and there. The men arrived looking very truculent, cigarettes hanging from their lips, and they stated their case and made a very poor one. Mr Young again asked the works council each in turn whether they were satisfied with the explanation. All agreed that they were not. So the tear-arses were given a week's warning and departed. The meeting then broke up, having lasted nearly 2 hours and K returned to her lathe purple in the face. At dinner time today there was no Biffo and the first violin, late of the Palladium and the Hippodrome, was conducting. Old gossip Joe told us that Biffo has 'packed up' as he has taken umbrage because he does all the work of the conducting, whilst Mr Payne steps in and conducts the plum shows like the Command Performance and the Aldershot. Much publicity has been given in the Press in inspired paragraphs over the Command Performance, with a special boost for Mr Reynolds Payne, and also for a member of the orchestra who used to be Tauber's pianist. No mention at all of Mr Biffo, who has quite a name in the BBC and in any case does all the conducting in the factory. We sympathise with him for being very much annoyed and he is certainly a great loss as he is a sublime trumpeter.

Tuesday 18 April
Els is becoming a proper tear-arse in her present job and goes rattling along at speed. Today she had an amusing comment from Stan when she asked him to

grind up her tool because the surface of her work looked to her a bit rough. He did so and said with a grin that many people would have considered the job had already got a very good finish! All the works council feel a bit fradged today. The tear-arse trouble is rather on their minds. Yesterday they had reason to hope that the men realised they had been very silly and would be glad of an opportunity to climb down. But today K learned that the men had been elected to the union with only one dissentient vote and the whole matter was going to be put before the Trades Union Executive Council. Old Brother Cayzer, one of Morrisons' inspectors, is inciting them and there is sure to be a lot more trouble.

Wednesday 19 April
An alert last night 1 a.m. Spasmodic firing and one very heavy bomb shook the house. The noisiest we have had here. A huge fire could be seen over Purley Way, near enough to see the flames. Today K went off to ask Mrs Barford if she would deliver some notes to the sub-council representatives in No. 2 Factory. She agreed to do it willingly, but said she didn't know who half of them were. As she has been in Morrisons five years K was astonished.

Everyone talking about last night's raid. A lot of damage was again done in S. Croydon. It must have been a very heavy bomb. Bill Brazier, who lives at Purley, helped to dig 6 people out of their shelter which was covered with debris. The big fire we saw is rumoured to have been the Selsdon Park Hotel.

Thursday 20 April
A short alert, mercifully before we had gone to bed. No gunfire or planes. Els had a frightful day, as her job went wrong. The rate-fixer came and stood over her for some time as the job is to be re timed. This nearly gave her a heart attack and she was hot and fevered. Unfortunately, while he was there the job went pretty well, so she will probably not get a good time allowance and the job will therefore be hours in debt. Hilda and Muriel had some sort of a tiff and seemed not to be on speaking terms all day. These bosom friendships which alternate with 'not speaking' are a feature of factory life.

Monday 24 April
After all the woes and groans over E's job, she has been given a most generous timing on it, so she feels that 'creating' is the thing. Grumbling is rife in the factory over the cold water in the cloakrooms, even though everyone knows that fuel has to be saved. The lack of hot water really is very trying as the oil and grease simply won't come off in cold water. It just gets loosened a little and is then wiped off on the towel. The result of this is the most appallingly filthy towels imaginable. Today Jimmy Dale and K visited Mr Payne to see if he could persuade Mr Proctor to get his 25 per cent gas cut in any other way. Mr Payne fully sympathises with the workers, and thinks it is a most dangerous economy as it might easily lead to an outbreak of skin diseases.

Tuesday 25 April
Today we heard that Mr Fitt, our elderly inspector, had a lucky escape last week when a heavy bomb landed in the road just outside his house. Luckily he and his wife were in their shelter, but their house is demolished and they are both suffering from blast shock.

The punctuality figures are now very much improved. This has been considerably helped by the moral suasion of the workers themselves. One of the men in the m/c shop has rigged up a great metal gong and beats a welcome to each latecomer. Everyone turns and stares and grins at the culprit, who, purple in the face, brazens it out, but makes an effort to avoid this publicity in the future. May Nolan, who is nearly always late, sneaks in at the other end of the shop hoping to avoid the gong. But a second gong has now been erected at this end too and she has since managed to arrive in time.

Wednesday 26 April
An alert last night, but no guns, and soon over. The raids seem to be mainly on the coasts just now. Today K was in utter gloom as Stan put her to work on a lathe right at the bottom of the shop, where there is no life at all and no one to talk to. The lathe itself is a nice one but it doesn't make up for the lack of amusement and she was bored to tears all day.

Thursday 27 April
Last night we had 3 alerts, one almost as soon as we had finished supper and two more during the night. No incidents and we hear it was the coast again. They are attacking the concentrations for the Second Front. The factory is full of rumours of how the invasion [*of Europe*] will affect civilian transport and facilities. The Home Guard have orders to report immediately the show begins and old Joe is thoroughly worked up about it all.

Saturday 29 April – Sunday 30 April
Everyone keyed up expecting the Second Front to open this weekend, but nothing happened, though the air offensive increases every day.

Monday 1 May – Friday 5 May
We find we have made no entry in the Industrial diary this week, a thing which has never happened before. It is partly tension waiting for the 2nd Front to open, and everything else seems so trivial. Added to this we are completely browned off. We don't like our work, nor our fellow-workers, nor Stan, nor anything to do with the factory. So there is nothing to stimulate us to write when we come back in the evening. K is still exiled to the bottom lathe, and is suffering from melancholia.

Saturday 6 May
Something has actually happened today! K has had a row with Hilda. Her selfish pouncing on the electric lathes has infuriated us for weeks, and today the climax

was reached when Hilda refused to give up the lathe to Muriel, as H had pounced on it when Muriel was out for a single day. She then proceeded to tear through her job so that she needed K's gauge for her next operation and K was so incensed with her for being so mean to Muriel, that she refused to share with her as it would have meant walking up and down the shop every two minutes. They both stormed up the shop to interview Stan and Rapley and in the end Hilda had to wait 1½ hours for K to finish with the gauge. Stan promised Els she should go on the electric lathe as soon as Hilda had finished her job, but E has heard this story before and is not very hopeful.

Monday 8 May
Just as E expected Muriel went on the electric lathe, and E remained on her old bone-shaker, but the worm at last turned and E complained sadly to Stan of his broken promise. He said rather grumpily that he would put her on an electric lathe tomorrow.

E was suddenly summoned to see Mr Payne, and found he was holding an unnotified Sick Club Committee, to explain that the fund is pretty well bankrupt and that he had been financing it for weeks . . . he wasn't prepared to go on any longer and was proposing, with the committee's agreement, to send a letter to each member explaining the position and cutting the benefits by half as from next Monday. E said that she didn't think Mr Payne had any right to be financing the Sick Club. She considered the committee should have been informed before. She also said she thought there should be a general meeting of the Sick Club before the benefits were altered and that a General meeting had been proposed last autumn but nothing had been done. Also that a Balance Sheet must be produced for the members. But Mr Payne is quite hopeless and E hates to be connected with anything so badly run and would like to resign if it were not for leaving the sinking ship. Mr Payne is a most unsuitable man to be a welfare officer – he is so vague and unbusinesslike.

Tuesday 9 May
To E's amazement this morning Stan set her up on an electric lathe, so she hopes to remain there for a bit with luck.

Tonight we attended a meeting of union members, convened by Cayzer. Only about 20 present, but not surprising as he only notified people this morning. The meeting was ostensibly to elect 2 shop stewards, but the plan behind it is to eject the works council and put up a Joint Production Committee in its place. Jeering remarks were made by one man about 'The works council, bless its little heart!' and, obviously, feeling is very high over the rate cutting! However, K and Costello were both present, and did not allow criticisms of the works council to pass unchallenged. K gave a statement as to how all the double time business arose and showed that the council's original idea was that bonus should be unlimited, but of course this is not happening. We all agreed that a Joint Production Committee would have more power than a works council as then management and workers would be on equal terms. We are very glad we attended this meeting as K was able to speak up for the work done by the works council. Unfortunately, we both dislike Cayzer very much, with his snidey, pompous voice, though we think he is quite in the right in trying to get a Joint Production Committee.

Wednesday 10 May

A tremendous amount of betting goes on in the factory – and there are 3 workers who are bookies. They do a flourishing business. Our Irish May Nolan, as might be expected, is always at it, and to our surprise we find that Kath Thorpe is also an addict. This girl is so dreary and uninteresting that we have never even mentioned her before, and we could hardly believe that this prim, self-satisfied little creature would do anything so dashing. We hear that Joe Moroney always puts on £10 bets.

Today at tea May had a passage of arms with Hilda Carter and told her off roundly. When Hilda and Muriel left the table, May commented that Hilda was a very bad influence on Muriel.

Saturday 13 May

Still so depressed that we have made no entry in the diary for days. Factory life has become very irksome to us, and the days are dreary. Some long time ago there was an appeal for women drivers for the Second Front, and this made K very restless, as she pined for a change of scene and occupation. Els is not good at seeing in the dark, so there was no hope for escape for her, but anyway K decided that the firm would never release her, so she did not ask to be allowed to volunteer. Then there was an appeal for women bargees and Els really did pine for this, as all her life she has longed to drift along the canals of England in a barge. However, she also decided that she would be thought too old. So here we both are, still at Morrisons.

Monday 15 May

The poor works council is still to the fore. Brother Cayzer told Costello today that the Metal Bashers and Welders were willing to elect a shop steward for their section if all the AEU Members of the works council would resign. This seemed to us quite illogical and barmy. In any case there is no good in getting rid of the works council unless a Joint Production Committee is permitted by the management. It would simply leave the factory with no committee at all and we should be worse off than ever.

We had an interesting meeting at the union tonight with plenty of political discussions. A great sheaf of applications for membership came up. 'Shall we deal with them singly or 'en block,' asked the chairman. 'Oh – en block', we all chanted in unison.

Wednesday 17 May

K reckons that all her hopes and plans for increased production by unlimited bonus earnings have gone by the board. The management continue to cut times on jobs sent in 'under double time' and so everyone has now lost all faith in the unlimited bonus talk and they take good care not to send in their jobs too quickly.

Thursday 18 May
Elsie has had a miserable time for the past ten days as her pivot pin job would not go right. However, at last all is going well and she is 'making a good job of it,' as Stan would say.

Saturday 20 May
K hasn't done any work since Friday morning as Fred is setting her up on a new job, very tricky. She started off about 11 a.m. and was incredibly slow.

Monday 22 May
works council for K. She and Costello did most of the talking. The question of X-ray facilities for all the workers was brought up again, but the management have set their face against it and we got nowhere. On the whole a pretty amicable meeting. Questions about ARP, ventilation and hot water were all referred to Mr Proctor again. At which the workers groaned inwardly as he is an obstructionist.

Tuesday 23 May
The works council received a written reply from Mr Proctor today. All the suggestions and appeals were vetoed and in a very rude, blustering manner. K was in a rage and felt inclined to hand in her resignation from the W. Council forthwith. Hordes and hordes of planes went over today.

Wednesday 24 May
Consternation reigned this morning as a rumour went round that the annual holiday had been cancelled. Everyone went rushing round collecting information and production certainly suffered for an hour or so. Finally, the rumour was traced to one particular section who have been asked to volunteer for fire watching during the holiday week. They will get their holiday later on in the summer. More hordes of bombers over this morning. The invasion seems very imminent and we hardly expect to get our Whitsun holiday. Passenger trains are being drastically cut.

Thursday 25 May
At dinner time today the Ministry of Information film *Let's Finish The Job* was shown in the canteen. The place was crowded to suffocation as all the windows had to be shut in order to put up the blackout and every worker in the place was there, including all the office. It was really a very wonderful film, designed to show by illustration how every excrescence, however minute, on the body of the plane sets up resistance to its passage through the air and in consequence slows up the speed. It was very cleverly devised and must have been planned by

a skilled engineer. The right and wrong ways of doing jobs was also shown in an amusing and narrative form. The moral was that how we finish the job is all important. Old Els, who has so often wondered whether her slow, careful work was justified, came away inwardly uplifted as obviously you can't be too careful. They told us that rough finish can make a difference of 25 mph to a plane's speed.

Friday 26 May
[*K and E depart for their holiday weekend and spend their time in Hindhead and Milford lying in the sun.*]
Everyone anxiously expecting the Second Front every day, but the weekend passed quietly.

Wednesday 31 May
Today Hilda was so hot and so enraged with the management for not trying to improve the ventilation that she threw a spanner through one of the windows in a temper! The resulting hole was a great improvement. K went to the union and was amazed to hear that Joe Moroney was being 'excluded' for non-payment of dues and the secretary said that he had frequently asked him to pay up.

Thursday 1 June
K told Moroney, artlessly, of this shocking sad story and he appeared to be appalled and said it was quite untrue and anyhow he would see 'Brother Seckyterry' and put the matter right. Poor Els felt miserable in the afternoon with a bad headache and when she got home found she had a temperature. So back to bed she went with flu for the fifth time in two years.

Friday 2 June
Elsie spent the day in bed, sweating gently with a horrible head. Bradford and Stan told her not to hurry back but to take the weekend off anyhow. K was in a fever all day as her job wouldn't go right and she expects to get them all back from inspection.

Sunday 4 June
Heard on the wireless that the 5th Army are on the outskirts of Rome.

Monday 5 June
Rome has fallen. E still not feeling up to much, so decided to stop at home one more day.

Tuesday 6 June
Terrific horde of planes went over about 6.30 a.m. We hadn't been at work long before Stan told Els that there was a rumour that the 8 a.m. news had

announced paratroop landings in France and bombardment of the coast. This whisper began to go round the shop, but it was followed a few minutes later by another rumour that this was only a German announcement so probably not true. Everyone was in a state of tension and wondering when we would get something official. Finally, K went off to ask if we could have the news on the loud-speakers at 11 a.m. This was agreed to and all the machines were shut off at 10.55. Everyone was holding their breath with anticipation. A voice came on the air, but it was only Mr McGiveney reading the appeal to aircraft workers made by Sir Stafford Cripps a few days ago! This was an almost unbelievable anti-climax and we returned to our machines feeling flatter than flat. However, a minute later the news came over the air and we heard that the Second Front has really started [*D-Day*]. An attack by sea and air had been made in Normandy. Everyone tremendously keyed up. It seemed to take people different ways. Poor Lily, whose boy is in a corvette, was in tears most of the day. Some seemed to be too much excited to concentrate on their work, whilst others were stimulated into working faster than ever. Everyone waited anxiously for more news at 1 p.m. during the dinner hour. But the wireless was not turned on, much to everyone's disgust. The clamour was so insistent that K went up again to ask if we could have it every day at dinner time for the present. At 3 p.m. the machines were again turned off and we got the next bulletin. All seems to be satisfactory at present and troops are pouring on to the beaches. The capture of Rome seems to be quite second-page news now.

Wednesday 7 June

K spent the whole day peering over people's newspapers and propped up one on her lathe to read while she worked. The news went on at dinner time today and we learnt the initial landings were very successful in spite of bad seas. Everyone seems more subdued today. We all feel that yesterday's success cannot continue and terrific counter attacks will soon be coming.

Thursday 8 June

News continues good in spite of very bad weather. Heavy seas have held up reinforcements. Laurie and Ron came in to spend the evening. They keep hens now and we are going to register with them in future. It will be a great boon to us, as we seldom get our quota of eggs.

Friday 9 June

K continues to read Lily's Daily Sketch surreptitiously from cover to cover all the time she is working.

Saturday 10 June

We chased all over Croydon to find a cinema with Invasion News and finally pedalled all the way to Purley in order to get a decent film as well as the news. To our utter disgust there were no invasion pictures, not even Rome, and we felt completely swindled.

Monday 12 June

An uninteresting day and ended with a badly attended sub-council for K. [*She*] is feeling more and more disheartened and depressed with the powers-that-be at Morrisons. She think the works council is utterly useless. The management just use the workers' representatives to cover their own unpopular actions. They either refuse any of the workers' requests or agree to them and then do nothing at all about it. They evidently regard the works council as a safety valve to keep the workers quiet, and think there is no harm done by letting them talk for an hour once a month.

Wednesday 14 June

Three alerts last night, the first since the invasion. No guns or planes near here. The whole factory has gone quite mad over the Derby and Oaks. Bets and sweeps going on everywhere. Betting in the factory seems very much on the increase. Everyone spends far too much time and money on it and many read racing books on form during the breaks.

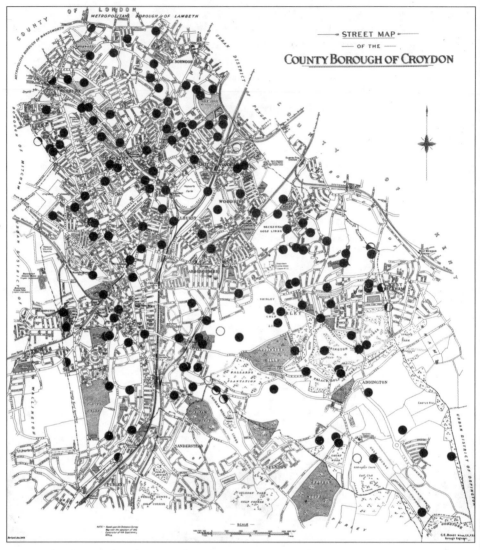

A map showing V1 bombing in Croydon, 1944. Purley Way is in the bottom left-hand corner. Duppas Hill Road and Common extend from the top of Purley Way to the right. The V1 bombs killed 215 people and seriously injured 705 in Croydon. Over 1,000 houses in the borough were destroyed and many more were badly damaged. Taken from W.C. Berwick Sayers, ed., *Croydon and the Second World War*, published in Croydon by the Croydon Corporation, 1949. (*Local Studies Library, Croydon Central Library*)

CHAPTER FOUR

Doodle-bug Alley

Friday 16 June
On firewatch last night and to our surprise the alert went at 11.30 and we rushed out to Duppas Hill. A very peculiar raid which we couldn't understand. No fighters were up and no gunfire, but a good many very heavy explosions were heard and several planes roared overhead very low. It went on for hours and we got colder and hungrier every minute, as we have to stand on the steps of the shelter, with nothing to sit on and no cover over our heads. Hour after hour went by and still no all clear. Finally the dawn came and still there were gun-flashes and intermittent firing. At about 4 a.m. what seemed like a very low plane swished overhead and released a bomb about ½ mile beyond Waddon station. Terrific explosion and a great flash and sparks and debris flew up in every direction. We were worried as it looked very near Laurie's house. At 6 a.m. we came in even though the all clear hadn't gone. We cooked breakfast with frequent interruptions caused by heavy gunfire and low flying machines. We finally went off to work in our tin hats and on arrival were sent straight to the shelters. The factory Home Guard had been on duty all night and the first person we saw was our dear Joe Phillips looking very tired and green. He is highly excitable and was obviously very much worked up. We soon learnt that this peculiar raid was not being made by bombers, but by pilotless aircraft, fired from France [*V1s*]. This information was startling, and as the weather was very stormy and lowering, the feeling of tension was acute. When the all clear went at 8.30 a.m. Mr Proctor addressed us over the microphone and explained that these raids were expected to last all day and might be continuous. The factory siren would give warning and we were then to go at once to the shelters, unless the 'crash' warning was sounded, in which case we were to throw ourselves on the floor immediately. Everyone was very excitable and a good bit of time was spent exchanging experiences. Poor May was in tears with anxiety worrying about her sister and baby and finally went home, but returned quite calm after dinner. The rest of the day was spent in bobbing up and down to the shelters a great many times. It certainly interfered with production, and even our mealtimes were much interrupted. After 3 p.m. there was a lull. During one of the longer alerts, our shelter became very musical, Pansy leading the latest song hits in her rasping contralto voice. Our shelter is full of young girls mainly under 18. They are as gay as larks and boisterously high-spirited. They keep us well entertained with their songs and quick repartee. There is a pin-drop hush while Pansy sings her song and then everyone joins in the choruses. Sally (our Gracie Fields) is

also there, but could not be persuaded to sing to us, though she was extremely amusing. 'Oh nao'w,' she said 'Panse is the artist,' and nothing would shake her. By the end of the day, having not been to bed since Wednesday and having stood on our two feet for the best part of 36 hours, we were pretty well whacked. We went to bed about 7.30 and had a couple of hours good sleep before the alert went. We took a mattress down to the ground floor and dossed down in Mrs Brooke's front room for the night.

Saturday 17 June
A very disturbed night, with masses of these pilotless planes roaring over. They sound like a train on the Underground rushing into a station and are quite terrifying. You hear them coming in the distance getting nearer and nearer. Then there is either an explosion or the noise diminishes in the distance. We lay on the floor with a couple of tin hats over our faces and got what rest we could. K's swollen feet and legs were aching so much that she couldn't sleep and worked herself into such a state that, in her imagination, London was left with hardly one stone standing upon another and all the communications for the Second Front destroyed. Els was so deadly tired that she slept moderately well. Soon after 5 a.m. two came down within ½ mile, and one caused a big fire. However, the NFS and ambulances were soon on the spot and it was quickly under control. We felt better after breakfast and we had a peaceful morning at the factory and got a good bit of work done. Hilda Carter arrived looking very much shaken by her experiences, emotional and near tears. After work we put on our best clothes and set off for London. Another alert went just as we were starting, but we decided to continue our journey. We had been invited to attend the reopening function of the repaired Cecil Sharpe House, and though we didn't really approve of this jollification with the Second Front in progress, we wanted to go and see our old friends . . . who gave us a great welcome. During the demonstration another alert went, but no one took any notice. Londoners seem quite unmoved by all the excitement and merely dodge under cover when the gunfire gets close.

Sunday 18 June
Had a lovely day. Els and Tommy Adkins had lunch together at Martinez, whilst K and Tony Buzzard also lunched there at another table. When Tony had to return to work K and E went to a News Reel to see the latest invasion pictures. And so back to Croydon. London was pretty empty today. We imagine most people were having a good sleep to make up for the recent bad nights. We heard that Croydon had had a very noisy night. The worst gunfire they had ever had.

Monday 19 June
Practically no guns last night. But a good number of P-planes [*pilotless*] over. The house was shaken a good many times. As soon as we arrived at Morrisons there was a violent crash and a pane of glass fell out at the back of the

building. We all rushed down to the shelters and were up and down five more times before 11 a.m. After this there was a fair amount of peace except for another alert in the middle of dinner. Mr Proctor made a maddening speech over the loud-speakers, complaining of the way people dawdled going to the shelters. He repeated himself many times till everyone lost all interest. Everyone rather gloomy today, and some even rather jittery, especially old Joe Phillips, whom we could hardly bear to talk to. Balloons are now visible in great numbers towards Kent.

Tuesday 20 June
A fairly quiet night and we slept pretty well on our hard mattress on the floor. We were awoken once or twice with bumps, but nothing seemed very near. Everyone more cheerful today and the weather clear and sunny – consequently fewer 'doodle-bugs' [*V1s*] over. Mr Proctor came down [*to*] the m/c shop and had a friendly word with all the women, to see that their morale was good. Masses more balloons up when we got back.

Wednesday 21 June
An awful night with flying bombs coming over in quick succession and dropping near enough to shake the house many times. We lay on the floor quaking and listening anxiously for the engine to stop, which is always a prelude to the bomb dropping. We got some sleep, but were woken up many times by the beastly things. It seemed to us the worst night so far. When we got up we found the day was lowering and stormy, with a thick blanket of low cloud. We could hear the brutes buzzing overhead, but could see nothing. No all clear until the middle of the morning and we were up and down in the shelters many times at Morrisons. However, not much time is lost, because as soon as the bomb is heard to drop we get the factory all clear and go back to work again. At lunch Joe was incredibly depressing with his horrible stories of casualties and wreckage. We hear that a block of flats near the main road was hit, but miraculously there were no fatal casualties.

Thursday 22 June
Another awful night. We slept at intervals, but in the middle of the night there was a period when four or five came over together and others followed in quick succession. The house shook many times. From 5.30 – 7 a.m. there was another heavy attack and bombs fell about every 4 minutes and we had many interruptions to cooking our breakfast as every time a bomb roared over the house we switched off the gas and rushed downstairs. Mercifully there was a lull soon after 7 a.m. and we cycled off to work with our tin hats. When we got there we found the night shift had kept a tally of the number of bombs and red alerts they had had – 25 bombs and 18 alerts! Up and down in the shelters all day and all the meal breaks interrupted too. On fire watch tonight and we contacted the Bellwoods and found that they have been sleeping in the public shelter on Duppas Hill all the week so we decided to go over there too and

take turns in the fire watch duty, so that we could get a little sleep if possible. There are 3 large trench shelters, well-built and dry, cut into the hill. You go down a flight of steps into them and there is about 3 ft of earth over the reinforced concrete. We managed to get a bunk each and laid these down in the passage.

Friday 23 June
Last night we went over to the shelter before 10 p.m. and got settled into our bunks to get what sleep we could early. We find our trench is occupied exclusively with the highly respectable middle-class house-owners from Duppas Hill. It was very amusing to hear all the various families arriving and bedding themselves out. Torches and hurricane lamps light up the gloom and husbands and wives argue and fuss according to temperament. The chorus of snores reminds us of the 300. Noises of children and fish and chip parties come from the adjoining trenches. It was a marvellous night and K sat on the hill in the warm night for most of her fire watch duty. But at 2 p.m., when E took over, the alert went and from then for about an hour and a half it was frightful. We could see the things coming over 4 at a time and bombs were falling all over the neighbourhood. We watched the red balls flying through the air and then when the engine cut out we ducked down the steps into the shelter to wait for the crash. Later it got a bit quieter and at 4.45 we handed over to Mr Bellwood and went back for an hour's sleep on our bunks. The all clear went as we got up and we collected all our things and went home. When we got to work we found the night shift had been in the shelters most of the night and 48 bombs had fallen. Lily arrived rather late and very much shaken as all the windows of the train had been broken by blast and some of the passengers had been cut. We learnt that Kath Weaver was in hospital. Her house was hit and she and her father injured and her mother was killed. She is a nice girl from inspection whose husband is a prisoner of war. Everyone is dreadfully sorry for her. Jim Sawyer went to see her in hospital and found her cut about the face and a tummy wound, but taking it all very bravely. We hadn't been in the place more than a few minutes before the alert went and we started rushing to the shelters. Luckily, it was some distance off. During the day various people were fetched away because their homes had been demolished and Costello went off to enquire about his brother who had had a bomb in his road. A good many interruptions during the morning, but after that there was a lull. A very good male voice choir . . . sang to us at the dinner break. They really were excellent and a more varied programme to suit all tastes. We couldn't help thinking how much nicer it would be if Morrisons did something like this instead of our grand professional orchestra costing £80 a week. A quiet afternoon but the alert went just before pay time and twice the queue had to break up and everyone scuttled to the shelters before all were paid. We decided to spend the night in the Duppas Hill shelter again as we certainly feel safer there and the rushing sound of the bombs is a bit deadened. We weren't able to get bunks, so took over a mattress and made ourselves pretty comfortable.

Saturday 24 June
A much quieter night for us and we got a good bit of sleep, only being wakened by the bombs which whizzed right over us. Another trench is now opened to accommodate some of the people who have been bombed out in West Croydon. The night shift recorded only 29 bombs tonight. We were up and down in the shelters several times before 9 a.m., but after that there was a complete lull and this lasted all day. It seemed uncannily quiet. Croydon was practically empty and everyone was listening in the unexpected quiet. There were many shops without windows. We think the majority of people don't like to be far away from their homes and shelters. The blast from these bombs all goes upwards and the earth is generally only penetrated a foot or two, so everyone feels safer if underground.

Monday 26 June
A fairly noisy night, with one terrific crash which shook the shelter. We learnt afterwards that it was in West Croydon near Purley Way. However, E slept through it and we are quite snug in the public shelter. Our work was very much interrupted today and we were up and down to the shelter many times, including twice at dinner and twice during the tea-break. Els had a maddening day rectifying some work which had been very badly made by another operator who has since left. She felt furious about this as it was really a job which Stan should have done. We are both looking forward to our week's holiday and longing for a good night's rest. [*E abandons her previous plan to see friends in Henley and instead will go to Hindhead with K.*] Having had such a time here lately we think we'd rather stick together, as it's impossible to find out what is happening in other parts of the country.

Tuesday 27 June
Deluging thunder showers most of the day. Lots of interruptions for flying bombs and we were running backwards and forwards to the shelters most of the day. However, luckily we have only to stop a few minutes each time. We are greatly amused by the young 'part-stamping' girls who are in our shelter. They are mainly under eighteen and they all adore our handsome Dennis Ellis and they will go to any lengths to get near him in the shelter. We've seldom seen such flagrant man-hunting. One of them was overheard to say 'Oh! I do love Dennis. Doesn't he roll his lovely eyes and wouldn't I like to sit on his knee?' When we got back from work the alert went continually and the buzz-bombs were flying over about every 4 minutes. We couldn't settle to anything – but had to rush downstairs every few minutes.

Wednesday 28 June
After such a noisy evening we were relieved to get a fairly quiet night – we got plenty of sleep. After all the heavy rain some of the shelters are very wet and have streams of water running down the passages at the sides. We are extremely lucky to have chanced on a dry trench as we have no bunks and have to put the

mattress flat on the concrete floor. Today was full of interruptions and bombs came over continuously and we were up and down at frequent intervals all day. During the afternoon we had a 'crash warning' but very few people recognised the signal and most of them started running out to the shelters, but the bomb passed over before anyone could get there. Luckily, the explosion was a long way away. Bernard asked Mr Proctor if he would organise a different signal for the crash warnings, but he pooh-poohed the suggestion and said 'he didn't anticipate many crash warnings!!' He is the most obstinate pig and nothing will budge him when he's once made up his mind.

Thursday 29 June
Noisy at intervals, but we slept fairly well. There was not the usual all clear at about 5.45 a.m. and we had to cart our bedding back to No. 25 with the bombs still arriving. Luckily, nothing fell near at that time. We are getting heartily tired of never getting our mid-meal in peace, but having to leg it out to the shelters several times whilst we are trying to eat. Hilda has not been seen for several days. Her nerves are in a bad way, and as she is shortly going to Lincolnshire to join her husband, she is trying to get her doctor to say she must go immediately. All the bombs seemed to fall in or around Croydon today, and during the morning one fell near W. Croydon station. May rushed home to see if her sister was all right and found all her windows gone, but the sister and baby quite safe. We had so many interruptions today that K entirely forgot it was her birthday until she came home at 5.30 p.m. and found a lot of letters and parcels for her. Spent the evening packing for our holiday and went over to the shelter early to try and get some sleep before fire watching.

Friday 30 June
We were lucky not to get the alert till just after midnight. It was a wonderful still night and we watched the bombs coming in from the coast with a great display of flak surrounding them. We went off duty at 2 a.m. and were awakened by a terrific crash about 4.30. Everyone in the shelter bounced out of their bunks and we went up to see what had happened. We learnt a bomb had fallen on the far corner of Duppas Hill, among the allotments, not more than 150 yds away. A lot of windows were blown out on Duppas Hill and we found that our front door glass had all gone and the lock had been blown off. Luckily, all the windows in our flat were unharmed. During the morning Hilda came in to say goodbye as she had got her release. She was thankful to be getting out of London as her home was badly damaged on Tuesday when *two* bombs fell within 50 yds of it. We had a record number of interruptions today and had 18 red alerts. We were amused to hear the young part-stamping girls discussing their holiday plans. If it was fine on Sunday they were going out cycling and if it was wet they would all go up to London! So bombs obviously make no difference to them. Everyone is pleased to be getting their annual week's holiday, but it seems sad that so many of them have made no plans to go away. We rushed home to change and collect our suit-cases and two bombs fell in the neighbourhood, though not very near, while we were getting ready.

We accomplished the journey to Haslemere very easily, in spite of a long wait at Sutton. As the train took us further and further out of the danger area an uncanny quiet seemed to descend on the countryside. When we arrived at Haslemere we felt as if we were sleep-walking. What we had come from seemed like a night-mare and it seemed quite incredible that it was only 40 miles away. Hindhead and Haslemere were completely peaceful and no one appeared to be thinking about bombs or alerts.

Saturday 1 July – Sunday 9 July
[*K and E enjoy a restful week's holiday.*]
    Found all well at No. 25, but another bomb had fallen on Duppas Hill on Saturday night, more or less in the same place as the previous one, and two houses are demolished and many more quite uninhabitable, with terrific cracks in the walls and windows and ceilings gone. Every leaf was stripped from the trees and bushes so that it looks like winter. We have lost the skylight in the scullery, but during the summer we shan't mind this as it makes it much lighter. We found [*our*] space in the Duppas Hill shelter has been usurped, but luckily we were able to have Norman Bellwood's for this week as he is away on holiday.

Monday 10 July
Back at work once more in 'Doodle-bug Alley', as this neighbourhood is called, and the factory seemed rather empty. A good many are still away. We had about 6 red alerts, but this was far less than just before the holiday. We managed to get a good bit of work done, but felt rather disinclined for it. Those who had not gone away said they had had an awful holiday. May and Lily both looked worn out as they had spent most of their time rushing from one shelter to another. We were glad to find Joe Phillips in much better spirits. He seems to have got over his deadly fear and now takes things more philosophically. During the evening we had several bombs near.

Tuesday 11 July
A pretty quiet night. We slept well on our hard mattress and only heard a few distant bumps, but the day made up for it and we had about 14 red alerts and bombs falling near. Two disturbances at dinner, but luckily we had just finished our meal before we had to leg it to the shelter. We were amused today to see that Dennis has shaken off his youthful admirers and now sits himself down by Lily, who holds a minor court among the boys. The two little adorers look very woe-begone. Alert on and off all day and just succeeded in getting supper before a succession of bombs came over. One fell near enough to shake the house considerably, and we saw the column of browney-grey smoke rising up from the direction of Purley Way. We hear it fell in the sewage farm, and we saw the ambulance and light rescue party go off.

Wednesday 12 July
A very good night. No alert until 7.15 a.m. just as we were leaving for work. As we neared the factory we heard a bomb coming up and we saw the night shift

going down to the shelters. The gate-keeper called to us to hurry. We rushed
in to put our bicycles away and as we were going to the shelter we saw the
p-plane right overhead sailing over the gas works. Its engine had shut off, but
mercifully it was still gliding along. Suddenly it dipped down and there was a
heavy explosion. Almost immediately a column of smoke rose in the
Thornton Heath direction. After this we had a few more over before 9 a.m.,
but then there was a blessed lull of over 5 hours, and we had uninterrupted
meal breaks and got a fair amount of work done. There still seems to be a lot
away absent. In the m/c shop neither Muriel nor Kath Thorpe nor Peter
Catford have appeared since the holiday and May has not been seen since
Monday afternoon. We wonder if she has evacuated herself with her sister
and the baby? During the afternoon the lull was compensated with interest as
we had 17 over in a quarter of an hour and then another batch later on.
Several fell in the neighbourhood and sounded fairly near. The all clear had
not gone when we were due to go home, but we luckily got back before any
more went over. A very much interrupted evening with a good many going
right over the house. We also heard 3 explosions in the direction of the
balloon barrage, so were glad to think they were destroyed before they could
do any damage.

Thursday 13 July
No alert last night and it was reported that there were no p-planes over England
at all. Only a few red warnings during the day, and during these we only heard
one bomb go over. Certainly a much quieter day. Masses more balloons
appeared. We can see about 300 straight ahead from our window in Duppas Hill.
The sky looks as if it had broken out in a rash.

Friday 14 July
On fire watch last night. A quiet night, but at 1.15 a distant alert went, so we
went out to watch, but there was nothing doing except away on the coast a
distant gunflash. During the evening we had a very funny little drama with the
only really educated people in our shelter. They are a most obnoxious party of 3.
Husband, peevish wife and still more peevish daughter by name Watkins. They
are quite determined that whoever is uncomfortable or goes short of anything
it shall not be any of them. While we were away on our holiday we were
dispossessed of the floor space for our mattress and since we have been back
we have been sleeping in Norman Bellwood's plot. All this week we have been
wondering what is going to happen to us when Norman returns. We have got
the shelter marshal's permission to cut down the legs of the pair of 3-
decker bunks, so that the top one shall be habitable and not quite so
impossibly close to the ceiling. This of course means that the present
occupants of the bunks will be nearer the floor and all this caused a great deal
of whining from the Watkins, and much stout support of us from the Bellwood
party who came out of the fracas very well. Mr Bellwood suggested that Miss
Joyce Watkins might occupy the bunk above her two parents, but this would
not do at all. Mr Watkins thought it would be much too stuffy and unhealthy

for Joyce up there and Mrs Watkins simultaneously announced that it would be much too cold and draughty for her. But when it was made quite clear that we two were prepared to occupy the top bunks (even though we are not very keen on them) Mr Watkins announced that 'strictly on the understanding that the two Miss Church Bliss's occupied the upper bunks' they withdrew all objections, though the thought of being 9" nearer the ground causes them much misgiving.

A fairly quiet day in the factory. A good many red alerts, but only 3 or 4 bombs thundered over. There was a lot of low cloud today and Mr Proctor announced that everyone must be very quick getting to the shelter as spotting was very difficult. On one occasion the tail of the queue was not under cover when the bomb went over. They had had to come all the way from the canteen. Mr Proctor made a round of the shelters and K asked him if we could pop into any shelter when coming from the canteen (we have the furthest to go.) He said we must only go to our own shelters as space was very limited. Later in the day he announced over the loud-speakers that to enable those in the canteen to get to cover the blue light would be switched on and off several times to indicate that the red warning would probably be going in a minute or two. This happened several times during the afternoon breaks and worked very well.

Saturday 15 July – Sunday 16 July
No alert at night and a quiet morning and we both got a lot of work done. The factory was very empty. Absenteeism is very bad these days. [*K and E spent the weekend in Kingswood.*]

Monday 17 July
We were glad to find our space in the shelter was still available for us, though we learnt that we nearly lost it by being away for the night. The 'inimical fascist' Watkins's caused another disturbance last night, as Mrs W., at about midnight, suddenly found an earwig and let out a squeal. They made a great fuss chasing after this poor insect, and K muttered to E in her piercing whisper 'Earwiggo' and then dissolved into convulsive snorts in which Mrs Bellwood joined. Peace had not long been restored before another row started among the fish and chip family in the next trench. Finally, even they tired and peace reigned once more. Two batches of bombs in the night, fairly noisy, especially in the early morning just as we were preparing to pack up our bedding and return home. However, the all clear went before we had to leave. A very quiet day, complete lull after 10.30 a.m. Very hot.

Tuesday 18 July
Last night was a bit noisy, several bombs in the neighbourhood, one *very* heavy one which shook the shelter, said to be at Wallington. As soon as we arrived in the factory the red went up and we spent the first half-hour in the shelter. Our own bombers were droning over head so it was very difficult to know what was happening with the planes. One fell in the main road between

Croydon and Purley and gave several of our people rather a fright as they were cycling to work that way. Stan says he only missed it by about 3 or 4 minutes. The rest of the day was completely quiet. The blue alert went on and off several times but no red materialised. This is always a cheering sight as it probably means the bombs were destroyed before they reached London. Stan says he would like to evacuate Winnie and the little girl, as the child is becoming nervous, but he knows no one to whom he could send them. Els wrote off to Eric to see if by any chance he had not yet had billettees and if whether he would take them in.

Wednesday 19 July
A rather noisy night last night. The p-planes seemed to be coming over off and on all the time. During the day there was a good deal of up and down to the shelter with red alerts, but only one explosion at all near. In the afternoon there were no more reds, though the blue went on and off a good many times. K went over to the capstan section today as they were short of women, and there is a particular job to be done which can be done twice as fast on the capstans as on the centre lathes.

Thursday 20 July
Very noisy night. At one time we heard five or six of the brutes in the air at once. Very much interrupted morning, though only one bump fairly near. In the afternoon there was an unearthly lull which lasted all the time. The factory had a visit from Mr G. R. Strauss MP representing Sir Stafford Cripps. He met the works council for a few minutes and then addressed all the workers in the canteen. He came to congratulate Morrisons' workers on their morale and on their good records for production & attendance during the present blitz. He said he had come from Sir Stafford to find out if there was anything he could do for us. This was greeted with a shout of laughter. He said this area was one of the worst, if not *the* worst, and he fully realised what a time everyone was having. He said that we were every bit as much in the front line as the soldiers in Normandy and the civilian casualties to date were much the same as in Monty's army. He also reminded us that Hitler, by concentrating on the manufacture of p-planes, had been unable to produce the air support which his armies in Normandy needed so badly. He spoke very well in a simple, straight-forward manner and the workers appreciated his visit. Saw in the paper this evening that the 24 hrs ending yesterday evening was the heaviest p-plane attack so far. We believe Hitler was 'showing off' to the neutral press agents who had been invited to visit the p-plane bases in action.

At night in our public shelter E goes off to sleep pretty quickly and hears none of the chatter of the arriving families, but K gets a lot of amusement out of them. One nice woman sits on our bunk and gossips to K about the inimical Watkins Family. Everyone loathes the daughter (Miss Haw-Haw as she is known to the occupants of the next trench – who can hear her piercing la-di-da voice holding forth on art and culture). K had a further passage of arms with her on the subject of the light, and Miss Haw-Haw recounted the whole story to her parents when they arrived, regardless of K lying in her bunk only a few feet away!

Friday 21 July
On fire watch and we had an awful night with many bombs coming over from 11.30 p.m. to 7 a.m. We were on duty from 2–6 a.m. and spent a cold 4 hours on the hillside. We went straight off to work and found that the night shift's tally showed 51 bombs and 20 red alerts. A record. The day continued in the same strain and we hardly got any work done as the red alerts kept going up and we were for ever snatching up our bags and coats and rushing down to the shelter. By the end of the day we had had 36 bombs near enough to shake us and one very near at the back of Trojan's factory. They had damage and casualties but none fatal. It's really been the worst 24 hours since the blitz began, but somehow we are getting acclimatised to it and we certainly feel much better able to put up with it than when it started five weeks ago.

Saturday 22 July – Sunday 23 July
Another bad night. The night shift's tally was 38 bombs and 18 red alerts, but we didn't hear much of it, as we were too tired to be kept awake. The morning was an improvement – but still fairly active. We rushed off after work to Henley [*spent weekend with friends and had great difficulties getting home*]. Got in just before midnight, fumbled about for our shelter clothes and finally turned into our bunk, clambering past our snoring companions. One of our factory boys, Billy Brown, was very kindly keeping guard over our bunk and was prepared to occupy it for us if we didn't turn up. The alert went just after we'd settled down. Els heard from Eric, but he couldn't manage to take in Winnie Wallace and Valerie. They hope to go to Devonshire with Mrs Wallace's sister.

Monday 24 July
We slept well last night though there were bombs coming over at intervals. The day was remarkable for a complete lull from 6 a.m. – 3 p.m. With so little interruption we managed to do a good bit of work. K is still on the capstans and finds Len Quirk a most considerate chargehand, always ready to help, and anxious to look after the bonus earnings of his girls. At dinner time today we saw Biffo back in the band to our great surprise. But he did not conduct. We had a visit from some bigwig who appeared to be an ENSA organiser. Mr Payne infuriated everyone by turning out the usual conductor and taking over himself. There was an audible boo at this! Our ex-policeman Graham then told us that no one in Croydon could bear Payne at any price. He was an unutterable blackguard and was always out for his own advantage. Early in the war he had an ARP job, distributing Anderson shelters from the Town Hall, with the result that hundreds of poor families had to go without while many of the rich were conveniently supplied with them. Graham did not say whether this was knavery or incompetence, but implied that it was knavery.

Tuesday 25 July

A pretty quiet night at any rate in this neighbourhood. All day we waited for the blue alert to go up in the factory, but to our amazement no alert all day. This is the first blank weekday since the p-planes started on 15 June. We even had *Music While You Work* during the afternoon and everyone looked so pleased and happy.

Today we received a personal letter from Sir Herbert Williams, our local MP, in answer to one from us. We had asked him to look into the billeting arrangements made for the blitz-repair workers who have come to Croydon from the West Country. We met two of these men while on fire watch last week and they told us that 40 of them were miserably uncomfortable in a boarding-house on Duppas Hill. Besides not getting enough to eat and the place being very dirty, they have no shelter accommodation and have to sleep on the top floors. They would like to come to the Duppas Hill shelters, but they have no bunks or rugs and the floor is very wet. So they sit out on the hill all night and get very little rest. We suggested to Sir Herbert Williams that a full complement of 3-tier bunks should be supplied to the Duppas Hill shelters and that these men should be issued with army blankets. He says he will take the matter up with the Town Clerk.

Thursday 27 July

Everyone got a good bit of work done today as we had no alerts till 3.30 p.m. To make up for the time lost recently in the shelters many people have been asked to do overtime and the men have been put on weekend work. Mercifully, they have not asked us. We think this policy is very short-sighted as everyone in this neighbourhood has been working under a great strain during the past 6 weeks and aircraft is no longer a no. 1 priority production. When we got home we had an awful evening with buzz-bombs. We were trying to cook supper, but they came over in quick succession and kept dropping all round us within an area of about ½ mile. There was one on the railway line just beyond Waddon railway bridge, one by the aerodrome, one in Wallington, and one behind the factory. All this within a space of about 5 minutes. So that we thought the next one must come on the house. We abandoned all thought of supper, but in the end there was a lull and we continued our cooking.

Friday 28 July

On fire watch last night. It started badly with a batch of bombs coming over together, one falling in Old Town, the other side of Duppas Hill, and giving the shelter a terrific shaking. After midnight it was quiet. When we got to the factory Els was put onto a difficult new job, the one Mrs Hazelgrove used to think no one could do but herself. E was in rather a fever about this especially as the red alerts kept going up and we had to rush to the shelters, so she found it difficult to concentrate. K has now been on the capstans about 10 days and has rather enjoyed the novelty. The day goes much more quickly with a change of occupation. She has also enjoyed having Len Quirk as a chargehand. He takes immense trouble with his girls and is always at their beck and call. It certainly shows up Stan's laziness and inertia. However, today Len fell from grace. K's work went wrong and he didn't seem able to put it right and he finally disappeared from the section for a considerable time. K fumed all day and at last sat down in despair & read a book.

Saturday 29 July
A bad night, hordes of bombs came over in batches and they told us at the factory that the control room gave up plotting them and declared it a blitz. However, a pretty quiet morning followed. Len Quirk not in at all today, so K besought Stan to come and help her. This he did and with great efficiency and success managed to put right the job which had baffled Len yesterday. So K has put Stan back on his pedestal! He certainly is a much better engineer than Len who, kind and energetic as he is, is very often slapdash and makes a god of speed. The alert went soon after lunch whilst we were sitting working by our sitting-room window. Almost at once we heard a bomb come roaring along so rushed downstairs. The front door was open and we were just in time to see two soldiers who were walking in the road suddenly fling themselves head first through the hedge into the ditch opposite the house. A second later the bomb thundered over and fell with a terrific explosion and then came the crash of falling glass. This was followed immediately by two more bombs falling near enough to shake the house. We found our sitting-room windows gone, most of the glass falling outside the house, though some covering the place where we had been sitting. One piece was embedded in the table, and the poor Brookes lost most of their remaining windows on the ground floor, and there was plaster down all over the house. We found the bomb had fallen just beyond Waddon railway bridge about 150 yards from us as the crow flies. The mess was indescribable and there were roofs and windows damaged for some distance round. We found the factory was all right and we left a message for the mobile squad that we should be glad of their help to mend our windows, though we hardly expect them to come . . . having seen the frightful mess up the road where Rapley and Reg Green live. Old Mrs Brooke seems to stand up to the racket awfully well. She is alone in the house all day while her daughter is out at work. Her reactions while the bombs are actually roaring overhead are peculiar and nearly drive us dotty. We are usually crouching on the stairs, trying to take what cover we can and Mrs B. then chooses this moment to embark on a long and involved story about how the newspaper boy has not been calling at his usual hour for the past 3 days, but will doubtless be doing so in the future! We spent the rest of the day sweeping up the flat and repairing the window with ARP material.

Sunday 30 July
Another rather noisy night. Instead of being the first to leave the shelter at 5.45 a.m. we were the last and had a good lie-in. Quiet domestic morning. An alert directly after lunch and almost immediately 3 came over and dropped in quick succession in the near neighbourhood. Miss Brooke's repaired window blew out again. She commented that everyone called this place Doodle-bug Alley, but she

considered a more apt name would be Doodle-bug Dump. We had a visit from 'Chippie', our Works carpenter of the mobile squad. He examined our window and said the frame would hold all right and that we'd made a good job of the repair. He dealt with Miss Brooke's window also and she was most grateful. He told us that Rapley and Reg Green's houses were both badly damaged yesterday and they had been all day helping to repair it.

6.30 p.m. Another batch of bombs has just arrived, one landing on the electric works. We have no light and rumour varies from 'very bad damage' to 'only a cable gone'.

Monday 31 July
No electric light all the evening, but it suddenly went on again at 2 a.m. Our public shelter has recently had a proper electric light system installed, and so we have revelled in being able to read while lying on our mattress. Last night, of course, we were back to the old dim religious gloom of candles. After our very noisy weekend there was a lull from bombs all the morning and only a few reds in the afternoon. A lovely evening and we spent it sitting on the hillside. Our very nice neighbours in the shelter, Mr and Mrs Barker, told us that when our 18-year-old factory boy, Billy Brown, came to occupy our mattress for us at the weekend when we were away he gave us an unsolicited testimonial. He said that we were such kind ladies and very popular in the factory and always such conscientious workers, never late and hardly ever away! For some time we have worried about our poor Fred who has been away ill with a duodenal ulcer for 10 weeks. We have repeatedly asked Rapley and Stan for news of him and finally we got Eddie Cook to go and make enquiries. It appears he is out of hospital now and better, but still not able to return to work. His wife has just had a second baby. Eddie can't imagine what he is living on as all his Sick Club benefits are now finished and he thinks he must be in a bad way. The m/c shop made a collection for him, but it only produced about £4 as it went round at a bad time in the week. K buttonholed Payne today to see if the firm would do something for him as he has been there about 5 yrs. However, Mr Payne said there were no funds to meet a case like this, and so nothing could be done as it would create a precedent. K came back very much disheartened, but Els thought why not go beyond Mr Payne and let K put the case direct to Mr Young. Stan and Eddie thought this was an excellent idea, so long as they hadn't got to do the asking. K then spent the afternoon mentally composing words and phrases suitable for Mr Young's ears.

Tuesday 1 August
A very quiet night. But the alert went again at 7 a.m. and we had a sending of bombs while we were trying to get breakfast. Only one dropped very near and shook the house and blew the front door open. During the morning K wrote a note asking for an interview with Mr Young and later she was summoned to the presence. She told Fred's sad story, and assumed that Mr Young wouldn't like one of his old employees to be in want, and Mr Young agreed to look into the case, and so we hope the firm will send him something. A quiet

morning, but several red alerts in the afternoon. One bomb fell nearby Payne's factory again.

Wednesday 2 August
Bomb at 4 a.m., but otherwise a quiet night. Another disturbed breakfast with several bombs falling in the neighbourhood. A great upset in the m/c shop today. We were told that MAP were possibly going to evacuate compulsorily some of Morrisons' machines, together with their operators, to the Preston branch. Bradford went round asking everyone whether they would be willing to go. This caused a great deal of talk and speculation. We said we would consider it, provided we could find somewhere to live and make some satisfactory arrangement about our furniture. The general feeling is that if we don't go voluntarily the NSO will compel us, and of course it is quite possible that any day Morrisons may be damaged and then we should all be sent off anywhere in England willy-nilly. We feel we should be better off going away with a nucleus of people that we know than just sent off into the blue, possibly not even together. Anyhow, it is all very unsettling.

Thursday 3 August
A very bad night last night. They seemed to be going over continuously. We managed to dodge back from the shelter in a lull about 6 a.m. and found the front door burst open. We had not a long enough interval between bombs to get breakfast, but managed to get some bread and jam and later got a kettle boiled. When we got to work we found they had had the worst night yet – twenty six red alerts and 64 bombs dropped. The control room said they had had nothing but interruptions by red alerts. Before dinner time we were down in the shelters 18 times, but not a great many bombs came over. After dinner there was a lull and we managed to get a good deal of work done.

Still a good deal of talk in the machine shop about the possibility of going to Preston. Mr Lines sent a message down to us to ask if we had decided, as they required two more to make up their numbers, and we said that we would go, provided the firm was willing to make satisfactory arrangements about moving our furniture and finding us accommodation. We understand that the firm is prepared to move our furniture, and Mr Lines is reported to have said that there is no difficulty at all about accommodation. This fills us with gloomy forebodings, as we are sure that anyone who makes a sweeping statement like that can know nothing whatever about it.

Friday 4 August
On fire watch last night, but only a few bombs came up the Thames estuary. It was a perfect evening with a great harvest moon and a clear sky. Billy Brown came and sat with us during our duty time and kept us amused gossiping about the factory personnel. He thinks our Stan is a 'proper gentleman' – by which he means that he doesn't put on airs because he is a chargehand.

When we arrived at the factory this morning we had the most wonderful surprise. There was a notice on the board signed by Mr Young stating that as a

mark of appreciation for long services any employee who had been with the firm
4 years and had a good record, would, in the event of illness, be paid full basic
wage for 6 weeks and half basic wage for a further six weeks. This of course is a
direct outcome of K's appeal to Mr Young on Fred's behalf. We could hardly
believe our eyes that such a wonderful thing had happened for Morrisons'
employees, and all through our action, Els having had the bright idea that K
should appeal personally to Mr Young and bypass Mr Payne. The whole factory
hummed with the news, and Stan said gracefully 'We owe that to Kath I reckon,'
and Ron and Eddie rushed at K with whoops of joy. They both want to organise a
deputation of workers to say 'Thank you' to the directors. Bernard thinks it is the
best thing the firm has ever done, and not only extremely generous, but very
nice also, as it will tremendously affect the workers' feelings towards the
management. Joe Moroney came over in high fettle and couldn't imagine why
the management had suddenly done this until K told him the whole story. His
factory also wants to join the deputation of thanks. It has made a very nice elated
atmosphere to start a Bank Holiday weekend and we personally feel we have
justified our existence in Industry if we never do another hand's turn. The
general feeling is that Mr Young and Mr McGiveney are pretty good employers,
but they are usually blockaded by Hurst, Lines and Payne.

Saturday 5 August – Monday 7 August
Lovely weekend [*in Hindhead*] and wonderful news from Brittany and Normandy.
The Germans are falling back everywhere. We found on our return that there
had been another bomb on Duppas Hill, nobody injured, fortunately, but a good
deal of damage done.

Wednesday 9 August
A quiet night here. An alert while we were making breakfast and five bombs
came over, one dropping on the far side of Duppas Hill. After that it was a quiet
day and we got a lot of work done. K is still working on the capstans and finds it
dirtier but cooler than on the centre lathes under the glass. She is still rather
enjoying the novelty of working the many gadgets and handles. Els is at last
beginning to get up speed with her difficult job and is enjoying it.

Thursday 10 August
Quiet night, no alert until 4 a.m. and then only a few bombs over. No alert all day
until 6 p.m. when two more bombs came over, one roaring right over the house,
but not dropping anywhere near. Very hot in the factory, but we both went racing
away on our jobs. K spent most of the afternoon chasing round the factory
getting volunteers to be 'blood donors' for Sutton Hospital. If 100 people will
volunteer, the hospital will send their mobile van and the whole thing can be
done in the factory. This has been in train for some weeks (at the request of the
works council), but through a misunderstanding, and the chargehands' inertia,
Mr Young had only received 34 names and he was preparing to call the whole
thing off. However, when K went round to see the chargehands herself she soon
got the required 100.

Friday 11 August

On fire watch last night, but a quiet night as no bombs came over this neighbourhood. A marvellous starlit night. We lay on the hill and really enjoyed it. We set off to work early and got in just as the red alert went and several bombs came down. After this all was quiet for the rest of the day, though the blue went up several times. Poor K is finding capstan life very hard on the hands and is covered with small cuts. She hopes to get back to the centre lathes soon. Terribly hot in the factory today and we all dripped. What a pity some of these bombs haven't smashed the machine shop windows. We grill under the glass and everyone grumbles. Elsie is doing double time on the job which Mrs Hazelgrove was always so conceited about, and has come to think that there is 'nothing in it' as Stan always says of the more tricky jobs!

Saturday 12 August

The personnel of our shelter on the hill is changing. Mr and Mrs Bellwood have gone for a week's holiday and their place has been taken by a very nice family who were bombed out last weekend: father, mother, little girl and an adorable baby. The father is a wonder and distressed us very much one night by calling out in his sleep 'Help! Help!' We suppose he was dreaming of all the horrors he has seen. Our shelter marshall, Mr Harvey, causes us great amusement and a good deal of irritation. He is an almost unbelievable figure of fun, aged about 50, retired and rubicund, and wears a straw boater and a white cotton Norfolk jacket. In fact he resembles a period illustration of 'a bicycle made for two'. He has a hearty and jocose manner and roars with laughter at all his own jokes. When he makes his nightly tour of the shelter he has a quip with each occupant in turn. We get much chaffed because we lie side by side on our single mattress, each rolled up in our separate blankets like a couple of cocoons. He used to call us his 'pin-up girls', but now we seem to be the Heavenly Twins. Every night he rallies us about reading in bed and when we are writing up the diary he rates us for doing our prep so late – and what will teacher say. When we walk back across the hill in the mornings we are interested to see that the REME men from the next house do not sleep indoors, but all lie head to tail wrapped up in their ground sheets in a long slit trench at the foot of the hill.

Today K was rather annoyed because Len has jockeyed her into staying another week in the capstan section. She went grumbling to Stan about this and he told her that Len had already said that 'he wished he had a few more like Kath in the capstans'. Len obviously finds it a nice change to have someone who will take trouble to get the job right and not just be content to whirl the handles regardless of accuracy.

Sunday 13 August

Yesterday we had a charming letter from Ronald. We had written to him telling him of Morrisons' most generous sickness benefit to their employees of four years standing. We were rather touched by this note.

Dear sisters (of Mercy). Well & truly done. This is just the sort of achievement which you – but no other worker at your firm – can bring off. You will always be proud of the memory.

Amongst our other correspondents lately has been Sir Herbert Williams, MP for Croydon. We have been trying to interest him in the poor sleeping accommodation available in the Duppas Hill shelters. We have had several letters from him explaining that there were many other shelters in Croydon fully equipped with bunks which were not being used and he seemed content to let the matter rest there. However, we wrote again to suggest that if the other shelters were not being fully used they ought to transfer the bunks to Duppas Hill where there was a terrific demand for them. He replied yesterday to this and informed us that he had spoken to the Croydon Town Clerk who would look into the matter. With so many bombs around here more and more families require shelter accommodation, and many of them are sleeping with only rugs between them and the cold cement floor.

Monday 14 August
Last night there was the most almighty row in our shelter. Mr and Mrs Bellwood returned from their week's annual holiday to find that one of their bunks had been given away to another man by Mr Harvey. They naturally felt rather aggrieved about this as Mr Harvey had told them before they left that it would be quite all right. . . . Now all he would say was that the Bellwood family must separate and one of them go into the upper shelter. Altogether there was a row royale and high words on all sides. Finally, the other occupant appeared (the father of the nice bombed-out family) and he saved the situation by saying he didn't in the least mind moving if he could be found another bunk somewhere else. So off he went, with one lilo on loan, and Mr Harvey surpassed himself by saying as he swept off 'How nice it is to meet a gentleman among all these people!! and I hope the lady might say thank you!' While all this was going on there was also a family row in progress amongst the Watkins because father had let the cat escape, so altogether it was a jolly evening. A fair number of bombs over in the night and one very loud explosion woke everyone. More also in the early morning while we were having breakfast. But after that a complete lull all day. To our surprise Fred returned today looking extraordinarily well and gay as a lark. During the day he came up to K and thanked her most charmingly for speaking to Mr Young on his behalf. The firm had sent him money for all his absent weeks, delivered by a girl from the office together with a letter from Mr Young. Fred said he could hardly believe his eyes and thought for some time it was all a mistake. He said that as soon as he realised it really was for him he began to feel better in health at once. Len was full of delight today because K's job card came back with 'no scrap' on it. Apparently, this happens very rarely in the capstans and he says he likes to comment upon it to the operator when it does occur.

Tuesday 15 August
Pretty quiet day, but two or three red alerts while we were in the factory, and two dropped very near soon after we got home. Very hot day and we dripped. At dinner time we heard that there had been another Allied landing in the south of France. K spent the whole morning sulking as Len took her off her job and made her finish someone else's horrible job, and she spent the whole day messing about with it as it wouldn't go right. When the good news about the landing came through she realised it was no day to be so childish!

Wednesday 16 August
A completely quiet night, but the warning went at 5.30 a.m. though none came over. Many warnings on and off all day, but not many bombs got through. The day started rather badly by the control room not giving enough time when sounding the factory siren, and the bomb cut out and fell within ¼ mile of the factory when many of the workers were still running to the shelters. When they heard it coming some threw themselves down wherever they were and poor old Lou hurt her knee and was much shaken all day. K has finished her hateful job and spent the day roaring away on the capstans in double time. Els also had a record day – in spite of the heat. Most tiresome evening – as the alert kept on going and we couldn't get supper cooked or anything else done. We wasted a lot of time listening and dancing attendance on the wretched bombs. When the gas is on it drowns the noise of the approaching bomb, so one of us hangs out of the window while the other one cooks and when it comes near we rush downstairs to get away from the glass.

Thursday 17 August
A quiet night. The blue went on and off all day but we only went to the shelters two or three times and no bombs came near.

Friday 18 August
A quiet night. We were on fire watch, but the decree had gone forth that we need not keep awake, but must be on call should anything happen near, so we had a very good night. One alert just as we started for the factory, but otherwise nothing all day. The news from France is excellent. The American advanced patrol's 23 miles from Paris. K came back to the lathes, but very sulky because she finds herself on a horrible machine with a horrible job. However, she did not get started on it and moped about all day while Fred tried to get the machine right.

Saturday 19 August and Sunday 20 August
Quiet night till the early morning when we had a few over. All the rest of the morning there were no interruptions. K's job took nearly all the time to set up, but she got going just before the end. [*They spent the weekend in Kingswood.*]

Monday 21 August
A quiet day for us, though we hear London got a good many bombs from a different route. K had her job back on the lathes and is feeling very sulky. The news from France is wonderful.

Tuesday 22 August
A fairly quiet night, a few came over rather low. A very wet and cloudy day and we were up and down to the shelters many times. A certain number of bombs came over but passed on and nothing dropped near. After 3. o'c. in the afternoon we had no more alerts and got on well with our jobs. Still more good news from France.

Wednesday 23 August
The alert went at about 4 a.m. and a few bombs came over but passed on. During the day we had several reds early in the morning, but after 10.30 we had no more. It is definitely quieter in this area. They say the other routes are being made more use of now. At dinner hour today the wireless was put on for the news and we heard that Paris has been liberated by a large force of French Forces of the Interior and several hundreds and thousands of unarmed civilians. It came as a tremendous surprise to us, and everyone clapped and cheered, and the band joined the BBC in playing the *Marseillaise*.

Thursday 24 August
A fairly quiet night, but while we were dressing the alert went again and we had an interrupted breakfast, having to rush downstairs several times when bombs passed overhead. Deluging rain all the afternoon, and soon after we got home an absolute cloudburst descended, the whole place was wrapped in mist with thunderous rain. This coincided with an alert and soon the bombs were roaring over every few minutes. It really was terrifying, as we couldn't see them on account of the low clouds, nor hear them coming in time to rush downstairs. We had several dropping fairly near and heard the fire engine going out. Finally, we got sick of rushing up and downstairs and gave up the remainder of our supper and took knitting and sat in the hall. When the alert had been on over 2 hours we decided to take our things over to the shelter and turn in early. It was still absolutely deluging and we found the entrance to the shelter had about 8 inches of water in it. The occupants came in early tonight and we had a long conversation with Bill Brown, our boy from the factory, who normally sleeps in the adjoining trench. At present he is occupying the space where our nice neighbours the Barkers usually sleep as they are away on holiday. With Bill Brown sleeping near us we now get still more frequent visits from Mother Brown, who is a great gasbag and tells us endless stories of 'her Bill' and 'her Bet'. Bill himself is a cut above his parents and has a really remarkable singing voice.

Friday 25 August
Complete lull at night and also all day, with the exception of a brief alert at 7 a.m. Glorious sunny day. K in a rage with Stan as he was too lazy to make her a tool she needed for her job. Finally, she sat down in despair and read her book. Rumania has made peace with Russia.

Saturday 26 August
A lull all night and no alert in the morning, so that there has been more than 24 hours clear of alerts. This is the longest period free since the fly-bombs started.

We heard from Stan today that the night shift is finished, and the men are coming on days. This means that all the girls will have to go on the small awful lathes which nobody normally uses. Muriel and Lily were out today so don't know of this, but K and E are very much upset, and think that it is high time that they become redundant and got their release. K has put out a feeler to go back on the capstans, but it looks as if these also will be full.

Sunday 27 August
The alert went at 1 a.m. and bombs came over then and again at about 6 a.m., but after that there was a complete lull and we spent the morning laying on the hillside enjoying a rest. After lunch we cycled off to Beddington Park where Morrisons' Cricket team were playing another factory . . . many of the team were machine shop men, and Stan is captain. We see that the balloons have been moved from the Chipstead Valley, so suppose that the bases which supply that route have been captured.

Monday 28 August
We went in to work expecting to find the night shift men, but they didn't turn up, much to Rapley's annoyance. K was given a horrible job on the lathes and told Rapley she would just as soon be on the capstans. He jumped at this – so off K went and got just as horrible a job on the capstans; however, she is on a very good machine. Poor Els had a dreadful day as her job baffled Stan with tools not working properly and she never really got going all day. We had a number of red alerts in the afternoon and the blue was up from 3. o'c. onwards.

Tuesday 29 August
A quiet night. The night men came back today and were on the carpet with Mr Hurst for not having come yesterday. However, their excuse was that they were only told about the change over at 5 a.m. on Saturday morning and had already made their weekend plans. Rapley got even with them by not taking the girls off the good lathes and left the men with the bad ones. Els was taken off her nice job which was given to one of the men. Stan was evidently quite determined that Els should not lose the job altogether, and spent the whole day getting paraphernalia together and setting the same job up on another lathe. Unfortunately, it is not nearly such a good machine, so the job is more likely to go wrong, and Els is nervous of it. K spent the whole day drowned in oil and getting more and more miserable. As people seem to be falling over each other in the machine shop with all the night men back, E and K went to Rapley to see if the firm would care to give us our release. We thought he would jump at it, but not at all, he said there was heaps of work for all, and in any case he didn't want to lose us. Though there were some he would gladly see the back of, he said the firm couldn't release us as it rested with the NSO. The alerts were on and off all day and there were several reds. One bomb fell fairly close, and the Home Guard were detailed for a repair party. In the evening we were thoroughly interrupted [*as*] the alert went about every ¾ hour and several bombs came over each time. In the end we went over early to the shelter, and as

we went there a bomb with enormous streaks of flame went right over our head and crashed a mile or two away. The fly-bombs seem to be using an old route again over our hill.

Wednesday 30 August
We both had awful days. Els's job wouldn't go right till nearly the end of the day and K was again drowned in oil. Her stockings and shoes are saturated with it and she is determined to get 'dirty money' for the capstan girls when they work in oil. Several alerts in the morning, and one or two reds.

Thursday 31 August
The blue alert was on and off all day and we had red warnings, but no bombs came within earshot. The news is marvellous. The British and Canadians have swept forward 65 miles in 48 hours. They are pushing on through the fly-bomb bases.

Friday 1 September
On fire watch last night, but no alerts. Complete lull all day. K finished her horribly oily job and was 5 hours in debt on it! She has asked the rate-fixer to come and re-time it. There has always been trouble over this job as it has a very tight time allowance on it. Most people have got fed up with it and either removed themselves from the section altogether on account of it or gone off the job. K is determined to stick to the job and get a fairer time allowance on it. The news continues to be unbelievably good. British, Canadians and Americans sweeping in everywhere. All the old 1914–1918 place names are coming into the news again. Verdun is captured and Amiens and Abbeville are only a few miles ahead.

Saturday 2 September
The lull continues. No alert last night, and a quiet morning. It seemed strange not to have alerts at the back of one's mind. K had a tempestuous morning. Mr Tickle, the rate-fixer, came down to see her about the rotten job and was extremely rude to her, refused to re-time the job and more or less told K she was 'going slow' on purpose so that more time would be given. K was in an absolute rage over this and dashed off to interview Bradford and tell him of Mr Tickle's accusation. She was in such a temper that she finally burst into tears and there was Bradford patting her shoulder and telling her 'not to take on so'. He assured her that she and Elsie were two of their best workers and never left their machines. Rapley then joined the party and he was astonished to hear what Mr Tickle had said. They neither of them like Tickle and were dying for K to charge him with 'being insolting' (*sic*). However, K's only anxiety was to get the job timing corrected as she knows that she has a very good case, and if she can't fight for it no one else will be able to. There are thousands and thousands of these little beasts to be done and it will be a continuous source of trouble unless the injustice is put right. Jimmy Dale then got involved in the fray as shop steward and was sent off by Bradford to interview Mr Tickle. Altogether there was

a pretty good rumpus in the m/c shop and we got several very emphatic, unsolicited testimonials to the effect that 'Elsie and Kathleen are very conscientious workers and never leave their machines'. It now remains for the whole question to be brought up before the Rate Revision Committee. Luckily, Mr Young is chairman of this and Jimmy Dale is one of the workers' representatives, so K thinks she will win her case.

Sunday 3 September
The Allies crossed into Belgium today and Patton's US army is rumoured to be behind the Maginot Line.

Monday 4 September
We heard today at dinner time that Brussels was liberated. Everyone in the factory cheered and clapped. It seems very queer to have had a complete lull from flying bombs for 4 days and to find that one isn't automatically keeping an eye out to see if the blue is up yet. Old Joe Moroney has had a blazing row with his inspector boss, the objectionable Willis Hole, and he has asked Mr Lines if he can come off inspection and go on the benches. . . . So now [*he*] has to clock in and queue up for the canteen like all the rest of us. Costello thinks he probably hasn't been very wise, but Irish Joe wouldn't worry about that. K is engaged on making Stan a glorious pair of striped football stockings – royal blue and white for Morrisons' colours.

The Pas de Calais area is now liberated, so we hope not to have to spend many more nights in the public shelter, though we really have a great deal of amusement out of our sheltered life.

Tuesday 5 September
We hear that the fly-bomb lull was broken by a few coming over from Holland, but nothing came in this direction and we decided to sleep at home tonight.

Wednesday 6 September
The first night in our beds for over eleven weeks and we revelled in it. K's only complaint was that the uninterrupted night passed too quickly, as she has been accustomed to waking up at frequent intervals when in the shelter. Works council today, the first for 3 months, owing to the fly-bombs. Mr Young told us how he had been down to interview the naughty part-stamping girls recently – when they had downed tools because they had not received a promised rise in pay. They were very pert with him and when he told them they would get their money next pay day, they said 'Huh! We've heard that tale before – and who are you, anyway?!' The works council shrieked with laughter at this, but it only goes to show how little the directors are personally known to the workers. Mr McGiveney came to the meeting and talked on Morrisons' postwar plans for about 1½ hours. The firm hopes to make prefabricated houses of aluminium on aircraft manufacture principles. He seems to have got the ear of Sir Stafford Cripps and is chairman of the AIROH Committee (Aircraft Industry Research on Housing). He says the Portal steel houses will be a flop as there are not

enough gigantic steel presses in the country for mass production, and the aluminium house will keep the aircraft industry in full employment on work which they are already trained to do. Sir Stafford Cripps has said that 90 per cent of the aircraft industry must stop making aeroplanes after the war, and yet there must be no more mass unemployment. So, naturally, Mr McGiveney's idea appeals very much to him. K has never seen Mr McGiveney at close quarters for so long before and took a great fancy to him. His enthusiasm over his houses, and his amused enjoyment at meeting so many bigwigs and nobs nowadays was very engaging.

Thursday 7 September
All the balloons have disappeared and this area is evidently no longer considered very vulnerable. The report on the fly-bomb attack was announced today, over 8,000 bombs launched . . . 2,300 reaching the London area, a million houses damaged, 23,000 of which are beyond repair.

Friday 8 September
Jimmy Dale had to attend an AEU meeting last night, called to discuss Morrisons' action in time cutting. This has all arisen over the row with the tear-arses. Jimmy was told he was not to sanction any more time cuts and the whole matter is still causing trouble.

Sunday 10 September
Very heavy coastal gunfire on and off all day. After lunch we went to watch Morrisons' team playing the 'Acc. and Tab.' at cricket. We were invited to tea with the team, and they seemed to like having us as supporters.

Monday 11 September
To our horror this morning we didn't wake till nearly 7.30. We bounded out of bed and rushed off to work without washing or doing our hair or having any breakfast and arrived in time as usual! K finished her loathsome oily job and it now remains to be seen whether she will be able to get the time improved on it. She has now gone to work on a very small capstan and doesn't like it much. Els started another tricky job, but thinks she will be able to earn a good bonus before long.

Tuesday 12 September
At 6.30 a.m. there was a loud explosion which sounded fairly near. Also another at about 9 a.m. No one seemed to know what they are. This month the election of the new council takes place and nominations have been asked for. None of the present council wish to stand again, as for various reasons they are all fed up. Costello thinks the whole council is a waste of time, as it achieves so little, and also considers that the management have put the onus of several unpleasant things they've wanted to do onto the works council. K heartily agrees with this, but thinks that the factory was definitely worse off before there was a council, as now the workers do, at any rate, have direct access to the management.

Wednesday 13 September
K asked Nancy Deacon if she would stand for the council, but found her rather unwilling. She says the council already has had 'the cream of the workers' on it and if they are fed up and unable to achieve much, what hope would there be for anyone else. Mr Tickle arrived by K's machine today, obviously keen to bury the hatchet. He intimated that he would see that K got a bonus on all her jobs, but said the time on the job was not to be officially increased. K said this wouldn't do at all and told Mr Tickle she would see Mr Hurst about it.

Thursday 14 September
After several false attempts K got her interview with Mr Hurst. Mercifully, he was in a very good temper and listened amicably to all K had to say and agreed to enquire into the job with a view to increasing the time allowance. At the end of the interview K suddenly asked whether she & E could have a week's holiday in the near future, as they felt they needed it. Mr Hurst hummed & ha'ed a bit, but finally said he thought it could be arranged at the end of September.

Friday 15 September
Another fairly distant explosion today. However, no one makes much comment. Billy Brown got his army papers today and goes for his medical on Monday. K caught her foot in yet another hole in the factory floor and sprained her ankle slightly.

Monday 18 September
Today was the closing date for the nominations to the new works council, but only Bert Runacres from inspection was proposed and none of the old council wish to stand again. We heard that the explosion we had heard on Sunday was at Purley Oaks. The crater was not very large, but a great deal of damage was done by [*the*] blast. In the evening we went to the union, our first visit since before the fly-bombs. We hadn't been in the room five minutes before the whole house was shaken by a loud explosion which was said to be in the Streatham direction. A deadly meeting. The chairman is elderly and rather deaf and cannot keep the meeting together at all. It degenerates into small groups of muttering people. We were bored to tears and vowed 'never again'.

Tuesday 19 September
An alert at 4 a.m. and a fly-bomb fell before we could get dressed. Alarms and excursions today over the works council elections. Mr Young sent for K to enquire why the old council wouldn't stand again, and she had an embarrassing interview trying to explain that she didn't think the works council achieved much and was not held in any favour by the rest of the factory, largely owing to the activities of the Bonus Revision Committee. She said she felt she was largely to blame for this as the whole thing had arisen from her question about unlimited bonus earnings at the meeting with Mr Strauss. Then Mr Young sent for the rest of the works council and, while waiting for them to arrive, he confided in K that

he and Mr Hurst were diametrically opposed in their views as to how a factory should be run. Young believed in cooperation with the workers, whereas Hurst believed in the old-fashioned nigger-driving methods. When the others arrived he asked them their opinions also, and explained that he had great opposition from the other members of the management to the idea of launching a Workers Council, and he would be very sorry to see it fail as he was a great believer in direct cooperation between workers and management. He worked himself up into a choleric state and finally delivered an ultimatum to the effect that if there were no nominations forthcoming by midday on Wednesday the council would be disbanded and the liaison severed between workers and management.

K came down determined to get Nancy Deacon and Anne Shine to put up for election and spent the rest of the afternoon racing round trying to get nominations.

Wednesday 20 September
A distant alert last night, but nothing came near. Today a woman doctor from the Sutton Blood Transfusion Clinic came to take blood donations from about a hundred workers who had volunteered to be blood donors. By dint of ramping round the factory 3 men were persuaded to stand for the works council and Nancy Deacon and Anne Shine said they would also put up if K would allow herself to be nominated too. Nellie Barford also agreed to stand, so there will now be a proper election for the two women's places, though the men will go on automatically as there are 3 vacancies. K was touched to find that she had been nominated by Ken Peters and Eddie Cook, all the other women candidates had been nominated by women.

Thursday 21 September
No alert last night so we had a quiet night for fire watching. Just before 'pay out' Mr Young addressed us over the loud speaker on the subject of the works council. He spoke quite well, and said that unless at least 50 per cent of the adult workers voted he would wash out the works council altogether.

Sunday 24 September
Great anxiety over the airborne troops round Arnhem – the position for them looks very bad.

We had a talk with Ronald concerning our future plans. He thinks it is time we gave up factory work and suggests we do welfare work, as our inside knowledge of factory conditions and our humanitarian outlook specially fit us for this. However, when we asked how we were to get our release he admitted that it would be impossible unless we had a job to step into. Els might perhaps get it on the ground of age. As we neither of us feel we could take on any new job unless we had a good holiday first it all looks pretty hopeless.

Monday 25 September
Els' cold, which has lasted for a fortnight, seems to be a bit better. All the factory is streaming with colds – especially the m/c shop where 8 broken windows let in

a howling draught. K was indignant to find she had to do a ridiculously 'unskilled' job on the capstans and suffered badly from injured pride.

Wednesday 27 September

Today K heard that she had won her battle for an increase of time allowed for the horrible oily washers. This will be a definite help to every worker on the job, so K was very pleased. Another desperate long day. We were both utterly depressed and gloomy, probably owing to the bad news of the loss of the Arnhem airborne troops. Everyone's too easy optimism of the past few weeks seems to be evaporating rapidly. De Gaulle has said the war will certainly not be over by the spring of 1945.

Thursday 28 September

Today the 100 volunteer Blood Donors had ¾ pint taken from each of them. The Sutton Mobile Transfusion service brought their van and set up an improvised clinic at the bottom of the canteen. Ken Peters was amongst the first to go and he fainted away and did not return to work for the rest of the morning. While he was away his various friends produced from somewhere a bunch of white dahlias, which they laid on the concrete floor in front of his lathe and chalked in large letters 'Gone – but not forgotten. He done it for Briton (*sic*) R.I.P.' The lathe was then hung with crepe and visitors came from all over the factory to see this friendly effort. Luckily, Ken seemed quite fit again when he came back after lunch. When our turn came, K was rejected on account of having had pneumonia in the spring. They took a blood test and said 'not today thank you – it was so kind of you to offer'. E was much amused at the to-do that some of the young part-stamping girls made over the business . . . all of them worked up to a state of patriotic heroism. In fact, the whole factory was rather elated by the proceedings and there was a great feeling of camaraderie amongst those with the sticking plaster badge on their arms.

Friday 29 September

Today was the works council Election. Costello told E that he wasn't going to vote for K as he wanted to get a good 2nd woman onto the council. He thought Mrs Barford had been no use at all and was determined to get her replaced. E pointed out that if everyone thought like this, K wouldn't get on at all, but Costello said he was certain she would get in easily. May organised the collection of voting papers and reported that Kath and Ken Peters were going to be top of the poll! During the dinner break Mr McGiveney talked to the workers about Morrisons' postwar plans. They are to make aluminium houses, and this scheme has now had the blessing of the Prime Minister and Sir Stafford Cripps, so will go ahead shortly.

Saturday 30 September – Sunday 8 October

[*K and E have a week's holiday. While in Kingswood E went down with shingles. It was decided that they should stay for another week and that K should travel to the factory from there.*]

Monday 9 October
We got up at 5 a.m. and E cooked K some breakfast to fortify her for the 5-mile cycle ride to Banstead station where she could get a train to Waddon. All proceeded according to plan and K got to the factory early as usual. But to her horror she found that a sub-council meeting had been called for 5.15 p.m. which would mean she wouldn't be able to start back for Kingswood until about 7 p.m. There were many sympathetic enquiries for poor Els and much commiseration over the horrors of shingles. K also had many congratulations on being top of the poll. The sub-council meeting was quite well attended and Bert Runacres was made chairman and K was asked to be secretary again. It was agreed that the management should be asked to allow the workers' representatives to write their own accounts of the council meetings. Up to the present the bald (and often biased) minutes written up by the management don't give at all a fair picture of the proceedings. K was very late getting away and it was 7.45 before she collected her bicycle at Banstead station. [*The journey did not proceed well and culminated in K spraining her ankle.*] So that is the end of her journeys to the factory this week. As Mum said when she heard of the accident 'Really a blessing in disguise'. Dr Watson ordered bed for a week and 3 days' massage.

Thursday 26 October
An alert last night and one distant bump. Went back to work rather unwillingly, but got through the day pretty well. We are annoyed to find that none of the 10 m/c shop windows have been mended in spite of repeated requests to Rapley, the nurse and Mr Young in the works council. The draughts are appalling and E has to stand right in the howling gale.

Friday 27 October
Today Bill Brown got his calling up papers for the army. He has never returned the rug and lilo we lent him in the shelter during the fly-bomb period – in spite of frequent promises. A very good concert by the local NFS choir. We feel very affectionate towards these men, who came to sing to us last when the fly-bombs were at their height – and had a most soothing effect on our somewhat frayed nerves. Several heavy explosions were heard today, loud enough to be heard through the machinery noise, presumably rockets.

Sunday 29 October
An alert at 5.30 and one fly-bomb came over pretty near. The explosion shook all the windows.

Monday 30 October
Today there was a schemozzle at dinner time. Our Muriel was sent for to speak to someone at the gate and (according to the inspector girls who were watching) she was blackguarded by an irate and injured wife who roared at Muriel that she had been living with the woman's husband for the past 3 weeks and he the father of 10 children! She slapped Muriel's face and there was a good old dust-up.

This new light on Muriel simply astonishes us as she has always seemed devoted to her Reg and has appeared to have very strict views on morality. She was the girl who said she never went to dances as she didn't consider it decent to have another man's arm round her when she belonged to Reg. Within a few minutes of this K was regaled with a story of Bill Brown being completely unprincipled about other people's possessions. So it looks as if we shall have to go and fetch our rug and lilo if we are to get them back.

Tuesday 31 October
It transpires that Muriel's 'married man with 10 children' is none other than her Reg whom she has been 'going with' for seven years. May Nolan seems to know the whole story and says that Muriel has tried to assert that Reg was single – but May pointed out that only an injured wife would come round to the factory on a face-smacking expedition. So Muriel's defence petered out after this. Anyhow it has caused a good bit of talk in the factory. We feel extremely sorry for her, though the general opinion seems to be that horse-whipping isn't good enough for her. This morning we had fly-bombs over about 7 a.m. – and two more red alerts in the factory before 9 a.m. It seemed quite peculiar to be back in the old shelters again. After work we went to Bill Brown's home to requisition our rug and lilo. We had had a horrible feeling that he might have popped them, but luckily we got them back all right and no recriminations. Several more heavy explosions during the day and evening.

Wednesday 1 November
More stories of Billy Brown were told us again today. For the past month we have been trying to get the machine shop windows mended – 12 of them are broken and the draught, now that the weather has turned cold, is simply shocking. Today, all the women were in a ferment as nothing had been done about the windows and a howling wind was coming in. The question has already been brought up at the works council and to Mr Payne and to Rapley – with no result. Today, the carpenter came and knocked out all the remaining glass in 5 windows by E's lathe, and then went away for the rest of the afternoon leaving E to freeze. This was done either out of spite, because the men broke some of the windows intentionally in the summer, or to 'larn' K for being bossy. K was working some distance away off on the capstans so was not affected by it, but E who is often mistaken for K by people who don't know us very well, had to suffer. She got colder and colder and finally had to put on a coat to keep warm. Everyone was hopping mad about the whole business and threatening to down tools if something was not done about it. However, 5 mins before the end of the shift 'Chippy' returned, grinning evilly, and the windows were repaired.

While K was in the welfare office today she was amazed to see a huge printed poster advertising 'Morrisons Aircraft Factory Orchestra'. The slogan read 'The Factories to the Forces', and is obviously the poster which is used for their outside engagements. A clear case of *suggestio falsi* as everyone would imagine that the players are the factory workers themselves.

Thursday 2 November
More rage about broken windows, and K told Rapley that he had better do something about it before there was a riot. He then fetched Hurst and the windows were done forthwith. A loud bang could be heard above the machinery in the morning and another terrific crash at about 5 p.m.

Friday 3 November
Morrisons has advertised a dinner & dance for the workers next Tuesday, tickets 5s. Ron Allen was going round the machine shop beating up supporters as he has been told by Mr Payne that the tickets are going very badly, and Mr Young is furious about it and says that if it isn't a success he will never do anything again for the workers. This seems ludicrous. Why should we be blackmailed into going out when we don't want to? The older ones don't particularly want to go out in these times, and the younger ones probably can't afford 5s. In any case the workers come from far and wide. For us it would mean a four to five mile cycle ride . . . nothing would induce us to go.

Monday 6 November
K had a dreadful day with her job wrong all the time and she didn't know how to endure it.

Tuesday 7 November
Recently the works council have been on the ramp to get the management's permission to write their own report of the meetings for display on the notice board. Up to the present the management have written the minutes and the council have often been annoyed by the unsatisfactory results. At the last meeting K got permission to do this and Mr Young said she could have the secretary's verbatim report as a ground work, and the firm would type the minutes afterwards. So tonight poor K was sitting up in bed till midnight trying to convert Miss Barr's confused account to simple straightforward English, also to put a little life into the report.

Wednesday 8 November
K gave her minutes to Bert Runacre, the new workers' chairman. A very pugnacious little man, ex-regular soldier and ardent trade unionist. In the past he has always been rather critical of the works council, but is now beginning to realise what a struggle they have. He was delighted with the minutes and congratulated K on such an excellent and lucid report. But when he took them up to the office to be typed, Miss Barr nearly passed out when she saw the pages of stuff she would have to cope with. She said very acidly she would have to see Mr Young about it. She obviously thought that her verbatim report would be accepted by the workers as it stood, which was of course absurd. K expects to be on the carpet with Mr Young as he is rather partial to Miss Barr. Elsie had a new compliment today. She saw the inspector holding an inquest on one of her bits and rushed up to see if anything was wrong. The inspector said 'Oh no! There's nothing wrong with your operation. In fact it would give me quite a bit of

pleasure to find something wrong with your work!' Hideously embarrassed, E said she was glad there was some compensation in being so slow, but Harry said 'Oh you're not so slow'. So E is purring. An alert in the early evening.

Thursday 9 November

K thinks she was cut dead by Mr Young today, so fears trouble is brewing. sub-council tonight and a pretty good attendance. They were pleased with the full-length report and thought it a great improvement on the previous ones. K was co-opted onto the Shop Stewards' Committee. An alert in the early evening. We sat on the stairs and ate our supper but heard nothing fall near.

Friday 10 November

Churchill has announced that the Germans have been sending rockets over the country [*V2s*]. He said they had fallen in widely separated areas. This was in reply to the German announcement that London was being devastated by rockets. We heard 3 bumps during the day but not near. An alert in the evening, but we heard nothing.

Monday 13 November

K had a Shop Stewards' Committee in the evening. . . . It was an interesting meeting, mainly the same people as on the works council. K thinks Bert Runacres and the others are going to be very good, and Bert Runacres as chairman is much more support than ever old blarneying Joe Moroney was, with his chatter about 'final victory'.

Tuesday 14 November

An alert early last night – but nothing this way. Els has had some praise from Stan, who seldom deals in praise. He said he was *very pleased* with the way E was doing her difficult job. He had had to finish some off in overtime as they were 'wanted urgent' and he rattled them off in no time as he knew they would be correct and hadn't had to check up each one.

Wednesday 15 November

Three alerts last night. As the local siren seems to be mute just now we did not wake till we heard a fly-bomb roaring overhead, and fell out of our beds and crawled underneath them. The bomb fell in South Croydon. For the past two days K has been teaching a newcomer on the capstans. There is a general post going on in the shops at the moment, as some contracts are finishing, and other new work being started. The machine shop is up to its eyes in work. Stan says he is negotiating to get K back on the centre lathes, but says he will have a struggle as the capstans will try to keep her. He told E that K and Alice Trett were the only ones who were any good in the section.

Tuesday 28 November

We leave a blank for a fortnight as one day seems so much like another that we have not bothered to enter anything in the diary. We have had a few alerts, and also rockets, but none very near, though the explosions are often extremely loud.

Today we had a Canteen Committee meeting, and Kathleen and Ken Peters and Ron Allen were all invited too, as the works council had proposed that something should be done about canteen behaviour. Various complaints have been received about hair combed at table, make-up applied and powder and cigarette ash over the food. Mr Young had made a suggestion that a notice of 'Canteen Dos & Don'ts' should be put up, but Els, cogitating on this as she drearily applied herself to [*doing*] work, thought how little interest was taken of typed notices and how much they were inclined to annoy. So she thought that if a few rhymed couplets were inserted they might slightly amuse as well as edify.

At the meeting Mr Proctor entirely agreed that notices did very little good, so Els suggested that doggerel verses might be more telling and proceeded to read her little effort:

> All who stand in the Canteen queue
> Please read these hints –
> they're addressed to you.
>
> This is first of our appeals
> Never comb your hair at meals
>
> Nor is the Canteen the place
> To put cosmetics on your face
>
> Don't carry food for more than two
> It blocks the others in the queue
>
> If you smoke it isn't good
> To scatter ash on your neighbour's food
>
> If your cup has got a chip
> Don't let that part touch your lip
> But if the chips are far too many
> Take it back and show to 'Denny' [*Canteen Counter Hand*]

Mr Proctor was delighted with this and said he would get it lettered in the drawing office and have two copies put up, one for the canteen & one for the office staff.

Wednesday 29 November

Mr Proctor came round to Els' lathe today and asked for her rhymes. She felt rather giggly at the picture of a director of 600 workers contacting one of his grubbiest employees and asking for her verses.

Thursday 30 November
We hear that the Christmas holiday is to be from Friday evening till the following Wednesday morning. This makes a lovely long break. K is going to Mum's new flat in Brighton and Els and Millie also to Brighton.

We are still both very bored and tired with our work. Els has the consolation of making a very good bonus on her job. K is now back on the lathes, and seems to be doing any odd job that is wanted in a rush.

[*The diary ends abruptly at this point.*]

Epilogue

Although they made no more diary entries, Elsie and Kathleen continued to work at Morrisons until April 1945 when they were given official release. It is clear from the diary that the pair had applied for release before this date and had been refused. The changed situation was undoubtedly due to the declining fortunes of the aircraft industry. From its height in the period leading up to the Normandy landings of June 1944, the war effort began to wind down. Government contracts with Vickers for aircraft declined. It is very likely that women who wished to continue working were refused, as Morrisons were obliged, by law, to provide jobs for ex-employees when they were released from the services. As the women workers were engaged on a temporary basis they had to make way for the demobilised men. Eventually, the work for Vickers dried up altogether and the company could not be sustained. Efforts were made to diversify its products. Although Morrisons' Peterborough factory had some success in this direction, the Croydon factory continued to decline and closed in 1947. (Morrisons continued in Rochester for some time after this.) However, the closure does not seem to have caused too many problems for its workforce who were quickly absorbed into other local firms. For many years the site was occupied by a firm called Bailey Meters. The building was demolished in the 1980s to make way for retail outlets.

Both Elsie and Kathleen were in a poor state of health at the end of the war. There is some correspondence which indicates that Kathleen injured her back around this time and Elsie was suffering from pernicious anaemia.[25] While little is known about this both women are known to have returned to Benacre for an extended period of recuperation. They decided not to reopen the café and returned to paid employment in 1947 as joint regional organisers for the English Folk Dance and Song Society, covering a patch from south London to the south coast.[26] They also travelled extensively abroad for the society, including around eight trips to the USA, where they made many friends and also visited Stan Wallace who had emigrated to the USA and built up a successful engineering business in California. Elsie pursued her interest in dancing and travelled to Indian reservations while in America to watch and record Indian dances.

Elsie and Kathleen continued to live and work together until 1960 when Kathleen married an old friend from the folk dance movement, Tommy Adkins, who had been recently widowed. Tommy moved in with Kathleen in Milford and Elsie bought a cottage in Suffolk near to her sister Phyl and close friends from the folk dance world, later moving to a nursing home. Kathleen and Tommy travelled extensively and continued to make trips abroad on behalf of the society. Tommy died suddenly while they were in the Pyrenees in 1976. Elsie and

Kathleen remained close friends, and Elsie was staying with Kathleen in 1980 when she became ill and was taken to Guildford hospital where she died. Kathleen remained at Benacre and led an active life well into her eighties. During this time she expressed an interest in publishing the diary, but did not make much progress in finding a publisher. After she died in 1991 her stepdaughter, Alison Speirs, passed the diary into the hands of the Imperial War Museum.[27]

Notes

(Published in London unless otherwise specified)

1. R. Croucher, *Engineers at War 1939–1945*, Merlin 1982, pp. 148–74.
2. J. Jefferys, *The Story of the Engineers*, Lawrence and Wishart 1945, p. 212.
3. For details see P. Summerfield, *Women Workers in the Second World War*, Croom Helm, 1984, ch. 7, and C. Wightman, *More Than Munitions: Women, Work and the Engineering Industries 1900–1959*, Longman, 1999, ch. 7. I would like to pay tribute here to Penny Summerfield for her enormous contribution to work in this field.
4. P. Summerfield, 'The Patriarchal Discourse of Human Capital: Training Women for War Work 1939–1945.' *Journal of Gender Studies*, Vol. 2, No. 2, November 1993, p. 192.
5. The name Morrisons was always spelt without any apostrophe between the 'n' and 's'.
6. For details see R. Croucher (1982), ch. 1.
7. Interview Ken Peters, Warlingham, Surrey, 20 July 1999.
8. The diary, 13 June 1942, see also 21 July 1942 that gives the workforce total for clocking on as 470. Management and office staff would be in addition to this. The diary, 29 November 1944, states that Morrisons had a workforce of 600. This would be at its peak, as aircraft production declined from 1944.
9. The diary, 16 September 1942, states that 300 women were at Morrisons at this time.
10. Biographical information about Kathleen Church-Bliss has been obtained from Alison Speirs (interview, 25 August 1997, and subsequent correspondence) and archive material held by Mrs Speirs and the Vaughan Williams Memorial Library, English Folk Dance and Song Society (EFDSS), Cecil Sharp House, London.
11. Handwritten memoir by K. Church-Bliss for Roger Marratt, EFDSS, no date, but appears to be 1980s.
12. Biographical information regarding Elsie Whiteman has been obtained from her niece, Jane Salusbury (interview, 27 September 1999), and the archives of EFDSS.
13. Interview with Jane Salusbury, London, 27 September 1999.
14. The Mass Observation Archive is at the University of Sussex, see particularly *People in Production*, John Murray, 1942, and *War Factory*, Gollancz, 1943.
15. See, for example, P. Summerfield, *Reconstructing Women's Wartime Lives, Discourse and Subjectivity in Oral Histories of the Second World War*, Manchester University Press, 1998.
16. P. Summerfield (1984), reproduces the figures in the table on p. 196. It is also mentioned in S. Boston, *Women Workers and the Trade Union Movement*, Davis-Poynter, 1980, p. 205.
17. Elsie took five years off her age at this point. This fact emerges in the diary, 10 September 1942, and 29 September 1942.

18. I am not seeking to undervalue the problems of younger women workers, especially childcare and domestic burdens, but instead I aim to present a perspective which has not previously been the subject of historical enquiry.
19. There are several small, black notebooks written by Kathleen in the early 1920s which describe characters she has met in the EFDSS in similar colourful language to the diaries. These notebooks are now divided between the EFDSS archives and Mrs Speirs.
20. The issues raised by the diary are more fully explored in my forthcoming article, 'A new perspective on women workers in the Second World War. The industrial diary of Kathleen Church-Bliss and Elsie Whiteman.', consult author.
21. Interviews were conducted with four ex-Morrisons workers. I am particularly grateful to my interviewees: Gordon Crosby, Audrey Clarke, Ken Peters and Ken Thorough-good. Correspondence was held with a number of others.
22. Interview, Ken Thoroughgood, 17 August 2000, Shirley, Croydon.
23. Interview, Warlingham, Surrey, 20 July 1999.
24. For details see A. Calder, *The People's War 1939–1945*, Panther, 1971.
25. 'Dear June', letter/memoir from Kathleen Church-Bliss, 7 August 1985, EFDSS.
26. Reports sent in by Kathleen and Elsie during their time as regional organisers are held by EFDSS.
27. I am grateful to my oral respondents, mentioned in the introduction, for providing biographical information on Kathleen and Elsie and Morrisons post-1945 for this epilogue.